781.66 BRO
Brown, G., 1954-
Colorado rocks!

COLORADO ROCKS!

A HALF-CENTURY OF MUSIC IN COLORADO

D1602163

COLORADO ROCKS!

A HALF-CENTURY OF MUSIC IN COLORADO

G. BROWN

PRUETT PUBLISHING COMPANY
BOULDER, COLORADO

©2004 by G. Brown

All rights reserved. No part of this book may be reproduced without written permission from the publisher, except in the case of brief excerpts in critical reviews and articles.
Address all inquiries to: Pruett Publishing Company, 7464 Arapahoe Road, Suite A9, Boulder, Colorado 80303; www.pruettpublishing.com.

Printed in South Korea

10 09 08 07 06 05 04 03 02 01 5 4 3 2 1

Library of Congress Cataloging-in-Publication Data

Brown, G., 1954-
Colorado rocks! : a half-century of music in Colorado / G. Brown.
p. cm.
ISBN 0-87108-930-0 (alk. paper)
1. Rock music--Colorado--History and criticism. I. Title.
ML3534.B772 2003
781.66'09788--dc21

2003000911

Cover & Book Design by Dave Consulting

Cover Photographs by Stephen Collector Photography

Special thanks to Jock Bartley for use of his 1958 Les Paul and 1959 Fender Telecaster in both cover and interior photographs

To the memory of Lila M. Brown

Set List

liner notes

I thank my wife, Bridget, without whom I would have wound up like the lead character in the movie *High Fidelity*. Family and friends, too. Special thanks to George Krieger, my rock consultant, and photographer Dan Fong--without their input, this project could not have been completed.

I would also like to extend my gratitude to the editorial staffers at Pruett Publishing--Jim Pruett for setting some wheels to turning, Dave Langmead of Dave Consulting for his yeoman work, and copy editor Dianne Nelson for her careful checking of grammar and accuracy

Assembling the mass of material required for a book of this kind naturally calls for assistance and support from many organizations and individuals. Among too many to thank, I must at least mention Bill Amundson, Gil Asakawa, Bill Ashford, Ricardo Baca, Larry Baird, Chas Barbour, Jock Bartley, Roger Beatty, Tim Benko, Jay Blakesberg, Mark Bliesener, Geoff Bond, Laura Bond, Michael Booth, Ron Bostwick, Peter Boyles, Jeff Bradley, Brian Brainerd, Michael Brannen, Bill Briggs, Bruce Brodeen, Mark Brown, Suzanne Brown, Tim Brown, Kristen Browning, Lauren Calista, Tom Capek, Diane Carman, Meredith Carson, John Carter, Linda Castrone, Todd Caudle, Pete Chronis, Rich Clarkson, Doug Clifton, Kevin Clock, Steve Collector, Walt Conley, Paul Conly,Dennis Constantine, Tim Cook, Kent Crawford, Kelly Curtis, Chris Daniels, James Dann, Chip Davis, Duane Davis, Buddy Day, Jay Dedrick, Henry Diltz, Gayle Discoe, Mike Drumm, Bob Dubac, Tim Duffy, Jammie Durkee, Erik Dyce, Frank Edmundson, David Eugene Edwards, Ing van Eijck, Natalyn Embree, John Emelin, Steve Eng, Paul Epstein, Laura Eveleigh, Brent Fedrizzi, Gene Felling, Bob Ferbrache, Craig Ferguson, Barry Fey, Harold Fielden, Rich Fifield, Art Fine, Kevin Fitzgerald, Rickey Fitzsimmons, Nick Forster, Jon Frizzell, Richie Furay, Bob Galinsky, Jim Gallagher, Ginny Ganahl, David Gans, Rich Garcia, Mel Gibson, Greg Glasgow, Kate Glassner, Michael Goldman, Ira Gordon, Joshua Green, Rich Greene, Max Gronenthal, Jeff Guard, Neil Guard, Ted Guggenheim, Jeff Hanna, Mark Harden, David Hartley, Butch Hause, Tommy Hauser, Mike Hawkinson, Bob Haworth, John Hayes, Leslie Hazen, Vickie Heath, Vince Herman, Dave Herrera, Neil Hickey, Candace Horgan, Bruce Hornsby, Geina Horton, Bill Husted, Ariel Hyatt, Jimmy Ibbotson, Elana Ashanti Jefferson, Michael Jensen, Rob Johnson, Marty Jones, Peter Jones, Mitch Kampf, Alan Katz, Doug Kaufmann, Herb Kauvar, Jim Kauvar, Rick Kauvar, Kathyn Keller, Sean Kelly, Kevin Kennedy, Lisa Kennedy, David Kirby, Kevin Knee, Steve Knopper, Dick Kreck, Alf Kremer, Jeff Krump, George Lane, Sherrie Levy, Huey Lewis, Mark Lewis, Michael Linehan, Phil Lobel, Carrie Lombardi, Doug Looney, Mary Ann Looney, Tom Ludwig, Kathy Lyle, David Mackay, Kyle Macmillan, John Macy, Sam Maddox, Dan Magoun, John Magnie, David Magoun, Tommy Malone, Rob Marshall, Jan Martin, Jason Martin, Jim Mason, Nancy May, John McEuen, Sam McFadin, Dennis McNally, David McQuay, Michael Mehle, David Menconi, Dick Merkle, Steve Mesple, Dee Ann Metzger, Laurie Michaels, Anne Millison, David Millman, Jerry Mills, Jason Minkler, Justin Mitchell, Kris Moe, Todd Park Mohr, John Moore, Pam Moore, Jesse Moreale, Chuck Morris, Mary Beth Morrison, Dean Myers, Jo Myers, Pete Names, Matt Need, Brian Nevin, Tom Noel, Michael Ochs, Mike O'Connor, Stan Oliner, Kelly Oliver, Barry Ollman, Scott O'Malley, Joanne Ostrow, Woody Paige, Kenny Passarelli, Bal Patterson, Zak Phillips, Lex Phillipus, Tom Pickles, Larry Pogreba, Pat Porter, William Porter, Sharon Poteet, Neal Preston, Trevor Price, Richard Ray, Nancy Rebek, Eric Reiner, William Reisman, Rip Rense, Harry Reynolds, Bob Richards, Dawn Richardson, Helen H. Richardson, Randy Robbins, Paul Robinson, Scott Roche, Eric Rollin, Pete Roos, Steve Rosen, Dave Rothstein, Leland Rucker, Mike Rudeen, Bob Rupp, Jay Ruybal, Bret Saunders, Sabrina Saunders, Henry Schmidt, Andy Schneidkraut, Andy Schuon, Ted Scott, Megan Seacord, Matt Sebastian, Clark Secrest, Jim Sheeler, Dan Sherman, Mark Shockley, Kevin Simpson, Mark Sims, Ray Skibitsky, Ed Smith, Larry Solters, Stan Soocher, Jim Sprinkle, Rob Squires, Dave Stidman, Bryant Stith, Art Stone, Gregg Stone, Andy Stonehouse, Don Strassberg, John Sunderland, Steve Swenson, Bill Szymczyk, Otis Taylor, Robert Taylor, Scott Taylor, Joey Teehan, David Thomas, Larry Thompson, Lois Todd, John Tope, Andy Torri, Hal Totten, Harry Tuft, Eddie Turner, Bruce Van Dyke, Rebecca Villanueva, Allan Vorda, Kyle Wagner, Scott Waknin, Tom Walker, Susie Wargin, Bill Warren, Bill Wedum, Kenny Weissberg, Dick Weissman, Eddie Wenrick, Jay Whearley, Ed Will, Kip Winger, Mark Wolf, Marty Wolff, Cary Wolfson, Rick Wurpel, Dolly Zander, Frank Zareno, Jordan Zevon, and Dave Zobl.

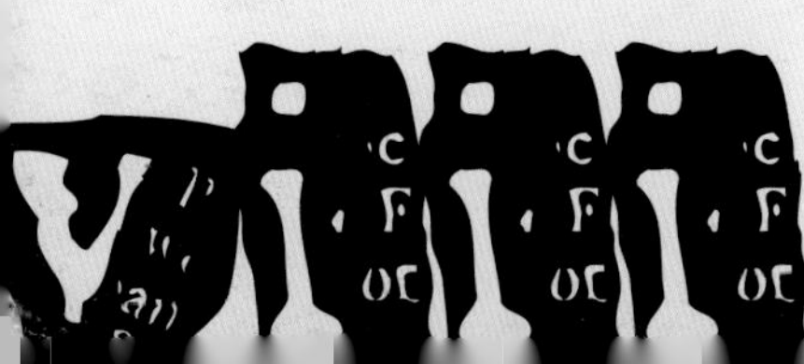

foreword

Colorado is a state of music lovers. Having been born here in 1965, I have been shaped, for better or worse, by the musical love affairs of those I have encountered in life. My earliest memories are of my mother listening to the radio. More than anything, I remember how strongly she felt about a song sometimes, how it really moved her—this more distinctly than the music itself. How and what people feel about a piece of music is what gives it its first and most important life. It is a shared experience, a social experience, and, in Colorado, I would say (partly with a chuckle) nearly a miraculous experience.

My childhood years were graced by a remarkable era in music, not just for Colorado, but globally. It has since been an evolution where we are always trying to recapture that very first high, serendipitously going on some great adventures of our own without realizing it. Rock 'n' roll is the attempt to retake that first virgin "blues" moment—every well-meaning rock guitarist wants to sit squarely at Robert Johnson's crossroads. Music conjures a secret link to the past, but in a way that is explosive, vital, and forward reaching. It's about living in the present, being present—being turned on.

What makes Colorado special as a cultural scene? You could say that the state has an identity crisis of sorts. Denver isn't Chicago or New York City. The West is so new; it lacks the regionalism that some older cities gave to music, like New Orleans–style jazz or Detroit soul. But there is definitely a rare affection and love for music that isn't found in many other places.

There has always been a thick stream of concerts of all kinds, in some of the most beautiful settings found anywhere. Anyone who has been to Red Rocks Amphitheatre or the Telluride Bluegrass Festival will find it hard to do better. Colorado has a history of far-reaching radio stations, including KFML, KBCO, KTCL, KBPI, KAZY, KQMT, and KCUV.

So with all this love, why have so few artists transcended the Mile High State to national success? The varied talent can be written in the palm of one hand: the Astronauts, Flash Cadillac, John Denver, Firefall, the Subdudes, the Samples, String Cheese Incident, and Big Head Todd & the Monsters. The list of long-running local bands is not much deeper.

However, I can cite major developments in Colorado music from my own experience. When we first started playing, there weren't many roofs for an "original" band to play under. The accepted notion was that if you were from Denver, you played covers. Everyone told us that we needed to move to New York or Los Angeles—to a "music town"—if we wanted to make it big.

Yet, as we performed around the country, I found that the "music towns" were not so musical after all. Of course, no one in the band ever found a good reason to leave Colorado. And, as it happened, we made it big anyway.

Which brings me to a point worth considering. It is always worth building your culture where you are—to be yourself. There are few things more valuable to a society than "folk culture." Always regional and personal, it grows out of artists having the courage to be individuals and reaching out to the neighbors. Folk culture is about making the apartment floor shake, so to speak, and about people being brought together. It is about taking risks—enough of them to get lucky. Every great movement in art has its origins in a supernatural or superfunky folk event—a local breakthrough. This happens all the time, everywhere.

But especially in Colorado.

- Todd Park Mohr
Big Head Todd & the Monsters
February 2004

preface

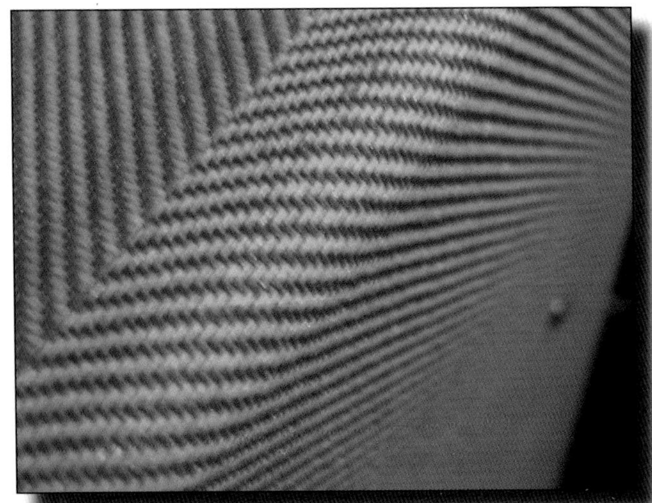

This book was born of two equal loves: my love for music and my love for Colorado.

Three decades ago, I was a young freelance music writer and Denver was still regarded as a cowtown nestled in the Rocky Mountains. It was a high-country retreat back then, an outpost of ski bums and nature lovers, oil tycoons, cowboys, and mountain men. It was the birthplace of Coors beer and home to a heck of a good rodeo. But on the national music radar screen, the city was but a blip that didn't reap the consideration of most Americans.

But all that has changed. *Colorado Rocks!* sketches the then-and-now picture of the Rocky Mountain region from my view—the window of music.

Questions arose continually about what to include and what to leave out. My original intention, in the name of historical completeness, was to tender an entry for every Colorado act that left behind a material document of its existence—i.e., at least one record for a nationally distributed label—and for the most important groups and players from other states and countries who certified Colorado's reputation as a music mecca.

This, however, was simply not enough. Therefore, *Colorado Rocks!* is a little more subjective than that. Hey, it's my book. For the sake of condensing, I mention many bands and musicians not under their own headings but as part of the commentary on more well-known entities to which they related in some way.

To cover the satellite factors to Colorado music—radio stations, halls and nightclubs, studios, and so on would have meant for an overly long, ungainly, weakly concentrated tome. Given enough perseverance and a voluntary publisher, a future book on the various persons and entities who provided the foundations of the general rock culture—those who interfaced between the musicians and the public—might fill out the picture. But first, I need a nap.

Most of the quotations in the various entries are words said directly to me, in conversations and interviews, over the course of twenty-six years of reporting for *The Denver Post*. All the writers and photographers represented here who offered the reality of the music in their own way have contributed greatly to the legacy of Colorado music.

More specifically, to all the people who listen, talk, and think about music every day and drive the scene—my everlasting thanks.

- G. Brown

Introduction

G. Brown walked into my office at *The Denver Post* in 1977, armed with a couple of record reviews and an attitude. "I can write better than your rock writer," he said. I was so taken with his confidence that I took a chance and assigned him a concert to cover, as a tryout.

Turned out, he was right; he could write better. And he knew a helluva lot more about more kinds of music than anyone who preceded him in the job. He appreciated that rock 'n' roll didn't arrive fully grown with Little Richard and Elvis, that Django Reinhardt, Slim Galliard, Louis Jordan, and dozens of others were there to lay the musical groundwork.

I hired him. Through rain and sleet and the dark of a rock 'n' roll night, G. covered everyone from Abba to ZZ Top in twenty-six years at the paper. He began as a college student and grew into an ooh-my-soul man.

Those years gave him a unique view of the rock world, particularly as it pertained to Colorado. He got to know everyone from the Who to who?, and his knowledge, background, and voluminous archives have come to fruition in this book, a look at five decades of popular music in Colorado.

Name any rock performers in the past thirty years and it's likely that G. crossed paths with them. In *Colorado Rocks!* he talks with Chuck Berry about the birth of the song "Sweet Little Sixteen." The reminiscences of rock's brightest lights frequently have a single undercurrent—Red Rocks Amphitheater, surely the premiere outdoor venue in the world. Brown and Bono recall the creation of U2's video at Red Rocks, perhaps the most famous and mystical rock video ever made.

In addition, there are home-grown talents who had a brief, shining moment and then faded back into Rocky Mountain obscurity. G. charts the sudden rise and tragic fall of Zephyr and its star-crossed young members. He knew and covered the Fluid and Christian rocker Steve Taylor, and he still enjoys a close personal relationship with Big Head Todd & the Monsters. He even retraces the strange journey of Coloradan Dean Reed, who, though virtually unknown in his homeland, became one of the brightest stars in music behind the Iron Curtain.

Brown demonstrates that, despite being isolated from "big-city" music markets, Colorado has an allure that draws megastars. It is illuminating to see how Stephen Stills views his days living near Ward, the isolated mountain town west of Boulder, and how those who remember him there recall that it wasn't always rock 'n' roll heaven.

G. and I have spent many memorable nights lost in the music—Dr. Hook at Ebbets Field, Joe Cocker at Mammoth Gardens, and Dan Hicks at Tulagi. And there was that special evening we ended up in the Boulderado Hotel room of two-thirds of the Roches. There was no rock-star orgy, just a night of chitchat so spellbinding that G. was inspired to give one of the girls his lucky softball ring. His diamond career quickly went downhill.

Ultimately, *Colorado Rocks!* is about the music. As the late Sam McFadin, G.'s close friend and shades-wearing front man for Flash Cadillac, the Fifties-style rockers, said, "What we're trying to get across is that there's a type of music—good-time, high energy—that has existed throughout rock 'n' roll history. Rather than being nostalgic about it, saying it's all coming around again, we just consider it to be all we know how to do. There are people who keep this kind of music alive."

Hail, hail.

- Dick Kreck
The Denver Post
February 2004

Dick Kreck

CHUCK BERRY

As a songwriter, Chuck Berry stood head and shoulders above all the stars of rock 'n' roll's early days. The majority of his output was self-penned, and during the second half of the 1950s he added new hits to his repertoire with almost every tour— compositions that gave rock 'n' roll a good deal of its language and style.

Several tunes were written from true-life experiences. "Sweet Little Sixteen," Berry's highest-ranking hit of the decade, was inspired after a Denver concert.

"I wasn't sweet little sixteen when I wrote it, of course," Berry said.

Berry had embarked on impressario Irving Feld's "Greatest Show of 1957" package tour, with Fats Domino, Clyde McPhatter, the Five Satins, LaVern Baker, and others. The event went through every region of the United States, including some— such as the northern Rocky Mountain states—that had never witnessed live rock 'n' roll.

"I happened to open the show this particular date at the Denver Coliseum, and while the other acts were performing, I walked around and signed autographs," Berry said.

"I noticed that there was this little girl wearing a big, flowery yellow dress running around and around the oval-shaped auditorium. I passed her six or seven times—she was searching for autographs a mile a minute, waving her wallet high in her hand.

"She never saw one complete act fully, and she didn't seem to care about who was on—she only cared about when they came off so she could get her autographs. And this made me think that she wanted things to remember."

Berry never got around to speaking with the girl, but he couldn't get her off his mind. He produced a great song about the teens who were buying rock 'n' roll, a celebration of everything beautiful about fandom.

"I wish I could have gotten her name. I was writing as I was looking at this kid, and I got several lines of 'Sweet Little Sixteen' that night."

Chuck Berry's "Sweet Little Sixteen," with pianist Johnny Johnson rocking at top form, sold more than one million copies. It reached No. 2 on *Billboard*'s pop charts and topped the R&B chart for three weeks.

DEAN REED

He never attained eminence in America. Even in Colorado, where he was born and raised, he was a virtual unknown.

But in the Soviet Union and other Communist bloc countries, Dean Reed was a superstar entertainer, bigger than Elvis Presley—so famous, shops sold his image alongside that of Joseph Stalin.

Reed graduated from Wheat Ridge High School in 1956. He briefly studied meteorology at the University of Colorado in Boulder and was known for his local performances. He dropped out and, thinking positively, decided to become a guitar-slinging folk hero. Capitol Records was fishing for fresh talent and signed him to a recording contract in 1958.

Reed made a few marginally successful folk-pop singles—"The Search" reached No. 96 on *Billboard*'s Hot 100 in March 1959—and he boasted a Colorado fan club of 6,000. By 1960, the good-looking innocent had gone to Hollywood for a screen test.

He played some bit parts in television and movies, but he was impatient with his lack of wealth, position, and fame. He heard that his song "Our Summer Romance" had hit the top of the charts in Chile and Argentina. He took off for South America in 1962, and his boyish, blue-eyed looks made him a teen idol.

But Reed was falling in love with leftist politics, and he became converted to the international peace movement. He traveled with his guitar and cast himself as a political good guy, picketing embassies and singing for the workers, who bought the slogans he stitched in between the songs.

The head of Komsomol, the Soviet youth organization, stumbled upon Reed. Komsomol was looking for something that could stop the mass defection of young Communists to the decadent music of the West. Melodiya, the state recording company, had never before released a rock 'n' roll record, but the handsome, honey-voiced Reed got a recording contract.

Hits in the Soviet Union followed—his signature tune was "Ghost Riders in the Sky"—and his albums sold in the hundreds of thousands across the Eastern bloc. The first Dean Reed tour of the Soviet Union in 1966 was like Beatlemania. His voice was light and he couldn't play the guitar very well, but the American singer electrified the Soviet kids, singing show tunes, wearing silky clothes, moving like a star. One of his concerts drew 60,000 fans.

The propaganda stories said that Reed was a sensation in his native land but that he had been brutally rejected for his politics. Dubbed "the Red Elvis," he was the only American to receive the Lenin Prize for art.

Reed played the global radical circuit, becoming friends with Salvador Allende in Chile and meeting with Daniel Ortega in Nicaragua, and he was frequently pictured in freedom-fighter mode.

ICIEMBRE

(Se confecciona con las opiniones
ue, por carta, llegan cada semana a
Ecran".)

	Votos
1.º DEAN REED	29.330
2.º ELVIS PRESLEY	20.805
3.º PAUL ANKA	17.548
4.º RAY CHARLES	7.260
5.º NEIL SEDAKA	4.800
6.º DION	3.220
7.º BRENDA LEE	3.21
8.º DANNY CHILEAN	2.90
9.º FABIAN	2.62
10.º FRANK SINATRA	2.57
11.º LARRY WILSON	2.38
12.º CHUBBY CHECKER	2.37
13.º EVERLY BROTHERS	2.07
14.º PAT BOONE	2.06
15.º PAT HENRY	1.98
16.º LORENZO VALDERRAMA ..	1.97
17.º CLIFF RICHARD Y CONNIE FRANCIS	1.43

A 1962 South American Hit Parade poll showed Reed trouncing Elvis Presley, 29,330 votes to 20,805.

The entertainer settled in East Berlin and was adored throughout the 1970s. He was mobbed when he appeared in public. He began making movies and starred in dozens of foreign-language spaghetti westerns. *Sing Cowboy Sing* was seen by a million East Germans.

But Reed missed his friends in Colorado. He wrote them long tracts about how the Communist system would improve people's lives. "Yet we lack certain things in East Germany—hamburgers, for example," he joked wistfully.

The Communist world changed in the 1980s, and Reed's time passed. In the age of glasnost, he was no more than a curiosity from the Cold War. He had kept his U.S. passport and remained an American citizen. In the fall of 1985, he returned to the United States for the Denver International Film Festival's showing of *American Rebel*, an American-produced documentary of his life.

It wasn't 1962 anymore. Rural Wheat Ridge had been eaten by Denver's urban sprawl. "The only buildings I recognize are those I've seen on 'Dynasty,'" he said.

Mike Wallace interviewed Reed in East Berlin for "60 Minutes." Reed thought it would be his ticket back to America, but he made a mistake by defending the Berlin Wall. His long-standing sympathies left him reviled by many in his home country.

In June 1986, the forty-seven-year-old Reed's story came to a mysterious end. He was found dead in an East German lake near his home. Accidental death by drowning was the official verdict. Reed's daughter later alleged that East German agents had killed him. His mother moved his remains to Green Mountain Cemetery in Boulder.

Reed liked telling the story of crooning "Ghost Riders in the Sky" for a grinning Palestinian Liberation Organization chief Yasser Arafat in Lebanon. 'His men danced around the table, their guns aloft. I said, 'Yasser, I always include "My Yiddish Momma" in my repertoire.' He said, 'That's okay, Dean—I have nothing against the Jewish people.'"

GARY STITES

Signed to the Carlton label, Denver-born-and-bred Gary Stites had a big hit in April 1959 when "Lonely For You" peaked at No. 24 on the *Billboard* singles chart.

"I grew up in Wheat Ridge, where my father owned a Gulf service station," Stites said. "He always wanted me to go into the business, but I hated working on cars, getting my hands dirty. I found that I could make more money playing music than I could in a real job."

When he turned fifteen, Stites got his start with the Rocking Rhythm Kings.

"Elvis Presley and Carl Perkins were starting to hit, and the rockabilly 'Blue Suede Shoes' sound was coming out. We played on a second-floor ledge at the Grubstake Saloon in Central City, which is now a casino. Every time we'd play a song, we'd ring a cowbell and drop a bucket with a rope on it down to the floor, and people would put quarter tips in.

"There was only one other rock 'n' roll band in Denver at the time, Del Toro & the Rockers. They were Mexican and had their own following on the east side of town. So I ran into some of the guys and we formed Gary Stites & the Satellites. The group took off like a rocket. We got bookings four, five months ahead. We played a lot of teen dances, sock hops, Elks Clubs, 3.2 beer joints.

"Because things got to poppin' so much with the band, I quit school in the eleventh grade. Stupid me—I was making money and said, 'Hell, I don't need an education, I'll just be a rebel on the road.'"

Stites met the program director at KIMN radio, the AM giant in Denver and friend of every teenager in town. The director said, "I really think you could get a contract to go national. You come down to the studio tonight." He then made a call to Joe Carlton in New York.

Carlton had been head of RCA Records' old guard A&R men, who hated rock 'n' roll and believed that they would wake up one morning and find that Elvis Presley had been a bad dream. But Carlton was dismissed, and he subsequently started Carlton Records. He no doubt thought, who could be his Elvis?

"I sang a song for him over the phone," Stites said. "It was on a Friday. He said, 'Can you be in New York by Monday?' I said, 'I certainly can.' They didn't want the band. I was eighteen years old, with my high-rising pants and white socks—I didn't know anything about the big time."

At that point, the song was called "The Diary of Love."

"Carlton told me, 'I love the song, but I don't like the title. I want you to change the lyrics.' If you listen to 'Lonely For You' real close, in the last half I say something about 'Help me write chapter four.' Well, when I was in the studio doing it, I got the lyrics on 'Diary of Love' and 'Lonely For You' confused, and I ended up putting in, 'Help me write chapter four.'

"Everyone in the control room was going, 'What the hell ...?' But they liked the way it came out and said they'd better not redo it because I had strep throat and my tonsils were swollen completely out of my head. They said, 'We'll just keep it; nobody will ever notice.'"

Stites' "Lonely For You" had the same gradually scaled lyrics that Conway Twitty had made famous with "It's Only Make Believe." He sang the song on *The Dick Clark Show*, the Saturday night extension of *American Bandstand* televised from New York.

"'Lonely For You' sold, but there was also a lot of hype—this was in the days of payola, whereby record companies won plugs and influenced disc jockeys. You could get an awful lot done."

Stites followed with several minor hits—"A Girl Like You" (No. 80, July 1959), "Starry Eyed" (No. 77, November 1959), and a cover of Lloyd Price's rhythm & blues classic "Lawdy Miss Clawdy" (No. 47, February 1960). He toured everywhere. But he could never build on the success of "Lonely For You."

"My brief little existence in the record business was not major by any sense of the word. But for a kid who grew up lower-middle-class, I thought I had the world by the tail until the bottom fell out—I went from $40,000 to $50,000 a year down to absolutely nothing. I wasn't smart enough. I didn't have people around me saying, 'You've got to put it away; you're going to want to do something else one of these days.'

"When you're a has-been at twenty years old, that's pretty hard to take."

Stites wasn't heard from again until his 1992 cassette "The Old Racetracker," recorded under the singular name Cloud and saluting his first love—horse racing.

JUDY COLLINS

Judy Collins is inextricably linked to the rise in the populist song movement that first swept the music scene during the 1960s. The world-famous folksinger claims Colorado as her home state. In 1949, her family moved to Denver from Seattle, where her discovery of folk music at age fifteen set her on a path that brought international fame.

Her early years in music gave her a taste for variety. At the age of ten, she began the study of classical piano with Dr. Antonia Brico, a woman teacher and conductor who had studied music with Sibelius and visited Albert Schweitzer every summer. Collins' father was a singer, composer, and broadcasting personality in Denver during the golden days of radio, and she appeared as a youngster on his KOA radio program, *Chuck Collins Calling*. Later, she became involved and influenced by the music of Woody Guthrie and Pete Seeger, and by the music of her ancestors in the ballads of England and Scotland.

By that time, Collins had traded the classical piano for a secondhand guitar, a gift from her father. A Denver East High School student, she started her singing career in the late 1950s, performing folk songs at clubs in Denver and various mountain bistros. Even at the age of nineteen, Collins had the special gift of turning folk songs into art songs.

"By the time I was discovered to be a folksinger, I already had a trail of Mozart, Cole Porter, and Frank Sinatra," she said.

"I'd never heard of folk music until listening to Jo Stafford and the Kingston Trio and Harry Belafonte sing it on the radio in '57. But I really got interested through Lingo the Drifter," a mysterious Denver character who had a folk music radio show in the mid-1950s.

On the night of March 2, 1959, Collins walked into Michael's Pub, a Boulder hangout where all the college students went to eat pizza and guzzle gallons of "horse-piss," which is what they called the 3.2 percent beer you had to drink in Colorado if you were under twenty-one. At Michael's, you could sometimes hear a barbershop quartet or one of the pop acts from Denver, but never a folksinger.

"I was with my guitar case, my hair cut short in a pixie. The room was filled with a noisy crowd, half of them a little drunk. The microphone sputtered and coughed, gave a

Judy Collins' piano debut, with the Denver Businessmen's Orchestra conducted by Dr. Antonia Brico, on February 19, 1953

high-pitched squeal. I climbed up onto the partially raised platform that served as a stage. There was some sparse clapping. I sat down on a chair, my guitar in my lap, and waited. The smoke rose from the dark, and lights were dim. Slowly people put down their beer glasses and looked at me. I looked out at them. It was a mutual dare—they dared me to show them what I could do, and I dared them to give me a chance.

"I sang everything I knew. When I finished singing, they started clapping and calling for more as soon as I stood up."

The folk craze, as it was named, was an entertainment distraction that caught America's fancy. In coffeehouses, folk music displaced the experimental arts of the 1950s. Teenagers congregated and sang along with and harmonized to intelligent lyrics. They behaved in a civilized manner and searched for an equitable link between music and the past.

In Denver, the place to play was the Exodus, the focal point for local beats, artists and poets and a sprinkling of button-down college kids. Denver's trendies gravitated there for art shows, poetry readings, and folk sessions.

"There was a dissatisfaction with popular music," she said. "People wanted to hear a story and a lyric they could understand. There was a throwing-off of all show business glitter. It was very important for people to get down to the idea of just a person with an instrument talking about issues or telling his or her own story."

With a voice that could electrify audiences with its crystal purity and wide range, it was not too long a step from Denver folk clubs to a record contract to major concerts.

A subsequent move to New York's Greenwich Village propelled Collins to international stardom. On her first albums in the early 1960s, she stayed mainly with clear-voiced readings of traditional material, as well as a sprinkling of folk-oriented writers (such as Tom Paxton, Eric Andersen, and Richard Farina).

But Collins began to make a transition, singing more and more of the music of her contemporaries, the young urban singer/composers whom she had been meeting in Greenwich Village since she had moved to New York from Denver. She was often the artist who was first to recognize the talent of new composers and introduce them to their audiences—Leonard Cohen ("Suzanne"), Randy Newman ("I Think It's Going To Rain Today"), and Joni Mitchell ("Both Sides Now" and "Chelsea Morning").

And she became the foremost American interpreter of the emotionally and musically expressive composer, Jacques Brel. In addition, Collins slowly began to write her own songs. The 1960s closed with her scoring a hit single in the Ian Tyson–written "Someday Soon," and the 1970s found her enjoying additional hits such as Stephen Sondheim's "Send in the Clowns" and a popular remake of the classic hymn "Amazing Grace."

Today, Collins ranks with the very few artists who can be said to have attained world stature, with a body of work to her credit of both commercial impact and artistic importance. Her reputation secure, she continues to explore and deepen her talents.

"I'm in Colorado from time to time, but I don't ever spend enough time in the place that's really important to me. I think Colorado is a metaphor for special, almost mythological places where we feel safe."

TOMMY FACENDA

In 1959, Tommy Facenda made the national charts with one of the most unusual—and difficult—novelty discs of all time.

Atlantic Records released "High School U.S.A." in twenty-eight local versions across America, each mentioning the names of specific major high schools in a particular city. Facenda, who hailed from Virginia, sang the verse over each time in the studio to add the name changes.

The effort picked up grassroots appeal, as kids in all the major markets listened to Facenda singing about their schools. The Denver version crammed in fifteen high school names. It referred to "Fort Morgan leadin' the band/Denver High was clappin' their hand/Englewood was doin' the crawl/Alamosa was havin' a ball/Walsenburg was hoppin', too/Well, I wanna do the high school bop with you …"

"I remember looking up the schools in the New York library," Facenda said. "I did most of the research, because I was the one that had to sing it. I had to put them to a rhyme and a beat in the song. It was a nightmare!"

Each regional version of "High School U.S.A." by Facenda was released on Atlantic with its own individual record number, from 51 to 78. The Denver single was Atlantic 77.

"On tour, I often got confused what version to sing in the town I was going to at the time. Back then we didn't have what were called concerts. We did rock 'n' roll shows—there might have been twenty of us on one tour package, and we all traveled together on a bus. Everybody else could just sing their same hit recordings all the time. While they were sleeping, I'd have a little penlight to study the upcoming town's high school name list."

"High School U.S.A." peaked at No. 28 on the pop chart.

"I was real fortunate and lucky because it was just the idea of the song—it sure wasn't me," Facenda said. "Anybody could have made it a hit."

THE NEW CHRISTY MINSTRELS

Before the Beatles emerged as pop's dominant power, Denver was a bastion of slick, commercial folk-pop, the soul and inspiration for groups like the New Christy Minstrels.

Randy Sparks founded the New Christy Minstrels in 1961. The large commercial folk group was unlike any group on the folk scene back then, starting out as a fourteen-member ensemble of singers and instrumentalists. Named after Edwin P. Christy's minstrel troupe of the 1800s (who introduced many Stephen Foster songs), the New Christy Minstrels were a barrage of color-coordinated blazers, starched petticoats, choreographed grins, and stage makeup.

Their success was immediate. Lined up across the stage, the group was a spectrum of ten colorful personalities. The arrangements creatively spotlighted the players in various "step outs" as duos, trios, and soloists.

"Everybody sang. Everybody played," the Kansas-born founder of the folk group said. It was an idea many inside and outside the group thought was crazy.

They were successful because their big sound was refreshing at the time and because members contributed original material. Their Top 40 hits were "Green Green," "Saturday Night," and "Today."

"They loved us. They played everything that I put out. My phone rang constantly —'Will you come to Denver?' The Back Porch Majority (a sort of farm club for the group) was huge there. I was really the man there. I put the Back Porch Majority in Taylor's Supper Club. It was a love affair."

"Denver" was bubbling under the *Billboard* Hot 100 in March 1963 at No. 127. But it was No. 1 on Denver's KIMN radio station for three weeks.

"It was one of our first records, and it immediately became a big hit in Denver.

"I say that in my shows—'I could write a song about Modesto.' I have done awfully well with geographical material—'Saturday Night in Toledo.'"

"Denver" was the first single from the New Christy Minstrels' second album, *In Person*, recorded live at the Troubadour in Los Angeles circa September 1962. "The people in the East Coast folk music hierarchy set the rules. If you did not follow what they said, you could not break into the business, according to what they said. So people sang all of the Woody Guthrie songs, anything that came out of *Sing-Out*, and they were instant hits because they were playing the game. Nobody wanted to hear anything from a writer.

Less than one year after debuting on the Troubadour stage in Los Angeles, the New Christy Minstrels had a Grammy to their credit.

"I started the New Christy Minstrels because it was a writing assignment.

"I was successful as a solo performer here and there with some of the greatest breaks you can imagine. But I couldn't get anywhere and save any money. I realized that writing was one of my long suits, but I could only record fifteen to twenty songs a year on Verve Records, so I needed another vehicle."

Sparks successfully used "Old Rosin the Beau" for his song "Denver."

"It probably came out of the music halls of Ireland or England. It's part of our heritage. We all own it together.

"If you did not have music that was old, nobody wanted to hear it in the folk tradition. If you wrote a new song, people were suspect of what you were doing and they rejected it out of hand. Very few new songs made it in.

"I looked at it very logically. Okay, we'll play a little game with them. I'll snag a public domain melody. People know they've heard it before, so they'll accept it. And I'll put new words to it and I won't violate any tradition. I'll make it chronologically correct.

"At the time, the No. 1 song in the country was 'Kansas City.' I said, that's neat, you can write a song about any location and it becomes successful there, and if you're good enough with it, it'll spread. I started looking at the map for places I could write about.

"It was an instant thing: 'Driving a rig out of Texas, full loaded and bound for Cheyenne.' I couldn't violate the timeline—it had to be as possible in 1880 as it was in 1960. And it worked.

"It was a good, up-tempo song, with Barry McGuire doing the 'Yeah!'s. It was a smash, but only in a few places."

The group radiated a contagious spirit that charmed their audience and the show-biz press alike. Andy Williams booked the group for his television show throughout the 1962–1963 season, and in 1964, the group hosted its own summer television show.

The New Christy Minstrels provided an early training ground for Kenny Rogers & the First Edition, some members of the Association, actress Karen Black, future Byrd Gene Clark, Barry McGuire, and Kim Carnes, as well as John Denver.

"I was the one who changed his name, and he fought it all the way," Sparks said. "He wasn't named after the city, or after his love for the Rocky Mountains. He was named after my song 'Denver.'

"This corny new kid named Little Johnny Deutschendorf came into my place. I said, 'I don't have room to put that on my marquee.' He said, 'Well, I'm not changing my name—I love my father, and he'd be really disappointed in me if I did.' I said, 'You'd better get used to it, because you can't market yourself with the name Little Johnny Deutschendorf.' You had to have a handle that people could spell and pronounce. I said, 'I'll give you a job beginning this weekend, but I need another name from you.' I gave him three days to think of one.

"Mike Crowley, a Back Porch Majority man, said to John, 'Let me give you a piece of advice that worked for me—if you keep the same initials, you won't have to buy new luggage.' So we were all looking for a name beginning with 'D.' 'Denver' was the first song I had sheet music done for. I had a piece of it above my desk. I looked up and said, 'What about John Denver?' He said, 'No, it's too close to Bob Denver' (known to many as the title character on television's *Gilligan's Island*; he also played beatnik Maynard G. Krebs on *The Many Loves Of Dobie Gillis* from 1959 to 1963). I said, 'Young man, if you play your cards right, nobody will remember Bob Denver.' And that's the way it worked out."

Sparks spent the next three decades with folk icon Burl Ives, as well as having his hands in a variety of businesses both in and out of the entertainment arena.

THE SERENDIPITY SINGERS

When Peter, Paul & Mary's 1963 recording of Bob Dylan's "Blowin' in the Wind" became an unofficial civil rights anthem, the identification of the folkies with the politics of progress was cemented. Though the music industry continued trying to capitalize on the folk boom, the music's implicit and explicit politics made many major corporations nervous, and a lot of effort went into developing purveyors of sanitized folk pop like the Serendipity Singers and the New Christy Minstrels.

"It was a period when the commercial folk music scene happened," Bryan Sennett of the Serendipity Singers said. "Folk music, of course, had been around forever. It still is. But that was the big commercial era for it."

The Serendipity Singers, a large folk-pop group organized at the University of Colorado, created a unique sound with the use of several guitars, banjos, bass fiddles, and drums. Virtually everyone in the group also sang.

"Ours was a conglomeration of different people who had worked in the Boulder area in different forms—duos and trios. We put several of us together. We should have done it earlier," Sennett said.

"The last group from Boulder was called the Newport Singers. I had signed the act with William Morris while we were still in Colorado. Seven of us borrowed $1,500 and we took it all to New York in the summer of '63 and added two more people, a duo that had been working out of Texas—a guy and a girl—we needed some highs in the sound.

"We changed our name and that's where we got started. We spent a lot of time at the Bitter End the first two months with a musical director. We were there night and day. It was my last go-round, by that time. I thought, if something doesn't happen, I'm going to law school."

The members of the Serendipity Singers were Sennett, H. Brooks Hatch, Lynne Weintraub, John Madden, Jon Arbenz, Robert Young, Michael Brovsky, Dianne Decker, and Thomas E. Tiemann.

Signed to the Philips label, the group reached the national Top 10 with "Don't Let the Rain Come Down (Crooked Little Man)"—No. 6 in February 1964, written by Ersel Hickey of "Bluebirds Over the Mountain" fame.

"Before that, it had been a traditional English nursery rhyme. We played with it and added things."

They followed with another major hit called "Beans in My Ears"— No. 30 in June 1964.

"It was banned in Boston, which always seemed to be the first place to take it off. Some television shows asked us to do something different. Understandably so—it was dangerous, trying to do that if you took it literally. Obviously, it was a statement about adults not listening to children," Sennett said.

"We did a bigger variety of music. The folk center was there, but we were doing Broadway things. We were trying to do a different sound. We mixed it up a lot. We were fortunate that we had a very visual act, a lot of talk, and blackouts along with it—everybody had some theater background.

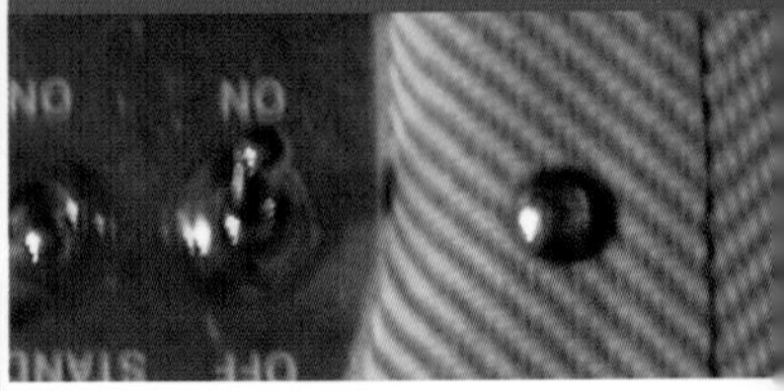

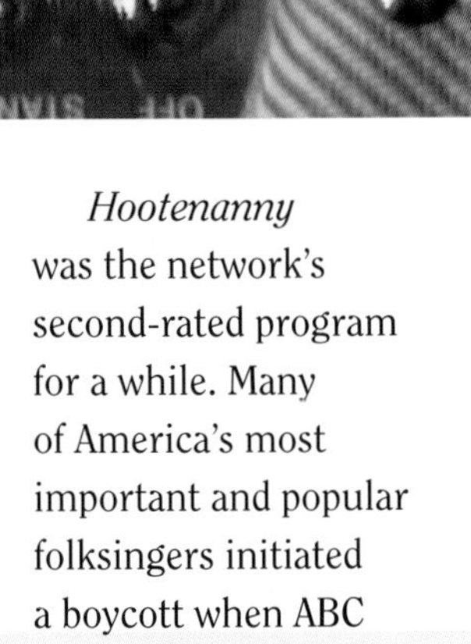

Hootenanny was the network's second-rated program for a while. Many of America's most important and popular folksingers initiated a boycott when ABC announced that it would not allow performers associated with "radical causes" to appear on its program.

"The main thing was instrumentation. People had all done different things—classical, jazz—and they brought all that together. A lot of times, folk music was new to a lot of people. When they first heard it, they would say, 'You're country & western!' The background of that music was interesting, and we did a lot of adaptation and arrangements of traditional things, to the point of not being recognizable sometimes."

Folk music made its television debut in the summer of 1963, when ABC-TV unveiled its weekly *Hootenanny* show. Each segment was taped at a different college campus, the audience consisting of students. Shows ran for a half-hour on Saturday night and featured four acts. The producers signed the Serendipity Singers and the New Christy Minstrels to alternate each week as the headline act.

"The whole college concert business grew up around folk music, where you sat there and listened, and *Hootenanny* helped that explode. It was a more rustic form of music, but it became more show business. It was a hard thing to do a remote from some college facility—technology wasn't as great, and there would be mishaps. But it was right in the thick of when folk music was popular. We were real fortunate to be on it."

By 1964, with the Beatles bringing rock 'n' roll back to America, folk music began to lose its popularity. By September, *Hootenanny* was history, after which the Serendipity Singers remained popular largely as a concert attraction.

"There wasn't just *Hootenanny*. There was a huge amount of variety television, and that was a big, big boost, especially if you were fortunate enough to get started. We did a lot of television, playing to millions—*The Bell Telephone Hour*, *The Ed Sullivan Show*, *The Andy Williams Show*, *The Dean Martin Show*. After *Hootenanny*, the network rock shows like *Shindig!* and *Hullabaloo* would play some folk music.

"We were pretty active politically. We did barbeques all over the country with young Democrats in '64 when Johnson ran against Goldwater. Hey, it was the 1960s."

Albums were *The Serendipity Singers* (No. 11 in March 1964), *The Many Sides of the Serendipity Singers* (No. 68 in June 1964), and *Take Off Your Shoes with the Serendipity Singers* (No. 149 in January 1965).

THE ASTRONAUTS

In the early 1960s, most surf bands were big California concert acts. But the Astronauts caught the sun, sand, and summer fun from Boulder, Colorado—a remarkable feat in that they were 1,000 miles away from the nearest ocean.

The Astronauts originally formed in 1960 as a trio, the Stormtroupers (named after bassist Stormy Patterson). Concern over the name's fascist connotations from Boulder's Jewish community necessitated a change. The guys opted for the Astronauts in honor of Boulder astronaut Scott Carpenter.

The Astronauts—Rich Fifield, Dennis Lindsey, and Bob Demmon on guitars, Patterson, and drummer Jim Gallagher (Fifield was the only member who hadn't graduated from Boulder High)—played to pre-hippie crowds around the University of Colorado campus circa 1962.

"We bought matching amplifiers and guitars, wore tuxedos and patent-leather shoes," Fifield said. "We did that whole pre-Beatles bit."

At the time, RCA Records was looking for an act to compete with Capitol Records' enormously successful Beach Boys, a West Coast surfing group scoring big on the national charts with songs like "Surfin' Safari." Even though they had never played surf music (or even surfed, for that matter), the landlocked Astronauts wound up with a long-term recording contract.

Amazingly enough, the ruse actually worked for a while.

"It was the strangest marketing scheme I'd ever heard of, and I've heard of a lot," Gallagher confessed.

The liner notes from the group's first album, *Surfin' with the Astronauts*, released in May 1963, explained it this way: "Fact is, they call themselves the Astronauts because they are the HIGHEST surfing group in the United States. And we mean like their home base is Boulder, Colorado, way up in the Rockies, just around the corner from the Air Force Academy and real live astronauts."

The Astronauts were the first Boulder band to make *Billboard*'s national charts—*Surfin' with the Astronauts* rose to a respectable No. 61. The album included "Baja," penned by Lee Hazelwood (better known as the writer of Nancy Sinatra's big hits). The single—a typical surf instrumental with a reverberation-heavy twangy guitar and driving drumbeat—occupied No. 94 on *Billboard*'s Hot 100 for one week in the summer of 1963.

On Denver radio, however, "Baja" reached No. 1 and earned the group a much bigger regional following. Like hundreds of other bands around the country, the Astronauts achieved a sort of working success, constantly touring a mind-numbing blur of colleges, gyms, and bars.

A local group of Astronauts devotees formed a fan club and petitioned to get the group on *The Ed Sullivan Show* to no avail. But the band appeared on television's *Hullabaloo* several times and also had cameo roles in the forgettable teen movies *Wild on the Beach* (also featuring Sonny & Cher), *Wild Wild Winter*, *Out Of Sight*, and *Surf Party*.

Unfortunately, the group could never build on the initial American chart success. Subsequent albums like *Competition Coupe* found the Astronauts trying on other styles like hot-rod songs. What really doomed them as a recording act was the 1964 British invasion.

"I heard the Beatles' 'I Wanna Hold Your Hand' on the radio and thought, 'That's it, we've had it—maybe I'd better dig out that dental-school manual again,' " Gallagher recalled. "They were so good and I was so elated to hear what they were doing. I loved it; it was the sound we wanted to get. That's what made it so hard on us."

Ironically, the Astronauts enjoyed their greatest success overseas. In 1964, RCA discovered that the Japanese were mad for the band. They outsold the rival Beach Boys, and five albums and three singles made the Japanese Top 10. "Movin'," titled "Over the Sun" for the Japanese market, hit No. 1. Five fifty-foot billboard statues in their likeness were hoisted in Sapporo.

"When we went to Japan for two tours, it was earth-shattering," Gallagher said. "We'd played

Astronauts Orbit Kampus (1964) was recorded live at Boulder's famous Tulagi and featured a cover shot with a snowy Boulder in the background.

the Midwest and done pretty well, but nothing spectacular. *Surfin' with the Astronauts* came out here in 1963 but didn't break in Japan until later. We had no idea how popular we were over there, or why.

"Then when we arrived at the Tokyo airport, 8,000 screaming kids were there. We kept wondering who they were waiting for. Then we found out it was us.

"One morning we woke up early and decided to go look around outside our hotel. We were accustomed to going where we wanted to go. We got about eight blocks and realized that there were forty kids following us at six in the morning. Pretty soon we were pressed up against shop windows signing autographs."

The Astronauts' conquest of the Rockies and the Orient meant little to the rest of America. They had to kick off the sandals, put away the woodie, and play with long hair. Nobody cared.

There was a time in Las Vegas when the Astronauts were mistaken for real astronauts. Five black limos met them at the airport and they were shuttled into individual suites in a luxury hotel. The jig was up after someone from NASA called the hotel to say that, as far as the government was concerned, these Astronauts were UFOs.

The Astronauts continued touring through 1966, but immediately after recording their final album (1967's *Travelin' Men*), the draft struck. Gallagher and Lindsey couldn't get out of it, and both wound up serving in Vietnam.

"The week I got my draft notice, we had been on the road and netted about $1,400 each after expenses," Gallagher mused. "Then the next month in the service, I think I made $90. Talk about depressing."

Others came and went until Fifield was the last of the original members. After he changed the band's name to Sunshineward and then Hardwater, the Astronauts were no more. They only played sporadic reunion shows over the years.

The longest concert swing the Beatles ever undertook was their first American tour, a thirty-two-day visit. The sixth stop was a performance at Red Rocks Amphitheatre in Morrison, Colorado.

It was the only performance on the itinerary that didn't sell out. Only 7,000 fans turned out to see the Beatles' one show in the famed 9,000-capacity natural amphitheatre. At the time, the distance of Red Rocks from Denver, coupled with no public transportation, was blamed for the unsold tickets.

Nevertheless, Denver, like the rest of the country, succumbed to Beatlemania in a tidal wave of sheer exuberance. Two hundred and fifty Denver policemen and auxiliary recruits were briefed on "Beatle invasion" strategies.

On the morning of August 26, 1964, a crowd bearing "I Love the Beatles" signs, Beatles hats, and Beatles pins began to gather for the group's anticipated arrival at Stapleton Airport. By noon, nearly 10,000 had blanketed a fenced area on an adjoining boulevard. At 1:35 p.m., the Beatles' chartered 707 touched down from Los Angeles, and twenty-four hours of pandemonium ensued.

Huge numbers of teens also descended on Red Rocks Park and the venerable Brown Palace Hotel. At 10 a.m., an estimated 1,000 were camped around Red Rocks, listening to transistor radios. Weather predictions called for rain, and emergency plans were made to transfer the show to the Denver Coliseum if necessary.

Nearly 5,000 sobbing and fainting fans mobbed the sedate Brown Palace's front entrance. Six girls and one harried policeman (who had been bitten on the wrist) were taken to Denver General Hospital for treatment.

Unbeknownst to the Fab Four, the Red Rocks concert was used to test a new ordinance banning alcoholic beverages, cans, and bottles in the park. Two years earlier, rowdies had hurled beer cans at Ray Charles, and other incidents had followed. The ordinance was passed in the summer of 1963 after a Peter, Paul & Mary concert.

At 9:30 p.m., the Beatles took the stage, and the quartet was indeed pelted—with jelly beans (reportedly their favorite candy), not beer cans. The audience was boisterous, loud to the point of drowning out all the performers, but polite.

The altitude was the only factor that proved troublesome throughout the Beatles' thirty-five-minute performance. Halfway through the first song, they were out of breath.

"We were all told it was high above sea water, altitude. We thought, 'Well, so? What's the difference?' We got there, and we started finding it a little hard to breathe, because we weren't used to it," Paul McCartney said. "I remember singing 'Long Tall Sally' and thinking, 'Hey, this is great—hyperventilation of the highest order!' 'Well, Long Tall Sally, wheeze, wheeze …' I was sweating, but I got through it. It was an interesting experience, physically.

"It was a lovely arena—it looked beautiful at night."

After the show, John, Paul, George, and Ringo retired to Suite 840 at the Brown Palace and visited for a while with Joan Baez, who would appear at Red Rocks two nights later.

"Joan used to hang out with us a lot back then," drummer Ringo Starr later recalled. "She would go on the road with us for a few days at a time."

The predicted rain finally arrived as the Beatles headed for the airport the following day. An estimated 3,500 people waited at Stapleton. Shortly after noon, the plane took off for Cincinnati, where the group was to perform next.

Verne Byers, the promoter of the Beatles' appearance at Red Rocks, said he had never even heard of the group before the booking, noting that they used their bowl-shaped haircuts as a "gimmick" to separate themselves from similar acts that were touring that summer, such as Peter & Gordon and the Beach Boys.

At $6.60, general admission tickets for the Beatles' show at Red Rocks were nearly $3 more than ducats for a recent concert by Igor Stravinsky, who was considered the world's greatest living composer. The 100-minute show featured the Bill Black Combo, the Righteous Brothers, Jackie DeShannon, the Exciters, and then a half-hour set by the Beatles.

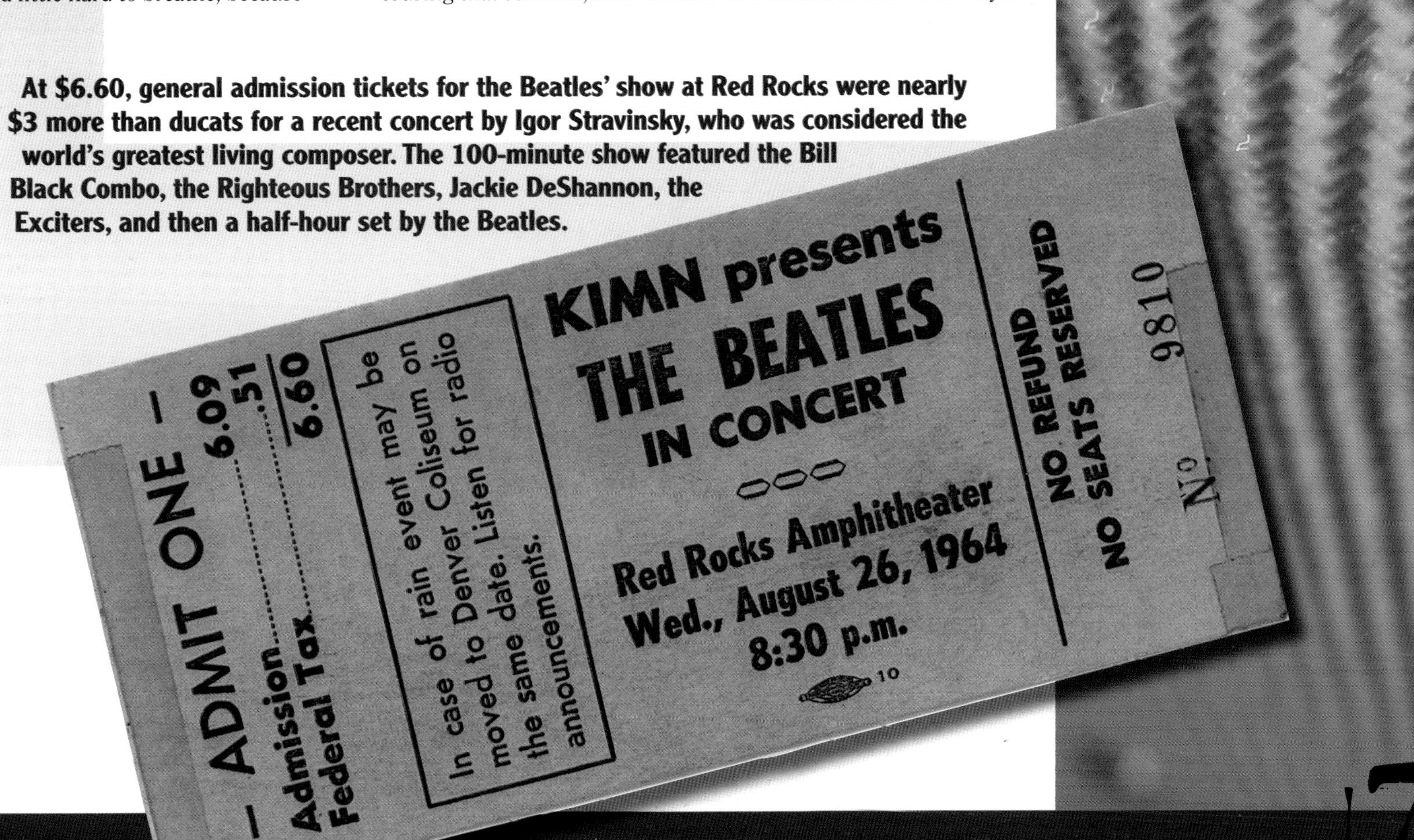

BOB LIND

Bob Lind was another Colorado "folkie" who found pop music success recording "Elusive Butterfly," a No. 5 national hit in March 1966.

While not a Colorado native, Lind called the state home. He graduated from high school in Aurora and attended Western State College in Gunnison. After three years of study, he flunked out and moved to Denver, where he became immersed in the folk music scene at clubs like the Exodus, the Analyst, and the Green Spider.

"It didn't last long—I'm talking about months. People think the folk boom of the early 1960s was an era like rock 'n' roll. It was really closer to the hula hoop—it just dried up," Lind said.

"But during that time, other strains of music were formed. There was a great split between ethnic or commercial. You either wore a striped shirt or you were funky .... There were people in Denver who would learn a Blind Lemon Jefferson song lick for lick from a record—nice Jewish kids singing black music. They did it well, but they frowned upon anybody applying any individuality to this music.

"And that's where it lost a lot of us. We wanted to express ourselves in these folk forms. So I began to write ...

"Here's my day in the summer of 1964. I'd get up at 10 a.m., put on a pot of coffee, take some uppers for some energy, sit down at the kitchen table with a pad of paper and a guitar, smoking cigarettes and drinking coffee, and write songs all day. At six, I'd fall into the shower, get something to eat, and then usually I'd have a gig or go listen to somebody else."

Late one night, Lind wrote a song called "Elusive Butterfly." It had vivid imagery and an extended, metaphoric narrative—"Don't be concerned/it will not harm you/it's only me pursuing something I'm not sure of/Across my dreams/With nets of wonder/I chase the bright elusive butterfly of love."

"There was a poem I loved by William Butler Yeats called 'The Wandering Aengus.' I wanted to write something that felt that way, that had the sense we feel of being alive most when we're searching or looking or chasing after something. That expectation is more life-affirming than getting the thing you're after. Other people call it the thrill of the hunt.

"It was originally five verses long, and I'd leave a lot of space in—it took ten minutes to play it. I played it for everybody I knew, but I didn't say, 'Man, this is my best song. It's going to be a hit. Millions of people are going to hear it.' It was just another song. I was thrilled by everything I wrote. I didn't know how crummy some of them were."

In the beginning of 1965, Lind left for San Francisco. The owner of the Analyst had made a tape of Lind and suggested he take it to record labels.

"The absolute first thing that happened, I took it to World Pacific (a jazz and international-oriented subsidiary of Liberty Records). The president of the label listened to it and they signed me. I said to myself, 'Gee, this is easy. That's all there is to it—you go to the record company and get a deal!' I had no idea that people struggled for years to get signed."

During the Christmas season of 1965, Lind's "Cheryl's Goin' Home" single had been out for about a month when a disc jockey at the Florida station WQAM flipped it over and flipped. Listeners did, too.

"Elusive Butterfly" became Lind's first and biggest hit, the kind of delicate song that until then had been thought to be too breathy, wispy, and lyrical to be commercial.

"It was my last choice as a single. I didn't have the slightest inkling of what would tickle the public's fancy."

Chart momentum was gone by the summer of 1966. Verve Records got hold of the acoustic demo tape Lind had made in his Denver days, overdubbed instruments, and released it as *The Elusive Bob Lind*. During the 1970s, Lind began easing out of the music business, concentrating on writing screenplays, novels, plays, and short stories.

THE RAINY DAZE

The Rainy Daze had a big Colorado-based hit of the 1960s—"That Acapulco Gold," an ode to marijuana crooned in Roaring '20s vaudeville style.

Started in 1963, the Rainy Daze played six nights a week at the Galaxy.

"We were a working band," lead singer Tim Gilbert said. "The idea wasn't to get rich and famous, although the availabililty of young women was way up on the list of reasons to do it. The whole idea was to play and make money, $350 to $500 a night.

"A band's identity was more determined by the covers you played than anything else. You had to play some Beatles, but we were more Stones, Yardbirds, Who, so people thought we were 'edgy.' We would periodically go into the studio and try to record an original song and become stars so that the pool of available women would grow!"

Originals were written by Gilbert and fellow Denver South High School student and lyricist John Carter.

"Everybody was going to the University of Colorado," Tim Gilbert said. "John was a roommate, a guy who hung around. It was a long time before I took him seriously. He has a great musical sense, but he can't carry a tune. When it became important to write original music, with people in Hollywood saying, 'If you're going to be anything, you've got to write your own music,' we looked at each other and said, 'Shit, who can do that?' John insinuated himself into that process. I had a micro-talent for writing melodies, and John was quite a talented lyricist."

In 1966, the Denver quintet—Gilbert, his brother Kip Gilbert (drums), Sam Fuller (bass), Bob Heckendorf (organ), and Mac Ferris (guitar)—issued "That Acapulco Gold" on the Chicory label.

"There was a song out at the time called 'Winchester Cathedral' (a No. 1 hit by the New Vaudeville Band, sung through a megaphone). A lot of what we did on 'Acapulco Gold' was reflective of that. It was 180 degrees from all the music we were playing."

The group was then signed to Uni, who distributed "That Acapulco Gold" nationally.

The song continued to dominate Denver radio in early 1967 and peaked at No. 70 on the *Billboard* pop singles charts. However, national sales and airplay were stymied once word got around about the song's real inspiration. The song was unceremoniously yanked from playlists.

According to Tim Gilbert, "KHJ was the 'boss' radio station in Los Angeles at that point. Every week, they'd print the Top 30 weekly survey. At one point, 'Acapulco Gold' was No. 1 with an asterisk next to it that said, 'Not suitable for airplay.'

"Radio stations didn't think it was inappropriate until Bill Gavin wrote in his tip sheet that if you played this record on the air, you did stand a chance of losing your license, because it did proselytize drug use. Which was fairly obvious …

"Carter and I found ourselves in Los Angeles in the spring of '67. I figured, hey, how often in your life are you going to have a record on the charts? I went back and got my degree later. We were sitting in a restaurant one day and George Carlin came up and shook our hands and said, 'You're the most courageous people in the United States.' There was a moment when we were at the head of the parade, all over this little song."

Tim Gilbert and partner Carter were asked to write a song for another Uni act. They scored a national No. 1 hit with "Incense and Peppermints" by the Strawberry Alarm Clock.

In the early 1970s, Spiro Agnew led a Nixon administration strike against rock lyrics. In a much-reported speech, he explained that "Puff the Magic Dragon" was code for marijuana and the "Friends" the Beatles were getting a little help from were illegal narcotics. His blacklist of twenty-two songs, compiled by a core of "concerned" generals of the Department of the Army, included "That Acapulco Gold."

"We had our fifteen minutes of fame," Tim Gilbert said. "It was a happy accident, or an unhappy accident. Ultimately, the song broke up the band. We got pigeonholed into that kind of a sound, and nobody wanted to play that music."

Carter went on to spend a dozen years as an artist and repertoire representative at Capitol Records, serving as a kind of staff producer and overseeing more than twenty albums, including hit records by Sammy Hagar, Bob Welch, and Tina Turner.

Rock promoter Barry Fey was one of the most influential people to emerge from the 1960s Colorado music scene. He moved to Denver from Illinois in early 1967 and, after a trip to San Francisco's Haight Ashbury district, contacted Chet Helms, manager of Janis Joplin's band, Big Brother & the Holding Company, to discuss bringing a bit of the scene to Denver. Joe Neddo of the band Böenzee Cryque informed Fey of a recently closed nightspot in Denver, a rectangular stucco building in an industrial stretch of Evans Avenue.

It became the Family Dog, named after the San Francisco collective that sponsored dances at the Fillmore and the Avalon Ballroom.

Fey became the local booking agent for the 2,500-seat concert hall, which opened on September 8, 1967, with a show featuring Joplin and Big Brother & the Holding Company and the heavy sounds of Blue Cheer. For ten glorious months, the Family Dog prospered, hosting an amazing roster of talent in its short life—the Grateful Dead, the Byrds, Buffalo Springfield, Van Morrison, Jefferson Airplane, Frank Zappa, Cream, and more.

Psychedelic images were hand-painted on the floor. Colorful posters and handbills prepared by San Francisco artists such as Rick Griffin, Stanley Mouse, and Alton Kelley were used to promote the shows. The most expensive ticket ever at the

venue, for the Doors on New Year's Eve 1967, cost $4.50.

But the club struggled to stay open, both financially and with mounting police pressure. The Denver police hated the idea of having a hippie club in their city and had done all they could to stop the Family Dog from opening. Helms and his people were subjected to a barrage of harassment and illegal searches.

It was Canned Heat's bad luck to show up on a Saturday night, October 21, 1967, just as the police figured they'd get one of the bands, and the bad press and legal troubles would carry over to Helms. Officers followed the band, a seminal influence on white urban blues, to a nearby motel at Santa Fe and Florida.

"I heard the story from the guys a hundred times," said drummer Fito De La Parra, who joined Canned Heat a few months later.

"The band didn't have any dope in Denver—everyone knew that things were tough there, so the guys showed up clean to play that gig. But the police dispatched a stool pigeon with some weed to the hotel to socialize and turn us on."

It turned out the stool pigeon was an old friend of Bob "The Bear" Hite, the band's singer.

According to Fito De La Parra, "Bear was raised in Denver before his family moved to Los Angeles, so he had made some friends there when he was a kid. So he trusted the guy, until he suddenly disappeared out the door and the cops came barging in to 'discover' a package of weed under the cushion of the chair where the 'friend' had been sitting. They busted everybody on charges of marijuana possession—still a big offense in those days. A judge wasn't available until Monday, so the band spent the weekend in the can.

"It was a terrible thing. To pay the price, the band had to sell its publishing."

The drama was immortalized in "My Crime," from the band's second album *Boogie With Canned Heat*:

> I went to Denver late last fall
> I went to do my job, I didn't break any law
> We worked in a hippie place
> Like many in our land
> They couldn't bust the place, and so they got the band
> 'Cause the police in Denver
> No they don't want long hairs hanging around
> And that's the reason why
> They want to tear Canned Heat's reputation down.

At the time of the Family Dog bust, Bob "The Bear" Hite said to a reporter, "To sing the blues, you have to be an outlaw. Blacks are born outlaws, but we white people have to work for that distinction."

The Family Dog began to falter when the club obtained an injunction forbidding police presence on its premises. Rather than benefitting the venue, news of the injunction resulted in diminishing patronage. After a short stint as the Dog, the club closed in July 1968. It enjoyed a much longer and successful run as a strip joint.

Paul Revere & the Raiders were a pop-rock group formed in Portland, Oregon, circa 1960 around Paul Revere (keyboards) and Mark Lindsay (lead singer).

"My good buddy, Drake Levin, was the guitar player for the Raiders," Phillip "Fang" Volk said. "We grew up together in Idaho and taught each other how to play guitar. We had a band in Boise that played at Paul Revere's teenage nightclub, called the Crazy Horse, in the summer of '63, after we graduated from high school."

From there, Revere hired Drake, and Volk attended college at the University of Colorado.

"I had a little fraternity band that played some of the parties," Volk said. "It was something we just threw together.

"A year and a half later, after Drake had been on the road with the Raiders and become a road warrior, he eventually talked Paul into hiring me for the band because we could do dance routines together. Paul had seen us at his club every weekend."

Volk replaced Mike "Doc" Holliday on bass. His toothy grin earned him the nickname "Fang."

"But they needed a bass player, and I was a guitar player. He called me in college and said, 'You'd better start learning the bass.' I wasn't very good at first ...

"I went right from the University of Colorado with my wing-tip Oxfords and my blue blazer and my grey slacks and short hair, looking like Joe College right out of the fraternity, to Las Vegas, Nevada, and joined Paul Revere & the Raiders at the Pussycat-A-Go-Go on the Strip. You talk about two different worlds colliding. It was an amazing metamorphosis.

"My fraternity brothers took me to the airplane and got me a little bit soused. They were sad to see me go, and you know how they like to drink. They almost didn't let me on the plane because I was a little bit nuts. In those days, you walked up a stairway off the tarmac to the airplane, and I jumped off that onto the wing, doing a little boogaloo. People didn't appreciate that ..."

Paul Revere & the Raiders went to Los Angeles in 1965 and got on a daily ABC-TV show called *Where the Action Is*.

"It ran five days a week for two years, which is a phenomenal thing for any band, to be in front of a national audience every day," Volk said.

"Even Columbia Records didn't realize the kind of popularity the show had given us. They said, 'Well, let's take the boys on a promotional tour, set up appearances at supermarkets and amusement parks.' They were shocked at the response. Every city we went to around the country, there were massive crowds gathered, riots. A couple of vehicles were destroyed when kids would jump on them trying to get a peek at us. They weren't ready for that."

Top 40 hits included "Just Like Me," "Kicks," "Hungry," "The Great Airplane Strike," "Good Thing," "Ups and Downs," and "Him or Me—What's It Gonna Be."

STEVE ALAIMO

Steve Alaimo was a purveyor of so-called "blue-eyed soul." His best-known hit, "Every Day I Have To Cry" (No. 46 in 1963), offered a good glimpse into the R&B rock style of the day.

Alaimo, who hailed from New York, eventually found his niche as a pop vocalist on Dick Clark's late-afternoon *Where the Action Is*, a popular show of the mid to late 1960s. It made stars of Paul Revere & the Raiders, the clean-cut house band, and younger teens could see "teen idols" like Alaimo, a regular on the show.

"Denver," written by Dan Penn & Spooner Oldham (who were responsible for the Box Tops' "Cry Like A Baby"), was a minor hit in March 1968. It made *Billboard*'s "Bubbling Under The Hot 100" charts, reaching No. 118.

"It was at the end of *Where the Action Is*—we did one of those big Dick Clark tours up in Colorado—and I met the woman that I ended up marrying later, in '71. Candy was going to Colorado Women's College. That's the reason I recorded 'Denver'," Alaimo later recalled. "Mark Lindsay of Paul Revere & the Raiders was my closest friend at the time, so I ended up naming my daughter Lindsey after him."

Ronnie Milsap's country version of "Denver" reached No. 123 on May 10, 1969.

Led Zeppelin took a calculated risk in leaving London to come to America in 1968. The band had no album out yet, response from the press in England was mild, and three of the group had never been to America before and didn't know what to expect.

But manager Peter Grant's strategy was simple—it was still worth the risk to go out and play, to see if they could create some excitement that might snowball into an avalanche. Grant had five years of experience in the United States with bands like the Yardbirds and the Animals. He felt he knew which American cities to make a part of that first tour, to maximize Zeppelin's exposure.

He saw an opportunity when the Jeff Beck Group, managed out of the same office, cancelled an American tour with Vanilla Fudge. He called the upset promoters and talked them into a new group.

"The agent said, 'Do you want to add another act, Led Zeppelin, for $1,500?'" Denver promoter Barry Fey recalled. "It was a sold-out show. I said, 'Why pay $1,500 for another act?' We settled on $500."

Then Grant had to convince the members of Led Zeppelin to leave their warm homes on Christmas Eve for parts unknown.

"I was twenty years old, and Christmas away from home for the English is the end of the world," singer Robert Plant later explained.

But Led Zeppelin packed their bags, ready to test America's waters. The band's flight from London departed for the Los Angeles airport on December 23. Plant was incredulous.

"L.A. was absolutely devastating for me," he said. "I was too young to go into any bars—not that that was the first thing I thought about. I had no idea what to expect—American TV in England was *Dragnet* or a U.S. cop thing. It was the first time I saw a twenty-foot-long car."

The morning after Christmas, Led Zeppelin headed back to LAX, boarding a TWA flight for Denver. That night they met up with their bass player, John Paul Jones, who had arrived on a separate flight from New Jersey, where he and his wife had spent the holidays.

They assembled downtown at the Auditorium Arena and began their first U.S. tour. Pacing nervously and biting their fingernails, Plant and drummer John Bonham tried to stay calm backstage.

"Colorado was so beautiful and gentle compared to L.A., but I was petrified by the hugeness of the venue," Plant said.

"Neither Robert nor John nor John Paul had played in a really big hall like that first performance," guitarist Jimmy Page recalled. "Since I'd toured with the Yardbirds, I was the only one who knew how big the places would be, even though we were only opening the show. I just tried to boost morale."

Led Zeppelin wasn't even listed in advertisements for its first U.S. concert—the bill was Vanilla Fudge and Spirit. The band performed an hour-long set on a revolving platform that night, introducing their powerful personalities and unprecedented sound—"Good Times Bad Times," "Dazed and Confused," "Communication Breakdown," "I Can't Quit You Babe," "You Shook Me," "Your Time Is Gonna Come."

After Led Zeppelin sprinted from the stage, Plant reached into a cardboard container filled with spareribs from a local restaurant.

"I couldn't believe that the promoter could charge for food backstage," he said, laughing.

Denver was only the beginning. Led Zeppelin spent the next year and a half on the road, including six separate tours of America that featured them as headliners on most nights, earning their fortune and a reputation for bawdy mayhem and excess. Between 1969 and 1980, the Zep released nine multi-million-selling albums and reigned as the No. 1 hard-rock band in the world.

DOUG LUBAHN/THE DOORS

The instrumental chemistry of the Doors was exceptional because, unlike virtually every other rock band of the mid-1960s, it was driven by a keyboard, rather than all guitars.

John Densmore (drums), Robby Krieger (guitar), Ray Manzarek (electric organ), and Jim Morrison (lead singer) were still looking for a bass player, but most of the players they rehearsed gave them a sound that was too full. The solution came when Manzarek discovered the thirty-two-note Fender Rhodes keyboard bass. He could control the compact model with his left hand while playing chords and solos with his right hand on the Vox organ. It became the bass for the Doors.

"The piano bass was okay for live work, but in the studio, it didn't record that well—it just didn't have any definition. It had a soft sound on the first album, so that's why I didn't use it after that," Manzarek said.

"When we did *Strange Days*, we said, 'Let's get some bass players in here.'"

The Doors used Doug Lubahn, who hailed from Colorado—a Golden High School graduate, class of 1965.

"In school, I got the gig as the bass player in the hottest band, the Carpetbaggers. But they didn't want me to stay because I had bad breath," Lubahn said.

"I was going to be a ski instructor. I was a fanatic. I hitchhiked up to Aspen for the summer, and a friend and I started skiing the glaciers. I was seventeen. I knew some of the local bands, and every night I'd sit in and play bass. A group called the Candy Store came to Aspen to play, and along with them came Mama Cass. She heard me and said, 'What are you doing here? You should come with me back to L.A. You should be playing for real.' I jumped on a plane in the spring of '66."

Lubahn joined Clear Light, a Los Angeles rock band. *Clear Light* peaked at No. 126 on the *Billboard* album chart in November 1967.

"All the musicians looking for stuff to do would hang out at a delicatessen called Cantors at night. These guys came walking through with a sign on their shirts saying 'We need a bass player.' I'd been staying in a basement somewhere. They took me to pick up my stuff, took me to their community house, and I ended up staying," Lubahn said.

"We had the same producer, Paul Rothchild, as the Doors. He said they needed a bass player for their records. He drove me up to Laurel Canyon. I played with them for a half hour, and they gave me the job. The first album hadn't come out yet. When it did, they became huge."

Lubahn played bass on the hit albums *Strange Days*, *Waiting For the Sun*, and *The Soft Parade*.

"Ray Manzarek would show me the bass part and then I would play it, adding my own little filigrees. I admired him so much, because he would come up with the most interesting bass lines, then he'd let me go have fun with it."

But Lubahn never played live.

"Paul felt it was better that they remain a quartet, visually, fan-wise. They didn't want to add or subtract anything, just keep it the way it was. I was happy to do it. It was great music, great fun."

Harvey Brooks came in about midway through *The Soft Parade*.

"Dumb me—they did that song 'Touch Me,' and I hated it. And I didn't think they were paying me enough money to do it, now that they were all millionaires. I got tired of the whole thing, so I told them I was leaving. They were nice about it, and they were anxious to get Harvey in anyway. It was amicable."

Lubahn moved to New York and played in Dreams, a jazz/rock group formed by Michael and Randy Brecker. In the early 1980s, he co-wrote "Treat Me Right" with Pat Benatar and played bass in Billy Squier's band on the heavy-metal rock guitarist's platinum albums *Emotions in Motion* and *Signs of Life*. He toured the world. He also played on Ted Nugent's 1984 *Penetrator* album.

The first and only Denver Pop Festival opened at Mile High Stadium on Friday, June 27, 1969. The three-day music festival was the first of its kind in Denver—promoter Barry Fey's shot at the big time. Woodstock didn't happen until three months later.

Admission for each day was $6, or concertgoers could buy a three-day ticket for $15. The festival ended up with 60,000 admissions. The lineup:

Friday—Flock, Big Mama Thornton, Mothers of Invention, Three Dog Night, Iron Butterfly.
Saturday—Aorta, Zephyr, Poco, Tim Buckley, Johnny Winter, Creedence Clearwater Revival.
Sunday—Aum, Rev. Cleophus Robinson, Sweetwater, Joe Cocker, the Jimi Hendrix Experience.

The year 1969 was a time for drawing hard lines. Civil rights demonstrations, antiwar protests, and student strikes were loose in the land, but it was the Denver Pop Festival that brought home to Denverites that, ready or not, the rock revolution was on.

In the late afternoon of June 28, the event changed from a musical episode to a panic. Tear gas intended for gate crashers outside Mile High Stadium swept over the west stands, blinding and gagging many of the 21,000 fans seated inside listening to Zephyr. Violence erupted in the audience, and police moved in with clubs and more tear gas.

On the festival's last day, the Jimi Hendrix Experience played its last concert. Rumors of an imminent split in the band had been supported by the announcement that bassist Noel Redding had formed his own band, Fat Mattress.

At a press conference in the afternoon, Hendrix announced a new bassist, his old army buddy Billy Cox, and a new approach: "A sky church sort of thing … I want to get the whole Buddy Miles group and call them the Freedom Express …" He added that Redding and drummer Mitch Mitchell weren't necessarily out of the band.

At the gig, Mile High Stadium was in an uproar. The stage was located on the infield dirt, and fans were bursting forth from the stands, desperate to get down close to the music. Hendrix clambered onto stage and launched into "Bold As Love."

Meanwhile, some 2,500 kids outside the stadium lobbed beer bottles, firecrackers, and rocks at police, who responded with clouds of tear gas. The battle raged for two hours, ending only when the gates were opened and those who wanted to went in to hear the music.

"We were just finishing our set when suddenly they let tear gas off and people started to panic," Mitchell recalled. "The road crew found us one of those two-ton panel vans, with aluminum sides and a top. The band got into the back, this huge cavernous space, and they locked us in."

To avoid the tear gas, people immediately swarmed onto the roof, which started to cave in.

Barry Fey's three-day music festival was the first of its kind in Denver.

"Suddenly we were very scared. We thought it was just a matter of moments before we were going to be crushed," Mitchell said. "We only had to drive about a quarter of a mile back to the hotel, but it took us nearly an hour—and there were still people on top of the van and hanging on the sides.

"We really still felt like a band, no animosity—we had all linked arms and shook hands, feeling that if we were going to go, we'd all go together. But Noel did fly back to England the next day to announce that he'd left the band."

Soon after the Denver Pop Festival, Hendrix went into virtual seclusion, and the Jimi Hendrix Experience name was no longer used. He delved further into experimentalism, recording an immense quantity of unfinished music before his sudden death in 1970. The only other full-scale album project released in his lifetime was with his all-black Band Of Gypsys—Cox and drummer Miles were basically a jam-rhythm section for Hendrix.

Rock concerts in city facilities were limited to the Denver Coliseum until 1974, when the first Colorado Sun Day was staged at Mile High Stadium.

Page 1. USE ON L.P. Jimi Hendrix Electric Lady Land -

the Cosmopolitan

DENVER, COLORADO 80202 • BROADWAY AT EAST EIGHTEENTH AVE • PHONE

Letter to the room full of mirrors . 4:30 – 6:00am Denver Colo. Sept 2nd. 1968 ... alone

let's see how .... " It wasn't too long ago, but it feels like, years ago, since I've felt the warm hello of the Sun... lately things .... " and then he was interrupted by the slow motion speeded up sound that sometimes cut so deep, that sound was from those chellophane typewriters ... Excatly. Constantly from the South side of those carpets and Sweet Rome was on my mind. "She gave so sweetly ...." And on he walked until after crowning Ethel the dog, the only Queen of ears, the sky cracked wide open and split many of his brothers and sisters heads all over the world . . . the approximate same) ....

WESTERN INTERNATIONAL HOTELS

On September 1, 1968, Jimi Hendrix wrote the liner notes to his *Electric Ladyland* album in his Cosmopolitan Hotel room after a memorable gig at Red Rocks Amphitheatre.

In 1969, it was beginning to dawn on people that most of the decade's rock icons weren't functioning. The Beatles hated each other. Bob Dylan had become a recluse.

The Rolling Stones were the only ones left, putting their talent on stage for the first time since 1966.

When the Stones had last toured and made their reputation, it was still basically as a pop group—they were obliged to do little more than fill theaters with shrieking teens. (In Colorado, Governor John Love had declared Rolling Stones Day on November 30, 1966.)

But in those three years, pop had evolved into rock culture and consciousness. The music was not only a thousand watts louder, it was also a thousand times weightier. The Stones had been portrayed as heroes and villains. There was public controversy over their drug busts, censorship battles, and their reportedly unconventional sex lives.

"The greatest rock 'n' roll band in the world" was jittery at the prospect of moving into arenas. The Stones assembled a traveling rock 'n' roll circus with the lighting and sound equipment that the rooms demanded. They even booked their own maintenance, publicity, and security staffs and their own supporting act, Ike & Tina Turner.

The opening gig was scheduled at the Forum in Los Angeles. But actually, the tour started the day before, on Friday, November 7, when the Stones flew to Colorado to perform at Colorado State University's Moby Gym in Fort Collins, about sixty miles north of Denver. It was a "break-in" concert—a rehearsal, though no one called it that. The performance had been advertised for three weeks, but outside of Colorado no one seemed to know of it. The Stones had asked that details of the concert go untold, in case something went wrong.

At sunset, the Stones got dressed in the Letterman's Lounge. And then Mick Jagger danced onstage and Keith Richards pumped out the opening chords to "Jumpin' Jack Flash."

Founding member Brian Jones had died in July of '69, and the tour showcased new rhythm guitarist Mick Taylor, who was instrumental in revitalizing the Stones. They concocted a brutal, salacious onstage sound. The set included "Stray Cat Blues," "Carol," "Love in Vain," and "Little Queenie." "Street Fighting Man" closed the show.

Fans weren't familiar with "Midnight Rambler," Jagger's eulogy to the Boston Strangler. The singer pranced around the stage, posing maliciously. He lashed the stage with his belt and thrust his crotch into the audience's faces. The audience response?

"They just sat there," Jagger later said. "They were, I think, too stoned to move."

Drummer Charlie Watts found America circa 1969 to be a radically different country than the one the Stones had previously entertained.

"People didn't scream anymore—the music was taken seriously," he recalled. "And you had proper amplification—suddenly you could hear everybody. Nobody had heard drums before. We must have sounded a joke before that. But in '69, you really had to be on top of it to play. That's how Hendrix and bands like Led Zeppelin came about."

The tour was a media event, but the Stones' satanic image came home to roost at California's Altamont Speedway. Prodded by the summer's Woodstock gathering, the band chose to stage a free thank-you-America concert. Members of the Hell's Angels motorcycle gang were appointed by the band to work security for the day-long event, and a young black man was stabbed to death just in front of the stage.

BEAST

Beast premiered in 1968 at the Calker Junction in Colorado Springs, where the septet was based for a time. Members included Bob Yeazel on lead guitar and Kenny Passarelli on bass for the first of its two albums, *Beast*, which charted for two weeks in late 1969, peaking at No. 195.

"I graduated early from East High School, then went to the University of Denver on a trumpet performance scholarship. I quit DU after a year when the Beast got a record deal," Passarelli said.

"David Raines was an R&B singer, like Mitch Ryder. He had that kind of throaty voice—he did the splits. The instrumentation had an R&B texture to it—Gerry Fike played a Hammond B-3 with Leslies—and part of it was funky, part of it was Motown-ish. But we weren't a straight-ahead soul band. We were doing original material, the majority Yeazel's, and it was more psychedelic. It was a real odd mixture."

A few members of the band connected with a rough group of people from Denver, which was called Crystal City because of the speed laboratories that were proliferating.

According to Passarelli, "We settled in the Black Forest, an area northeast of Colorado Springs, and lived on a farm, almost like a commune—a couple of guys had their old ladies. Word got out that these speed guys were going to use our farm to set up a drug lab. The feds grilled us on that.

"I was breaking away, hanging in Boulder a lot of the time. I got introduced to Stephen Stills, who was putting together a new group and looking for a bass player. He'd broken up with Judy Collins and was clearing out his head in Gold Hill. It was the first time in my life I thought, 'Maybe I have a chance to do this—someone's given me the green light to make it.'

"I had hepatitis and went down for six months. I freaked out. At nineteen, I thought I'd been offered the gig of my life and didn't get it. When I got well, I left Beast. They made a second record, continued playing through the Midwest, then fell apart."

Beast recorded both of its albums with Norman Petty in the Clovis, New Mexico, studio that recorded all of Buddy Holly's songs.

Passarelli went on to bigger success with Joe Walsh, studio sessions, and Elton John. Yeazel and drummer Larry Ferris put in an appearance with Sugarloaf in the 1970s.

ZEPHYR

Janis Joplin, with Big Brother & the Holding Company, popularized a style of music recalling the days of great black soul singers such as Bessie Smith and Billie Holiday, only with a much harder edge. In Boulder, feisty little singer Candy Givens and her husband, bassist David Givens, recruited drummer Robbie Chamberlin, keyboardist John Faris, and a special young Iowa guitar player named Tommy Bolin to play this same style in a band they named Zephyr.

"Our first performance was at a nightclub called the Sink back in an alley near the University of Colorado," David Givens said. "This may sound immodest, but it's the truth—we had no competition in Colorado. Right from the start, people treated us as if we were extraordinary."

Zephyr's music quickly developed as a curious mix of supercharged jazz-inflected rock and rhythm & blues underpinned by a strong keyboard sound. Givens' harmonica and vocals—from lusty growls to lacquer-thin highs—and Bolin's guitar were raising the roof in Boulder and Denver clubs and college haunts with a brand of blues-rock that a lot of Colorado kids had never heard before. The group lived the typical late 1960s lifestyle, headquartering at Candy Givens' mothers' house until Bolin wrangled an audition with concert promoter Barry Fey.

Fey liked the band (and especially Bolin, who was one of the premiere young guitarists in the country) and set up a showcase in Los Angeles. After playing the legendary Whisky A Go Go, Zephyr was signed by ABC Probe Records, recording their first album for the label in two days. The year 1969's *Zephyr*, the "rainbow in the bathtub" record, reached the Top 50. It was a fairly hesitant affair with a primitive studio sound and established Bolin as one of the hottest guitarists on the scene.

"The first record was recorded in two days," David Givens recalled. "Then a producer came in

and wrecked it. I liked the basic tracks—it was real spontaneous, especially Tommy's guitar work."

Zephyr gigged solidly through 1970 and 1971. The heavy blues-rock act performed at such noted rock emporiums as the Fillmores East and West and the Whisky A Go Go and opened for such luminaries as Jimi Hendrix, Led Zeppelin, Mountain, and Fleetwood Mac. But their recording career was held up after Probe folded. When they did venture back into the studio, it was for the Warner Brothers label, and recording 1971's *Going Back To Colorado* took place in the prestigious Electric Ladyland Studios in New York. Eddie Kramer, who successfully produced albums for Led Zeppelin and the late Jimi Hendrix, had heard the group in Colorado, guided them out of an ineffectual record contract, and put them on Warner Brothers.

"We'd been there a couple of weeks when Jimi Hendrix died. It fell to Eddie Kramer to try and make Hendrix's *Cry of Love* album sound finished. He felt the weight of trying to complete it. We were pushed aside right when we needed him to help us," Givens said.

Zephyr learned the music business through painful mistakes. Sad tales of managerial hang-ups and broken promises ensued.

"The hassles started. Tommy fought with the drummer, then the drummer came back, so Tommy quit, blah, blah."

Bolin and drummer Bobby Berge quit Zephyr in early 1972 for new pastures. Bolin formed a new band called Energy before leaving town to play with the James Gang. Zephyr persevered with a third album, *Sunset Ride*, featuring guitarist Jock Bartley, and even a brief reunion some years later.

Candy Givens graduated from Golden High School.

One of David Givens' fondest memories of her performing days was at the riot-filled Denver Pop Festival in August 1969: "The cops were tear-gassing people at the gate and the performers were getting gassed. Candy took charge. She said, 'We're crying anyway. We may as well do some blues.'"

Candy and David Givens, Bolin, and Faris came back together in 1973, with Harold and Mick from Flash Cadillac, as the Legendary 4-Nikators, playing oldies every Monday night at Art's Bar & Grill, out on Broadway in North Boulder. They packed the place and made more money than they ever had as Zephyr.

In 1976, four years after leaving Zephyr, Bolin died of a drug overdose.

Givens drowned in her hot tub after overdosing on quaaludes and alcohol in 1984.

"Candy was unique, the first female lead singer who could hang with the guys that I was aware of," Givens said. "Over the years, Candy was accused of copying Janis Joplin, but she was an entirely different kind of duck. True, she was brash and sang hard sometimes, and our records didn't often capture her at her best, but she was never a Janis clone to anyone with eyes or ears."

The Moonrakers were the most popular group in Denver during the mid-1960s with four singles hitting the local charts (the biggest being "You'll Come Back"). But Joel Brandes, Denny Flannigan, Bob MacVittie, Bob Webber, and Veeder Van Dorn couldn't break out nationally.

After several membership changes, the Moonrakers returned in 1969 with the Christian rock album *Together with Him*. The drummer on half the songs was Jerry Corbetta, who had played keyboards in the Half Dozen't and the Brambles as a teenager.

Corbetta returned to keyboards, and the band transformed into Sugarloaf (a mountain where one of the members lived). The Colorado rock quartet had a big national hit—"Green Eyed Lady" peaked at No. 3 on October 17, 1970.

"The Moonrakers and the Half Dozen't were seasoned bands. We played in nightclubs six nights a week for years. You honed your chops—you could play the songs in your sleep, with a shower or without a shower," Corbetta said.

"Bob Webber was the Moonrakers' guitarist, and he and I were fire and ice personality-wise. He's a real linear thinker—an aerospace engineer, 4.0 student. I was Italian, from North Denver—I played the accordion.

"But I knew music theory and harmony, and he respected me on that. I sat him down one night and said, 'If the Moonrakers can get a deal, I'm convinced that you and I could start a band and get twice as good a deal.' That was my simple, straight logic."

Before their debut as Sugarloaf, the band was called Chocolate Hair, and they cut seven songs. According to Corbetta, "Those were demos, but the record company said it was going to be our first album—don't make waves. I said we needed one more song. I thought I'd write better if I knew we were doing it for real.

"So I went back in my room and wrote the melody. It wasn't called 'Green Eyed Lady' at the time—I wasn't a lyricist. The guys in my band used to call my girlfriend, Kathy Peacock, the green-eyed lady. She was from Denver.

"We went out to Hollywood to record, and the singer never showed up that day in the studio. I sang the funky stuff in Chocolate Hair—I was trying to emulate Bobby Darin. So I ended up on the record."

Corbetta's organ solo in "Green Eyed Lady" is a classic.

"Jimmy Smith was my idol. I knew all of his songs, every lick he played. 'Green Eyed Lady' was a combination of his jazz and my rock influence. It's truly a jazz-rock song.

"I was taking private piano lessons. I was giving lessons. I was in the college jazz band. I was playing six nights a week. I was right in the middle of the music, my fingers were in shape, flying. So, boy, I just had the juice."

Sugarloaf—Corbetta, Webber, MacVittie (drums), and Bob Raymond (bass)—toured a lot and then faded away after two minor chart hits featuring new member Bob Yeazel (late of Beast).

But in trying to regain a recording deal, Corbetta was spurned rather imperiously. This resulted in an amusing song by Sugarloaf/Jerry Corbetta. In "Don't Call Us, We'll Call You," the CBS Records phone number and a general White House number were spelled out—touch-tone style—for the world.

"It was an attitude song. 'You got my number?' 'Yeah, don't hold your breath.'

"CBS changed its number. But three months later we got this official letter from the White House saying a gentleman from the State Department wanted to meet with us.

"This official-looking guy said, 'Look, we get over 50,000 phone calls a day, and we've heard this name Sugarloaf.' I said, 'Well, that's the name of my band.' He had to see the albums. I told him I was going to call my lawyers. I was really a cocky kid."

"Don't Call Us, We'll Call You" was another hit. It peaked at No. 9 on March 29, 1975. But the band quickly dropped from sight.

"Colorado has always been the little sister of Los Angeles, not Seattle or anywhere else," Corbetta said. "That's why all of the rockers came here. It is only a two-hour flight, it's beautiful, and you're a mile high already—what's not to like?"

Sugarloaf/ Jerry Corbetta circa 1975

STEPHEN STILLS

Searching for some peace from Crosby, Stills, Nash & Young in the early 1970s, Stephen Stills would fly in a Lear jet to airports in Boulder County that were near his cabin near Gold Hill, Colorado. Locals always knew when Stills was in town because he had a Mercedes truck, one of the few in the country.

"It was as far away as I could think of to get," Stills later recalled. "Basically, nobody up on that mountain gave a shit who I was or what I did."

Stills wrote many of the songs for his second solo album in the winter of 1970 while in Colorado.

Chris Hillman, then the Flying Burrito Brothers' lead singer and driving force, was bored and broke. He got a call from Stills to meet him in Miami. Stills wanted Hillman to bring along Burrito guitarist Al Perkins and fiddler Byron Berline. He had been visualizing a group that would bring together rock, folk, Latin, country, and blues. He also retained Dallas Taylor on drums, bass player Fuzzy Samuels, Paul Harris, and a young percussionist named Joe Lala.

When the Stills-Burritos amalgam —dubbed Manassas— congregated in the studio, something clicked. Rehearsals flowed right into marathon recording sessions that went round-the-clock and then some. According to engineer Howard Albert, the longest session was 106 hours straight.

"Manassas was such a terrific band—it had some structure and could play anything," Stills said. "I had a house in Colorado, but I took Manassas over to England to get good. We all lived at this little house out in Surrey."

The debut album featured the song "Colorado." Manassas shows generally ran close to three hours and built off the Burritos format, with an opening rock set, then Stills playing solo acoustic, Hillman and Perkins on bluegrass, then Manassas country, more Manassas rock, and an acoustic finish.

Down the Road, which peaked at No. 26 on the *Billboard* album charts in May 1973, was completed at Caribou Ranch Studios in Colorado.

"But I short-circuited there for a while," Stills admitted. "Things were moving too fast. I got a little crazed. Too much

On September 20, 1970, snow fell in the Rockies. Stills, at dawn, walked outside his cabin, guitar in hand, and posed for his first solo album cover photo.

In 1972, Stephen Stills based his band Manassas in Colorado. He also named his publishing company after the town of Gold Hill.

drinkin', too many drugs. What can I say?"

In 1972, Stills had married French singer-songwriter Veronique Sanson, and the couple became parents in April 1974 with the birth of a baby boy in Boulder's Community Hospital.

"When I was growing up in the Southeast, I hated the humidity and was totally addicted to air-conditioning. I discovered that in Colorado there was air-conditioning all the time, and I loved it," Stills reflected.

"Also, in Colorado, I met some real down-home people who had no particular illusions about who I was. To them, I was just Stephen. I liked that. It helped me sort out a few things and brought me back to an understanding that there's more to this life than just rock 'n' roll. I began to paint. I was a Rocky Mountain rescue volunteer, as well as an auxiliary fireman.

"But the high and dry does not agree with my throat, and I never did ski worth a shit, and now I'm paying for it. Both of my knees are completely trashed. I can't dance anywhere near the way I'd like to."

The Soul Survivors (left to right): Allen Kemp, Pat Shanahan, John Day, Bob Raymond, Gene Chalk

Nelson was determined to establish an adult identity and gain the respect he deserved as a musician. He put together the Stone Canyon Band around Poco bassist Randy Meisner.

"The Stone Canyon Band came together almost from a negative standpoint," Nelson said.

"I didn't know what kind of music I wanted to do. I couldn't verbalize it, really, so I just got to thinking how I started, the kind of music I liked. I was really fortunate in getting a unique type of style and then clicking with musicians who played along those lines. The first guy I found was Randy Meisner."

Meisner grew up on a farm near Scotts Bluff, Nebraska. He travelled throughout the Midwest, working the road and pursuing his musical ambitions. An affable, easygoing sort with a sweet, high voice, he cut his teeth in the Dynamics and arrived in Denver in 1966 to play a battle of the bands.

He linked up with one of the competing groups, the Soul Survivors—not the New York–based white soul group of "Expressway To Your Heart" fame, but a well-produced pop-rock act that scored two No. 1 hits on Denver's Top 40 giant KIMN ("Can't Stand To Be in Love with You" and "Hung Up on Losing").

"When they lost their bass player, they asked me if I wanted to jump ship and move to Los Angeles with them," Meisner said.

The name of his new band was changed to the Poor. Meisner and lead guitarist Allen Kemp slept on the living room floor of a one-bedroom apartment in East Los Angeles for eighty-five dollars a month. Gigs were few and far between.

"We didn't realize how much competition was out there," Meisner said. "My jacket was my first pillow. We really had nothing at all."

When Meisner took the job with Poco, the Poor broke up. With drummer Patrick Shanahan, Kemp moved to a cheaper three-bedroom house in Sherman Oaks and got a job washing cars. Meisner left Poco in a dispute over the final mixes to the country-rock group's first album. Upon leaving the band, Meisner was contacted about working with Nelson.

Meisner contacted Kemp and Shanahan, his buddies from the band that first brought him from Denver. Nelson got the band's name from a remote area of the Los Angeles hills he used to drive by. The sound was crisp and clear—Meisner and Kemp stacked their vocals on top of Nelson's in angelic harmonies.

Rick Nelson was the first teen idol to use television as a way to promote records.

In 1948, he joined his parents' radio show, *The Adventures of Ozzie and Harriet*, which moved to television in 1952 for a fourteen-year run. Eight years into the show, Nelson became an "overnight success" when he released his first single, "A Teenager's Romance" / "I'm Walking." Television's commercial power was unrealized at that time, and almost as an afterthought, a Ricky-sings-at-the-party sequence was aired. "A Teenager's Romance" sold a million copies the following week.

Nelson released an endless stream of hit singles such as "Stood Up," "Poor Little Fool," "Lonesome Town," "Travelin' Man," and "Teen Age Idol," to name but a few. By the mid-1960s, when *The Adventures of Ozzie and Harriet* went off the air, his hits began to dry up and his music was eclipsed by the British Invasion.

THE STONE CANYON BAND

Meisner quit and rejoined, then quit again to form a band with Glenn Frey and Don Henley. They hit it off so well, he decided to fly with the Eagles.

On October 15, 1971, Rick Nelson & the Stone Canyon Band were special guest stars at the Richard Nader Rock & Roll Revival at New York City's Madison Square Garden. The concert program acquired an integral place in Nelson's own legend.

"At sound check, everybody else was looking out of the '50s and doing just their strict old hits. Rick refused to do that. He wanted to do something different," Kemp said.

Nelson fed the Garden crowd pure nostalgia. But when he sat down at the piano and performed new material, he was booed off the stage for departing from the rigid oldies program, for having long hair, and for the general drugstore cowboy appearance of the Stone Canyon Band.

As a result of the experience, Nelson penned a song six months later featuring a mildly scornful mood and the resolute conclusion, "If memories are all I sing, I'd rather drive a truck." "Garden Party" climbed all the way to No. 6 on the *Billboard* pop singles charts, one of the most unprecedented comeback hits in rock history.

Rick Nelson & the Stone Canyon Band went through several personnel changes. Allen Kemp and Pat Shanahan went on to play with the New Riders of the Purple Sage in the 1980s.

Nelson died in a plane crash in 1985 at the age of forty-five.

Jimmy Buffett was raised in Alabama and never had seen the mountains until a friend from Colorado's Timberline Rose turned him on to the Rockies.

"I was a preacher of humidity and living in that swamp gas environment. I had been up to Montana to visit people, but I hadn't spent a long period of time out West," Buffett said.

"Denver was the first place I went on tour. I got out of humidity and came to the mountains to play. The Cafe York on Colfax was my first gig in Colorado."

Dressed in Levis and a cowboy shirt, his hair long, and with a distinctive southern-flavored accent, Buffett carried his two Martin guitars from the small coffeehouses to college campuses. There he entertained. "No flashing diamond rings, no skin-tight tuxedo, no Las Vegas marquees"—just sharing an honest talent with his audiences.

"I lived in a little sleazy hotel in metropolitan Denver, and then I went to the mountains, as everybody has done—up to Evergreen, Bailey, then Breckenridge, where I did the summer mountain circuit, having a glorious time.

"I wound up the tour in downtown Pueblo, not known as the most beautiful spot in Colorado. But seeing every side of Colorado eventually led to me settling there for a while."

"Come Monday" became Jimmy Buffett's first hit single in 1974.

"Circa 1971, when I was doing my mountain touring summers in Colorado, I'd gone out to San Francisco and was living in a Howard Johnson's in Marin County. I left my girlfriend, who later became my wife, in Aspen. I was thinking about her and I wrote 'Come Monday.'"

Buffett became an Aspen resident for many years.

"Most people always consider going to Colorado for the winter, but my attachment was a summertime thing," Buffett testified, having made yet another survey of Aspen's bars. "There's so much to do."

The song "A Mile High in Denver" appeared on Buffett's *Before the Beach* album.

In one of the most infamous events in Denver concert history, Jethro Tull appeared at Red Rocks Amphitheatre on June 10, 1971. Police fired tear gas cannisters to disperse a mob of 2,000 fans who were attempting to climb the barricades and get into Tull's sold-out gig for free.

Undaunted, the venerable British rock act played anyway.

"It was so polarized it was ridiculous," singer Ian Anderson recalled. "Those who disrupted things outside were just as much to blame as police for overreacting."

Rumors on impending trouble had flown in the days before the show.

"Some of the blame belonged on me," promoter Barry Fey admitted. "Tull was so big, I should have booked them for two shows.

"As it turned out, there was an unhealthy combination of people. Outside there were maybe fifty punks who wanted to start trouble, mixed in with 2,000 people holding cash, saying, 'Hey, take my money, let me in.' Then it came to, 'Okay, if you won't take my money, I'm coming in anyway.'"

The disorderly throng swarmed around the perimeter of the outdoor venue, walking over the bluffs and into the top parking lot. The first volley of tear gas was dropped by a police helicopter. Livingston Taylor, the opening act, was onstage, and once he got a whiff he began crying, "This is supposed to be music! What's going on here?"

At that point the encounter between gate-crashers and police erupted into a full-scale riot. Police cars were set on fire and hundreds of arrests were made.

"We were leaving our hotel to go up to the show when we received word that there was a problem," Anderson said. "We set off in our rented station wagons and were met by a police roadblock that tried to turn us back. We said, 'We're the band,' and we were told, 'There's not going to be a show. Go away.'

"We thought that was ridiculous, so we managed to find a back route on a dirt road. We still had to make a fairly aggressive effort to get to the site—we wound up running a roadblock—and when we got there, we realized there was trouble going on outside.

"I said, 'Look, if you don't let us go onstage, not only are there going to be 2,000 people outside rioting, but 9,000 poeple inside are going to go crazy as well.'"

Reluctantly, the authorities allowed Tull to take the stage, even though keyboardist John Evan couldn't see his piano through the tear gas. Anderson was magnificent, stalking the stage and playing his flute like a man possessed despite the circumstances.

"The gas made life very difficult in the amphitheatre itself," he said. "The wind blew a cloud of gas over the audience to the stage. We had to stop several times. I remember seeing babies being passed down through the crowd so they wouldn't be affected by the gas. It was a horrifying sight."

The show at Red Rocks Amphitheatre was drummer Barriemore Barlow's first date with the band. "Having slightly upset the police on the way up there, we had to be careful going down again," Ian Anderson said. "We were hiding under blankets in the back of a station wagon, licking our wounds. Our eyes were streaming; we were coughing. Barrie turned to me and asked, 'Is it going to be like this every night?'"

The rest of that summer's Red Rocks shows were canceled, and the debacle convinced Denver officials to ban rock concerts from the site until 1975, when soft-rock acts such as America were allowed to be booked.

10 THE EAGLES

The Eagles were the archetypal California band of the 1970s. Their name was synonymous with the country-rock movement that sprang up in Los Angeles.

But the band's first-ever concerts were in Colorado.

Linda Ronstadt's manager had an idea for a supergroup to back up his singer, coming up with the combination of Glenn Frey (a guitarist and singer from Detroit), Don Henley (a singer and drummer from Texas), Bernie Leadon (previously in the Flying Burrito Brothers and Dillard & Clark), and Randy Meisner (he played with Poco and Rick Nelson's Stone Canyon Band).

They eventually left Ronstadt and took shape as the original Eagles. In 1971, David Geffen (the head of Asylum Records, home of Jackson Browne and Joni Mitchell) got involved as manager. He provided expense money for the guys to leave Hollywood and get their act together so that they could come back and blow minds rather than develop in front of everyone's eyes.

They went to Colorado and got gigs in local bars. In Aspen, "Eagle" played two stints at the Gallery (four sets a night, legend had it) and the whole town got behind them.

Eagle was then scheduled to perform at Tulagi, the nationally famed 3.2 beer nightclub on Boulder's Hill, December 11-15. It was finals week at the University of Colorado, and attendance was fifteen to fifty people a night. The band got paid $500 for the five nights.

Yet Henley and Frey sat at the bar drinking pitchers of 3.2 beer, confident to the point of insisting that they were going to be huge stars.

"Oh, yeah, we were cocky little bastards," Henley said. "Those gigs were sort of our coming-out party."

Frey said they were matter-of-fact over the inevitability of success.

"We had it all planned. We'd watched landmark country-rock bands like Poco and the Flying Burrito Brothers lose their initial momentum. We were determined not to make the same mistakes. This was going to be our best shot. Everybody had to look good, sing good, play good, and write good. We wanted it all. Peer respect. AM and FM success. No. 1 singles and albums. Great music. And a lot of money."

The members dressed in the fashion of the time—ripped jeans with paisley patches. In Boulder, a beered-up patron kept screaming, "Play some Burritos, ma-a-a-an!"

"We're a new group with our own songs," Frey earnestly explained from the stage.

One night, the heat went out in the club. It was so cold that Leadon played with gloves on.

The band auditioned for producer Glyn Johns.

"He was this superstar producer who none of us had ever met," Henley noted. "He agreed to fly over from England and listen to us when we played Tulagi. I remember I got designated to drive to the airport to pick him up.

"It was a horrible, cold, snowy night, and nobody was at the concert. We were nervous and not very good, and Glyn passed. Later, he came to Los Angeles on a more casual scale when we weren't so keyed up about performing. He listened to us rehearse, singing harmonies with acoustic guitars, and that's what got him."

Within weeks, Eagle became the Eagles. The band went to London to record its first album, produced by Johns. *Eagles*, released in 1972, was a huge success, helped by the hit singles "Take It Easy" and "Peaceful Easy Feeling." The Eagles went on to become the most successful American music act of the 1970s with sales of more than fifty million albums worldwide.

Don Henley maintained a residence in Woody Creek, Colorado, for decades. "I fell in love with the place. Colorado was great back then, but it's changed a lot now. It's getting a little glitzy up there."

Glenn Frey still lives in Aspen. "After the shows at the Gallery, I swore if I ever made a dime in the music business, I wanted to have a house there. It's a good place to practice. If you can sing in Aspen's thin air, you can sing anywhere."

RICK ROBERTS/ THE FLYING BURRITO BROTHERS

In 1970, Gram Parsons left the Flying Burrito Brothers to begin a solo career. The band continued without replacing him for four months, gigging around the West Coast as a four-piece. In late summer, a newcomer to the Los Angeles scene was asked to join, and while none of the Burritos said so outright, Rick Roberts was the man chosen to fill Parsons' role.

"I'm a Floridian. I left college in South Carolina in July 1969 and was living in Colorado for a while. I arrived in Los Angeles on my mother's birthday, September 14. I was telling her and everyone else I was going to L.A. to become famous. Through every step of joining the Burritos, I would get discouraged and think about going back to Colorado."

Morale of the remaining original members was low. In 1971, Bernie Leadon left to join members of Linda Ronstadt's backing group to form the Eagles. Michael Clarke went to Hawaii, while Chris Hillman and Al Perkins left for Stephen Stills' band Manassas. Roberts reorganized the band and finished all the Burritos' performing commitments, and they played a tour of Europe.

Roberts recalled, "I was a raw rookie. Here I was given the opportunity to play with some of the people that I had grown up idolizing. Gram had drug problems; he eventually OD'ed. They parted ways on not so cordial terms."

Roberts' stay with the Burritos was mildly profitable, very productive, and an exceptionally valuable experience. He played on the final pair of albums by the group, contributing several compositions to the repertoire, including his best-known song—"Colorado," from *Last of the Red-Hot Burritos*.

"I wrote that song in California. I'd been out there for four or five months. I was nineteen years old. When I got to Colorado on my way out to L.A., I was stopping in order to see some friends of mine, but it turned out they had moved on. I ended up coming up to Boulder looking for a place to stay for a couple of days, to catch my breath. I ended up staying for three months and fell in love with Colorado.

"When I got out to California, that song came out of that. Sitting around one night, boy, I wish the hell I'd never left Colorado. Those were the days when University Hill in Boulder was really happening. I ran into the guys in Zephyr."

By June 1972, the group was no more, with Roberts staying with A&M Records as a soloist.

"I made my second solo album in Colorado with Joe Walsh, a couple of Poco people, Kenny Passarelli. I made that album for $12,500."

Linda Ronstadt's version of Roberts' "Colorado" bubbled under *Billboard*'s Hot 100 in 1974, reaching No. 108 in 1974.

DANNY HOLIEN

Danny Holien grew up in Cannon Falls, Minnesota. He came west to Colorado and wrote songs that inspired Denver's Tumbleweed Records to produce *Danny Holien* in 1972.

"A friend of mine had moved out to Colorado. He said there was all kinds of work, so we moved to the ghetto and starved for quite a while! We played some ski resorts, but it wasn't the big hot-shot clubs, it was on the edge. The whole band lived in a house together."

Tumbleweed Records was a small independent label owned by Bill Szymczyk, whose first major success had come when he convinced blues legend B.B. King to cut contemporary-sounding albums. The result was King's first major pop crossover, "The Thrill Is Gone," a hit in 1971. The producer went on to have great success in the 1970s, both as an A&R man and behind the board, signing and producing the James Gang.

"I decided to leave Los Angeles after a big earthquake," Szymczyk recalled. "A few of us record company people had bandied about the idea of starting our own label. Back in the early '70s, you'd get two hit records and you could do that."

Tumbleweed Records was based out of a funky old house just east of downtown Denver on Gilpin Street, with Szymczyk running the show.

"Gulf + Western owned Famous Music, which bankrolled us," Szymczyk said. The reason we went to Denver was that my partner Larry Ray's wife was from there. I had visited two times for a total of six days, but each time, I had an incredibly good time! Colorado was happening in a lot of ways back then."

Indeed, thousands of suntanned, blue-jeaned artists, poets, and just ordinary people had instinctively come to the state from New York, Chicago, San Francisco, and Boston for basically the same reason Szymczyk left L.A.—the big city just didn't make it.

"Everything was self-contained in that house," Holien said.

"They had a lot of money behind them. Most of it was blown partying and having a big time. That's what it takes to make money—spend a lot of money to impress a lot of people. But I saw the inner workings and didn't care for it too much. Nice people, but I thought everyone was trying to be big-time. Boy, did they spend a lot of money."

Tumbleweed released some very good albums in nice expensive covers. *Danny Holien* came housed in a luxurious die-cut jacket with a sixteen-page songbook.

"It was the first bunch of songs I'd written, for the most part. I was naive and green. It was a fluke. I'm not that aggressive of a self-promoter, but I just happened to meet a person who introduced me to Bill Szymczyk. I sat down and played a couple of songs for him acoustically, and he slapped his knee and said, 'Hot damn, let's do an album.' I said okay. It was that funny."

Holien's music was that of a poet, not a philosopher. "I don't want people to hear what I have to say," he said at the time. "I want them to hear what I'm saying."

Holien almost hit with a single called "Colorado," a quiet protest against the rape of the land. His song was very popular on FM stations in the 1970s. "Colorado" reached No. 66 on the *Billboard* charts on September 9, 1972.

"I hate to be a protest singer. Things just come up. I was in a house a block from the busy intersection of Colorado Boulevard and Colfax Avenue. I wrote it in a few minutes one day, a feeling—it's a nice little tune."

"Colorado" did better in Northern California—Salinas, Monterey—than in Denver.

"I was not very well known in Denver. I was playing around the fringes."

Joe Walsh, Joe Vitale, Rick Derringer, and Todd Rundgren played on another Tumbleweed recording for Michael Stanley, which included "Rosewood Bitters," a song that became a concert mainstay throughout Stanley's career, and "Denver Rain," an introspective ballad.

Holien and Steve Swenson also played on the solo album of Dewey Terry (of Don & Dewey fame), *Chief,* on Tumbleweed. Holien didn't want to tour, so Swenson teamed up with Don Debacker from 60,000,000 Buffalo, Dan McCorison, and others and formed Dusty Drapes & the Dusters—in essence, Boulder's first alt-country band.

But Tumbleweed was short-lived. The label folded in 1973.

"We lacked for nothing," Szymczyk said. "The Gulf + Western corporate structure went along with it for the first year, anyway, until we ran through a million and a half dollars—a lot of bucks back then!"

When the Eagles wanted a more rock 'n' roll sound, they hired Szymczyk, and the unprecedented chart success of the 1974 *On the Border* and 1975's *One of These Nights* albums made both parties millions.

Holien eventually moved back to Minnesota, then to Estes Park, Colorado, in the late 1970s and early 1980s with a band called Hoi Palloi. He then moved back to Minnesota and dropped out of the music business.

success of the band's first three albums brought wide popularity for such Walsh tunes as "The Bomber," "Funk 49," "Tend My Garden," and "Walk Away"—and endless touring.

As the James Gang became bigger and the big bucks beckoned, Walsh turned the other way. Encouraged by the Who's Peter Townshend (who admired Walsh's fretboard talent and asked the James Gang to open the Who's 1971 European tour), the Kent State alumnus made the difficult decision to begin again and go it alone, moving to the open air of Boulder County in Colorado. For months he lived in the mountains and practiced ham radio operations.

"I didn't get much help from my management or record company at the start of pursuing a solo career," Walsh said. "Moving to Colorado had a lot to do with my friendship with Bill Szymczyk, who at that point was an advisor helping me feel confident because I was scared to death."

"The James Gang was on tour and played Denver," Szymczyk recalled, "and Joe hung out with me and saw the Tumbleweed Records offices on Gilpin Street and what we were doing and said, 'This is kinda nice here.' He was making noises about quitting the band and starting his own solo career. I said, 'Well, if you do, move here.' He said, 'OK!' "

Walsh found an easygoing lifestyle in perfect accord with the music he was bent on making. At a time when he needed encouragement, Colorado challenged him and seeded a new perspective. Full-time exposure to the rural landscape and rustic lifestyle in the small towns of the Rockies was almost therapeutic.

"Rocky Mountain Way," the classic-rock nugget, is Joe Walsh's signature tune, a perfect vehicle for his soaring slide-guitar work and odd strangled tenor.

"It's about living in Colorado, having left Cleveland and the James Gang and having no regrets at all," Walsh said.

Before going out on his own in 1971, Walsh had made a considerable reputation as lead guitarist and lead vocalist for the James Gang, based in Cleveland. The

"I took an amount of time off and began forming an arrangement of players conceived in a way to express what I was hearing and what I thought a band should be. They were strange times and it was hard, but it took me back to basic survival, which is always very positive in terms of creative energy. When you have to get yourself together, you play differently from when you're rich."

In 1972, Walsh emerged from a long winter and spring in the studio with an album called *Barnstorm*, accompanied by drummer Joe Vitale, an old colleague, and bassist Kenny Passarelli, a newfound friend. The album—which included "Mother Says," "Turn To Stone," and "Here We Go"—showcased Walsh as not only an innovative, distinctive guitarist, but as a competent keyboardist and songwriter with impressive scope.

"When Joe and I were getting ready to do his first solo record, I had heard rumors of Jimmy Guercio's Caribou Ranch," Szymczyk said. "So of course I wanted to suss him out and see what was going on."

Guercio, producer of the band Chicago, bought Caribou, near Nederland, for a reported $1 million in 1971 and installed a studio by 1973. But Caribou served Walsh and Szymczyk before it gained fame as a destination studio.

"Guercio was going to direct a movie, *Electra Glide In Blue*, starring Robert Blake," Szymczyk explained. "He said, 'I'm not going to finish the studio because I'm not going to be here for six months.' We begged and pleaded with him. We definitely wanted to record there because it was only three miles from Joe's house. He thought it would be good if we could break it in for him while he was off making a movie, so he finished the room for us.

"But the downstairs was still dirt floors, there was no bathroom, and upstairs was two-by-fours. We used the studio, but it was a lot of DIY stuff."

For the road, Walsh built a larger version of the "Barnstorm" band, also called Barnstorm (with Rocke Grace on keyboards). He officially went solo with 1973's *The Smoker You Drink, The Player You Get*—its title growing evidence of his comic persona—which became the first Top 10 album of his career and went on to sell more than a million copies. Two songs, the radio hit "Rocky Mountain Way" and the memorable "Meadows," opened up an enormous audience for Walsh and the group.

"I always felt 'Rocky Mountain Way' was special, even before it was complete," Walsh said. "We had recorded that before I knew what the words were going to be, but I was very proud of it. That was pretty much one shot at it, all playing at the same time.

"I got kind of fed up with feeling sorry for myself, and I wanted to justify and feel good about leaving the James Gang, relocating, and going for it. I wanted to say, 'Hey, whatever this is, I'm positive and I'm proud,' and the words just came out of feeling that way, rather than writing a song out of remorse. It turned out to be a special song for a lot of people.

"It's the attitude and the statement. It's a positive song, and it's basic rock 'n' roll, which is what I really do."

Barnstorm parted amicably in 1975, allowing Walsh to produce Dan Fogelberg's first hit album, *Souvenirs*. The Eagles invited him aboard as guitarist-writer-vocalist-keyboardist, and Walsh gave the country-rock band a much-needed harder edge. It gave him enhanced visibility, and along the way he continued his solo career.

Colorado was where Walsh experienced some of his greatest musical triumphs—and a great personal tragedy.

A simple plaque adorns the water fountain in North Boulder Park: "This fountain is given in loving memory of Emma Walsh. April 29, 1971 to April 1, 1974." Walsh and former wife Stephanie donated the water fountain to the park in 1976 because it was a favorite playspot of their daughter, who died in a car accident. Walsh's 1974 *So What?* album also included another tribute, "Song For Emma."

"Joe was on the road constantly, and when he'd get off he'd spend more time in L.A. than he would in Colorado," Szymczyk said.

"When Emma died, that put the period on the whole deal. Stephanie went to pieces, and so did he, and so did I—I was her godfather, in the hospital when they had to take her off life support. That was a very dark time.

"Very shortly after that, Joe was permanently gone from Colorado."

Joe Walsh with daughter Emma and former wife Stephanie

Moving to Colorado from Los Angeles in 1971 was perhaps the singular most important element contributing to the Nitty Gritty Dirt Band's rise in status, commercially and creatively.

To attempt to chronicle the various manifestations of the Nitty Gritty Dirt Band is a bewildering task. Jim Ibbotson, Jeff Hanna, John McEuen, Jimmie Fadden, and Les Thompson came together as the Nitty Gritty Dirt Band in 1969. There had been four emanations of the band before that. The band was part of the very fluid California scene that flowered with the careers of Jackson Browne, Linda Ronstadt, and the like. NGDB was in at the beginning of it all.

They had some pop singles ("Buy For Me the Rain" and "House at Pooh Corner") and one massive hit (a 1971 cover of Jerry Jeff Walker's "Mr. Bojangles") and had been a pioneering band, straddling such diverse styles as rock, folk, country, and bluegrass.

It was taking part in one of contemporary music's most historic albums, *Will the Circle Be Unbroken*, the American music anthology put together by Dirt Band majordomo Bill McEuen, that the band really came together.

The ambitious three-record set saw them joined by old-time greats Mother Maybelle Carter, Earl Scruggs, Roy Acuff, Doc Watson, Merle Travis, Jimmy Martin (of Bill Monroe's Bluegrass Boys), Vassar Clements, and Norman Blake. Recorded live on a two-track machine, the amazing results marked an important point in the acceptance of long-haired "hippie" types by country music establishment figures.

"There was a country-rock movement born out of that big folk music scare of the '60s," Jeff Hanna said. "And all of a sudden, they were going, 'Hmm, let's see where we can go with this,' and coming up with this weird hybrid."

The Dirt Band was trying to decide whether to maintain one foot in pop or go with tradition. The band had played to enthusiastic crowds in Denver and Boulder during early tours. In 1971, they left Los Angeles to relocate in the Colorado mountains, settling into their respective wooded communities—Evergreen, Golden, and Aspen.

Then, at the suggestion of manager Bill McEuen, the Dirt Band outlined plans for recording a selection of traditional country numbers to be performed in conjunction with the original musicians. The band went to see the Earl Scruggs Revue at Tulagi in Boulder in 1972.

It was Scruggs' picking that had made the banjo a lead instrument over two decades prior and given bluegrass a distinctive style. Scruggs was still innovating, but it wasn't always easy. His Revue—featuring his hip-looking sons, Gary and Randy, and Vassar Clements, the middle-aged fiddler—used electric instruments and drums, and the band was often booed by traditionalists at bluegrass festivals.

"He had come to see us at a concert we did at Vanderbilt University," Hanna said. "Before he left the room we said, 'Would you think about playing banjo on one of our records?' And then months later, he played Tulagi. And we had come up with this idea ...

"The catalyst? Randy and Gary had been listening to our records—they were into this country-rock aspect. And having grown up in Nashville under the tutelage of the greats—their Sunday dinners with Merle Travis coming over—they saw the potential for something as well. And they nurtured this along with their father.

"Earl was our liaison."

The Nitty Gritty Dirt Band went to Nashville, gathering country stalwarts. Some of the stars were skeptical at first of the Dirt Band members and their amplified instruments. The long-hairs had their own preconceptions. Common ground was found when the traditional musicians saw how respectful the Dirt Band was toward them and their work, as well as how serious the members were about their own music. In a modest and self-effacing manner, the band allowed the spotlight to fall on the old masters.

The resulting triple album changed the direction of popular music. *Will the Circle Be Unbroken* brought a new appreciation for unadulterated folk and roots-country stars to rock listeners' ears. It elicited positive reviews from both the rock and country music press. *Circle* even sold well, an amazing achievement for a sprawling three-record set, and it produced the first gold album for Scruggs, Carter, Watson, Acuff, and others.

The geographical transition had brought an immediate host of fresh, attentive new faces to the front of stages, the personification of all the things the band stood for conceptually. The Dirt Band reflected the Colorado locals' consciousness, and it wasn't long before the new citizens of Idaho Springs and Castle Rock claimed the group for their own.

Subsequent album releases were peppered with country-flavored material, but still the Dirt Band was seen as more of a rock band than a country oufit. Because of its impressive history and

***Will the Circle Be Unbroken* featured the Nitty Gritty Dirt Band & a cross section of country music greats.**

outstanding live shows, the band was able to continue working. A couple of pop singles made the charts—1980's "Make A Little Magic" and "An American Dream" with Linda Ronstadt, both released under the name the Dirt Band.

The band didn't make any inroads into the contemporary country music world until Chuck Morris, whose attention had been steered to concert promotion, entered the management picture. In 1983, the band gradually forced its way onto country radio with a slew of Top 10 hits—"High Horse," "I Only Love You," "Partners, Brothers and Friends," "Soldier of Love," "Long Hard Road," "Fishin' in the Dark," "Modern Day Romance," and more.

The Nitty Gritty Dirt Band's "Colorado Christmas" remained a radio staple around the holidays. By the 1990s, the members had raised their families. Jimmy Ibbotson was the only member who remained in Colorado, in Woody Creek.

Keyboardist and vocalist Bob Carpenter (second from left) was based in Aspen in the 1970s with the band Starwood. He went on to join the Nitty Gritty Dirt Band.

REO SPEEDWAGON

Like other midwestern bands in the 1970s, REO Speedwagon was constantly on the road, eventually becoming a regional superstar. Lead singer Kevin Cronin and guitarist Gary Richrath wrote the classic rock staple "Ridin' the Storm Out" in 1973 when REO played Tulagi in Boulder.

"We were kids—twenty going on fifteen. We had a record deal, and we were goo-goo eyed," guitarist Gary Richrath recalled.

"In combination with that, we were romantics from Illinois where there's no hills—we hadn't been far enough west to see mountains. And we freaked. I remember we were driving across the plains and said, 'Shit, look at that stuff!' We were dying when we got to Boulder.

"Kevin and I were like two brothers. We did everything together at the time. We got a few provisions to go up to the Flatirons to hike around. Our tour manager said, 'You're not going up there'—a big blizzard was coming in. We ditched him and went anyway."

"We ended up getting lost," Cronin continued. "It started snowing, and we thought for a moment that we were goners."

"It was confusing for a couple of kids from the Midwest. We got nervous and scared and walked around in circles for an hour," Richrath said. "Then we saw a flagpole in a park and ran to it. Our road manager had brains enough to sit and wait for us.

"It was an inspiring moment, walking in the woods, hoping to get our asses out of there. The next morning I woke up and said to Kevin, 'I've got some lyrics. Let's work on them.'

"Kevin always says he knows a new hit when he writes one. I didn't quite see 'Ridin' the Storm Out' becoming the stalwart REO song of the '70s, but now you've got to give the song the respect it deserves."

REO Speedwagon's first million-seller was a 1977 live album titled *You Get What You Pay For*, and the "Ridin' the Storm Out" single reached No. 94 on the *Billboard* charts.

REO became America's No. 1 rock band in 1980, reaching a zenith with a carefully crafted blend of hard-rock and high-energy ballads.

"We weathered neglect from New York and Los Angeles music circles, critical drubbings, personnel changes, and years of opening-act status," Cronin said. "'Ridin' the Storm Out' was the one thing that held the band together for all of those years. It closed our shows for over a decade."

JOHN DENVER

Once one of the top five selling recording artists in the history of the music industry, John Denver will always be associated with the Rocky Mountains and the city from which he took his name.

In 1974, then-Colorado Governor John Vanderhoof proclaimed John Denver the state's poet laureate. Every year prior to his death in 1997, he returned to his Aspen home to host his own Celebrity Pro/Am Ski Tournament. Concern for the mountains and the environment at large spurred him to found the Windstar Foundation in 1976 as a research facility to study alternative solutions to food production, energy, and land education.

His explanation for the attraction?

"When I get to the mountains, I'm happy," he said. "That's all there is to it."

Henry John Deutschendorf, Jr. was born on New Year's Eve, 1943, in Roswell, New Mexico. An air force brat, his childhood was spent all over the Southwest, but his favorite times were spent on his grandmother's Oklahoma farm. The guitar that his other grandmother had given him at age eight accompanied him everywhere.

He took one year of lessons "to learn the basic chords," then joined a rock band in high school. Architecture was his official major at Texas Tech, but he spent more time playing than drawing. Folk music clubs drew him to Los Angeles midway through his junior year, where he renamed himself John Denver after his favorite city.

"I liked it because my heart longed to live in the mountains," he said.

In 1965, Denver was selected out of 250 candidates to replace Chad Mitchell in the Chad Mitchell Trio. During his three-year tenure with the trio he began writing songs.

A cheerfully optimistic image marked John Denver's 1970s heyday. He was a grinning sprite known for saying "Far out!" He insinuated himself into the public's consciousness with "Rocky Mountain High," No. 9 in March 1973.

"It's very much an autobiographical song. It came out of several things. One was finally moving to Colorado, that first summer of my twenty-seventh year, and making it my home. I'd been to Colorado several times. It was the Rocky Mountains, man—I wanted to live there.

"I did a lot of camping that summer, which had me getting back to the things I love most—the beauty of the land and the quiet of the wilderness—and just how precious it is to me. There was a trip during the Perseid meteor shower, which happens August 12 through the 15—a really spectacular night. I'm an amateur astronomer, and there's never been a better one.

"And there was all this stuff going on then about having an Olympics in Colorado. With the experience I'd had seeing some of the other places around the world, I was very much opposed to it.

"So those questions were going on in my mind—the experience of feeling like I'd found home, this glorious night under the stars, and then the problems that face any place where tourism is the primary industry, keeping development and growth under control and guided wisely. Out of all that came the song.

"I've never burnt out on it. It's fun to think of coining a phrase that gets into the language, and 'Rocky Mountain High' is in the language now."

Windsong (1975) was probably the most nature-inspired of all Denver's albums. It lent its name to Denver's newly established record label—formed, he said, to further Colorado musicians and his own self-taught knowledge of his craft.

Bill Danoff had been a folksinger working nights as the light and sound man at a club in Washington, D.C., where he met Denver, who was near the end of his stretch fronting the Chad Mitchell Trio. Soon Denver recorded Danoff's "I Guess He'd Rather Be in Colorado." The friendship between them was cemented when they co-wrote Denver's first smash hit, "Take Me Home, Country Roads."

Danoff and his wife Taffy were members of the band Fat City. They created the Starland Vocal Band, and they fine-tuned the clean-cut, all-American quartet's rich pop harmony sound before becoming the first act signed to Denver's Windsong stable. The first single "Afternoon Delight" was released, and nine weeks later the Starland Vocal Band and the label had their first and only No. 1 single.

Absent from the Top 30 since 1976, Denver's 1980s and 1990s output focused on a mature interest in the range of human experience, using his popularity to promote one of his favorite causes over the years, the environment.

"I look back at some of my old album cover pictures and I wonder who that guy is. I just don't feel like that anymore. I guess I've gotten past the picture that people had of long hair and the granny glasses, and I'm glad about that. The worst things that have ever happened to me have been what people said about my music—'the Mickey Mouse of pop,' or 'the Ronald Reagan of rock.'

"That's aimed at diminishing not only me, but all the folks whose lives have been touched by my music. I still meet people who use my songs in their weddings, who have played them while they're going through labor. But I know that it took going through all of those former years to get where I am."

In October 1997, John Denver died when his experimental aircraft crashed into the Pacific Ocean.

RICHIE FURAY

While walking down a road to his house near Nederland, Richie Furay wrote Poco's most distinctive composition—1973's "A Good Feeling To Know."

"It's that opening line—'Colorado mountains, I can see your distant sky.' When we were away on the road, flying from east to west and seeing the mountains, it was like, 'Oh, boy, this is home,'" Furay said.

"But that song devastated me. I thought it was going to catapult Poco into another realm of acceptance, yet we had a lot of trouble getting played on the radio at the time. We were too country for the rock stations and too rock for the country stations."

In the spring of 1966, Furay had formed Buffalo Springfield with Stephen Stills and Neil Young. The West Coast group had only one major hit (Stills' ominous protest song "For What It's Worth"), but Furay's songs made the rock band perhaps the first to experiment with a country sound.

The volatile group broke up in 1969, and Furay then formed Poco with Jim Messina (Buffalo Springfield's recording engineer who took over as the bass player) and Randy Meisner, along with ex-Coloradoans Rusty Young and George Grantham, who left Böenzee Cryque. Meisner left Poco to join Rick Nelson's Stone Canyon Band and later the Eagles.

In the fall of 1970, Furay and the remaining band members moved to Colorado. Messina departed after three albums to form Loggins & Messina, and Furay provided Poco with the rugged toughness of *A Good Feeling To Know.* The album reached No. 69 on *Billboard*'s pop album chart, but the title track failed to make the singles chart.

In September 1973, Furay, frustrated by the record's failure to generate the expected commercial success, left Poco to form Souther-Hillman-Furay, a ready-made supergroup put together by record mogul David Geffen. By all indications, success was inevitable. J.D. Souther was a masterful songwriter in the Eagles mold. Furay's roots were Buffalo Springfield and Poco, and Hillman's utilitarian prowess supposedly clinched it.

"Fallin' in Love," the group's sole hit, was written by Furay. It peaked at No. 27 on *Billboard*'s pop singles chart in 1974. But the band never jelled and evaporated after two years. Yet, while recording the second Souther-Hillman-Furay album at Caribou Ranch in Nederland, steel guitarist Al Perkins—a former Flying Burrito Brother and a member of Manassas—suggested Furay consider Christianity as an alternative lifestyle.

"When Chris Hillman wanted Al in the band, I said, 'No way—I know this guy's reputation. He's one of those born-again Christians with a Jesus sticker on his guitar. I don't want anything to get in the way of stardom.'

"But I couldn't deny his musicianship. And I couldn't put my finger on what was different and attractive. This guy was in the middle of rock 'n' roll, and he wasn't getting drunk or doing drugs or chasing women every night. But he was having fun, being creative, and enjoying music.

"When my wife left me, I hit the bottom. That's when I finally prayed with Al, and that's when I found God's plan for me. I had wanted to be a star, but stars burn out."

Injuring his hand while chopping wood near his Colorado home, Furay was forced to suspend his playing until his convalescence was complete. Nearly a year later, Furay re-emerged and pursued a solo career, one of the first rock stars to make Christian music for the general market. Three late-1970s solo albums failed to find wide acceptance, but "I Still Have Dreams" debuted on *Billboard*'s pop singles chart in October 1979 and peaked at No. 39.

Yet Furay severed his ties with a major label following a controversy over a song that had some spiritual content.

"They wanted me to compromise the lyric, which I couldn't do. It came down to the wire after five years. I said, 'I've tried, and it hasn't worked. What do you want , Lord?'"

In 1982, Furay abandoned his music and devoted himself to his chores as pastor for Boulder's 150-member Rocky Mountain Christian Fellowship. When Rusty Young orchestrated a Poco reunion in 1989, he urged Furay to give the rock world one more try. Poco's *Legacy*, Furay's first secular musical project in a decade, earned a gold record.

But the one stumbling block was the choice of songs dealing with sex. Having given his life to the Lord, Furay made no secret of his disdain for the rock-star life that clashed with his religious beliefs. He didn't participate in the second leg of Poco's tour.

FLASH CADILLAC & THE CONTINENTAL KIDS

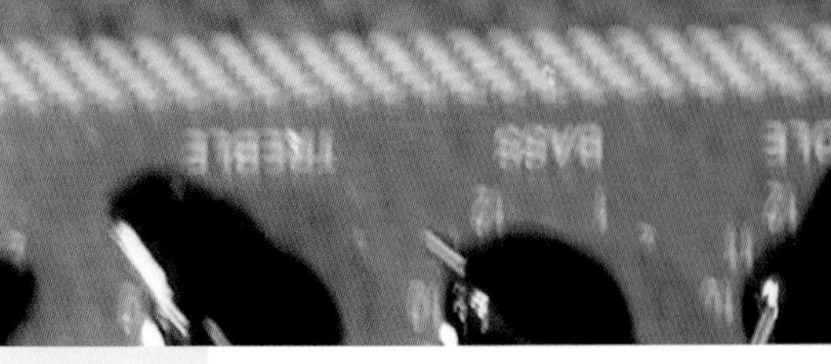

What band would audition its sax player with a four-part questionnaire: "Are you single? Do you drink beer? Do you play basketball? Can you play 'Yakety-Yak'?"

Only Flash Cadillac, the best-loved 1950s oldies band in America.

"Sha Na Na started up about the same time in New York. They were on the East Coast and got all the notoriety, but we may have predated them," original drummer Harold Fielden recalled.

Flash Cadillac & the Continental Kids was formed in 1968 at the University of Colorado as a means to pass the time, an oldies rock alternative to the then-popular hippie sound. Mick Manresa eventually signed on as the lead singer. As the original "Flash," he hid his oriental features behind wraparound shades and slicked-down hair.

Two of the first people recruited for Flash Cadillac were Tommy Bolin and Jock Bartley. "They had long hair—Tommy's was red, green, and purple—and the last thing they wanted to do was get a greaser haircut and wear tight pants and pointed shoes and do dance steps," Fielden explained. "So neither of them joined."

Word quickly spread about the neo-greasers' rabid live performances.

"It's hard for us to distinguish our actual first job because the first practice was a party—every practice was a party," keyboardist Kris "Angelo" Moe recalled. "And the first job was a party. So how do you distinguish a practice party from a job party?"

The first paying job came on February 9, 1969, but things got serious quickly. The lewd and rude Flash Cadillac shows at Tulagi became the biggest events in Boulder.

"The pressure was really on," Moe said. "Six months before, we were just another group of guys waiting for our book assignment. Suddenly, the whole town of Boulder was mobilizing every Tuesday night for some spectacular happening that we had no idea about—we were still trying to figure out the week before. We didn't feel in control. Everybody in town just decided, 'Well, Flash is playing, let's go do it there.' All of the loonies would show up. And let's not kid anybody—people took off their clothes all the time."

The "skin to win" rules for the twist contest, the "wild elephant" for guys (dropping trousers and pulling the pants pockets inside out), and other group participation bits were hatched by Fielden.

"You just can't match the old Tulagi days for sickness," Fielden said of Boulder's thriving late-1960s club scene. "*Playboy* named all the best party schools in the country, and they didn't include CU because they said they didn't want to lump the professionals in with the amateurs."

"We had the entire crowd choreographed and programmed in Boulder, and Harold wanted to see as much lewdness as possible," Moe said. "We didn't want to play a lot, and everyone thought we were trying to raise our prices, so they offered us more money! We would turn down everything unless it was for mondo bucks, so we were doing four times better than other local bands. So we figured we'd go to Los Angeles."

Exactly one year after their formation, the members of Flash Cadillac drove to L.A. to play a "hoot-night" at the legendary Troubadour. That day they called agents from a pay phone across the street. That night they came on last to a half-empty club and had the place packed and dancing on the tables.

"It was nice, because it proved we weren't just good in Boulder, we were good anywhere," Moe said. "All these guys in suits crowded into the dressing room after the show handing us business cards and saying they wanted to sign us.

"And we were saying, 'Well, we've got class tomorrow—we have to leave.'"

So the group quit school and hit the road. Within a year, Fielden and Manresa decided it wasn't fun anymore and returned to Boulder. Fielden became an attorney in the Denver area, but he and Manresa remained in pursuit of the ultimate gross-out, performing oldies sets with the 4-Nikators and backing up oldies acts like Bo Diddley and the Crystals when they came to town.

Having lost their singer and talker, the other members of Flash Cadillac made the big decision to make a go of it as a real working band in 1971. The first step was to find a new Flash. Sam McFadin, a Colorado Springs fan of the band, was the only person considered for the job.

"When I knew they were going to audition me, I went down in my basement and drank beer to see if I could still play Chuck Berry riffs behind my back. It was the only intensive training I got before I was out on the road."

Fronted by McFadin, Flash Cadillac gained instant popularity within the music industry. Flash Cadillac earned acclaim in the movies, appearing as the sock-hop band Herbie & the Heartbeats in George Lucas' *American Graffiti* in 1973, and also a scene with San Francisco rock promoter Bill Graham in Francis Ford Coppola's 1979 Vietnam epic *Apocalypse Now*.

And Flash Cadillac's work on television's *Happy Days* on March 11, 1975—the episode "Fish and the Fins" was written especially for the band—won the highest weekly rating.

Flash Cadillac also began recording albums of oldies and catchy 1950's-style pop originals, and the nightmares with record labels began. With the live show, the group never had a problem communicating its patented fraternity-style humor. It was on record that it didn't come across as well.

Flash Cadillac & the Continental Kids became the first band to perform on *American Bandstand* without having a record, in 1971.

The band's second album, *There's No Face Like Chrome*, was recorded using three different producers. In 1974, "Youngblood" was the No. 1 song in more than twenty markets, and "Dancin' (on a Saturday Night)" cracked the *Billboard* pop singles charts at No. 93.

"But they didn't know how to market what we were, they never let us take any chances," Moe said. "We recorded the greatest belch in the history of the world, and they'd say, 'There are ten other records with that.' Well, somebody likes it!"

Flash Cadillac gave the big time one more shot on Private Stock Records, recording minor hits in "Did You Boogie (With Your Baby)" (with spoken interludes by Wolfman Jack) and "Good Times, Rock and Roll." But a great version of "See My Baby Jive" (a hit for Roy Wood in England) was left hanging in January 1977 when the company's promotion staff quit over a salary dispute.

By that time, Flash Cadillac was looking for land in the Rocky Mountain area. The members—McFadin, Moe, Linn "Spike" Phillips III (guitar), Warren "Butch" Knight (bass), Dwight "Spider" Bement (sax), and the latest in a long line of drummers—purchased a little ranch near Woodland Park, outside Colorado Springs. All of a sudden, after years on the road, they found they had real lives to lead. Several of them got married, and the process of scaling down their careers began.

The ranch served initially as a rehearsal hall, but after several years the band built up the facility into a twenty-four-track studio. Several businesses were running at once—Flash Cadillac on the road, in the studio, and doing commercial work. The nationally broadcast *Super Gold* weekly radio program featured Flash Cadillac as the house band.

In 1992, the band was reborn performing with symphony orchestras across the country, one of the hottest pops concerts going, and easily the most fun. The symphony musicians got with it, getting old poodle skirts and letter jackets out of mothballs.

"What we're trying to get across is that there's a type of music Flash Cadillac plays—good-time, high-energy—that has existed throughout rock 'n' roll history," McFadin said. "Rather than being nostalgic about it, saying it's all coming around again, we just consider it to be all that we know how to do. There are people who keep this kind of music alive."

Flash Cadillac lost cylinders over the years. In March 1993, Phillips, who was known for his crazy on-stage antics, suffered a heart attack backstage after a show and died. He wasn't replaced in the band, and the use of nicknames was dropped. Moe retired to the studio while fighting a debilitating muscular disease. The heart and soul was taken out of the band when McFadin died of a heart attack in September 2001.

In the 1980s, Flash Cadillac was featured every weekend as the house band on the nationally broadcast *Super Gold* radio program.

QUEEN

A pioneering band in many ways, Queen assembled a brash, theatrical stage act well before glitter bands emerged as a potent pop vehicle.

In 1974, with a successful U.K. tour behind them, Queen was looking forward to bigger gigs in the United States as the *Queen II* album was released. On April 12, the band began its first American tour, supporting Mott The Hoople at Regis College in Denver. The English newcomers were received rather quietly at first. The audience had obviously heard of Mott but weren't too sure of Freddie Mercury wearing satin and nail polish. His outrageous on-stage theatrics set a new standard for rock showmanship.

By the end of the set, however, they were won over.

"It was wonderful," guitarist Brian May said. "After the gig, the most incredible bunch of people turned up and we had a party in the (hotel) room. I'd never been in a situation like that. In England, we had made very little ground. Suddenly, we were in a situation where there was a rock culture, and we were perceived as generating a new one, unwittingly close to the center of it. It was mind-blowing. I had so many incredible conversations. I remember the record company people being surprised—'This doesn't feel like Denver tonight.'

"From there on in, it was a constant high."

The U.S. tour was abandoned when May contracted hepatitis followed by a duodenal ulcer. The reversal worked to their benefit. They returned to England. What emerged from their enforced hiatus was a fresh group effort, Sheer Heart Attack, and the single hit "Killer Queen." Queen went on to international stardom, and the songs "We Will Rock You," "We Are the Champions," "Another One Bites the Dust," "Crazy Little Thing Called Love," and many others became mega-hits.

Intensely private about his personal life, Freddie Mercury never revealed how or when he contracted AIDS. He died in November 1991, only one day after publicly announcing that he was HIV-positive, a fact he had concealed from nearly everyone.

BOB SEGER

In 1976, after a decade of being rock's "Beautiful Loser," Bob Seger began his overdue breakthrough to stardom when his *Live Bullet* album went gold. *Live Bullet*, recorded at two sold-out shows at Cobo Hall in Seger's hometown of Detroit, featured versions of such early Seger classics as "Ramblin' Gamblin' Man," "Katmandu," "Turn the Page," and "Get Out of Denver." The 1974 single "Get Out of Denver" had peaked at No. 80 on the *Billboard* chart.

Was the tune based on a real-life Denver experience?

"Sorry," Seger grinned. "At that stage of my career, I tried to write a rocker for every album that would be fun to do live. 'Katmandu' was also done that way.

"I wanted to write a Chuck Berry song, and I liked the cadence of Denver in the lyrics—Albuquerque wouldn't fit.

"But I made it all up. I never got run out of Denver."

The song became a classic, covered in the next decade by Dave Edmunds, Eddie & the Hot Rods, and Dr. Feelgood.

EMMYLOU HARRIS

Emmylou Harris didn't really start writing her own material until she hit her fifties, with one exception being her heartbreaking paean to mentor Gram Parsons, 1975's "Boulder To Birmingham."

"It's not like I set out to write a song about Gram, but it was inspired by some of the feelings I had after his death," Harris said.

In the late 1960s, when the blues and British pop were all the rage on the rock scene, Parsons crusaded for country music's merits. Concocting his notion of "country soul" or "cosmic American music," the Georgia-bred singer-songwriter developed the genre that would later be termed country-rock.

Parsons' journey began when he was a member of the Byrds (he appeared on the countrified *Sweetheart of the Rodeo* album), and he later founded the Flying Burrito Brothers before releasing a pair of solo albums. Harris first came to prominence in the early 1970s, adding heart-tugging harmonies to Parsons' solo efforts. Her clear soprano perfectly complemented his lived-in lead vocals.

In the winter and spring of 1973, Harris toured briefly with Parsons in support of his last album, as the centerpiece of his touring outfit, the Fallen Angels. The performances established her as a decorous honky-tonk angel.

"Our first gig was in Boulder," Harris said of a show at the Edison Electric Company. "We actually got fired from that club —we forgot to work up beginnings, middles, and ends of songs!

"Then we went up to the mountains and played in Nederland. It was like seeing 'McCabe and Mrs. Miller'—two women were fighting in the parking lot. I thought, 'Yeah, this is for me.'"

Parsons' tragic overdose in September 1973 cut his life short and fixed him as a legend. It also marked the end of Harris' apprenticeship. Her debut, *Pieces of the Sky*, yielded the achingly beautiful original "Boulder To Birmingham," cowritten with Bill Danoff, who'd had major success as the co-composer of John Denver's "Take Me Home, Country Roads."

ELTON JOHN

In the mid-1970s, before the recording industry faced the economic crunch, the rage among top recording stars was to hole up at "destination studios." Wouldn't it be inspirational and less distracting, they reasoned, to record outside of the usual Los Angeles or New York circles?

So they packed up their bags and headed for Caribou Ranch, the legendary recording complex near the Boulder County foothills hamlet of Nederland, Colorado.

Before it gained fame as a destination studio, Caribou, in its idyllic setting nearly 9,000 feet up in the Rocky Mountains, was the largest privately owned Arabian stud farm in the country. The 3,000-plus-acre site also served as a dude ranch and a motion-picture set.

Owner Jim Guercio bought Caribou for a reported $1 million in 1971 and installed the studio in 1973. Then he transformed the place into an opulent retreat for pop music's aristocracy while developing an exclusive image for himself.

"We didn't run the place like a Holiday Inn," Guercio noted.

The life-in-the-fast-lane ambience that usually accompanies a recording session disappeared at Caribou. During the ranch's glory days, an entourage got full use of the facilities for a basic rate of $1,500 a day.

The studio was the main lure, but the lodging was equally seductive. The cabins, which slept up to thirty-six people, featured brass beds, lace curtains, leather-upholstered furniture, huge rock fireplaces, hardwood floors, dark cedar walls, and massive stereo systems. Steinway baby grand pianos lurked in the corners of several cabins.

To while away the off-hours, there was a comprehensive library of movies and games to chose from, an antique pool table for a quick game, horseback riding, or skimobiling.

But the favorite pastime had to be eating. A staff of friendly cooks remained on call twenty-four hours a day to prepare any snack or meal that came to mind. And every evening, there was a sit-down dinner with candlelight and wine.

What appealed most to Caribou clientele was the insulation from the usual rock 'n' roll circus. There wasn't a nightclub down the street, and artists didn't have to send for food or commute back and forth from a hotel or even worry about the laundry.

Record companies were only too willing to shell out the money during the mid-1970s boom years. Caribou gained additional prominence when Elton John recorded the gratefully titled *Caribou* in the spring of 1974.

"It really is luxurious," John raved. "The only thing you have to get used to is that it's so high up, you keep gasping for breath all the time."

Each of the flamboyant star's first eight studio albums had been made in Europe. John, always on the go, was in the middle of another of his traumatic periods because of the rigors of his commitments. Although many of his early albums were recorded quickly, the making of *Caribou* was particularly stressful, squeezed into the smallest time frame yet.

"We were under unbelievable pressure to finish the album in just over a week because we had to go right into a tour of Japan and

Australia," he said. "We wrote and recorded *Caribou* in eight days—fourteen tracks in all."

Caribou topped the album chart on both sides of the Atlantic, remaining in the *Billboard* Top 200 albums chart for more than a year. It spawned John's fourth million-selling single in eight months, "Don't Let the Sun Go Down On Me." The emotional ballad became a classic, yet it was the most troublesome track.

"I thought it was the worst vocal of all time," John said. "I said, 'I hate it ... so don't you dare put this on the album.'"

John recorded several other classic albums at Caribou Ranch, including *Captain Fantastic and the Brown Dirt Cowboy* and *Rock of the Westies*, which reached the No. 1 spot on the charts its first week out.

Bernie Taupin, the celebrated collaborator who put the words in John's mouth for three decades, said, "Some of my favorite work that we ever created was done at Caribou. *Captain Fantastic* is one of our finest records, and probably the most underestimated of our career.

"Oddly enough, it wasn't a particularly good point in my life. We were pretty whacked out in those days. I don't know where there was more 'snow,' in the mountains or in the cabins!

"But there were some great moments, like having Stevie Wonder drive me in a Jeep from the cabin to the studio. I think he set me up—he probably practiced it with somebody else. The funny thing was, I didn't pay any attention to it—a blind man driving didn't faze me at all!

"And spending time with John Lennon doing 'Lucy in the Sky with Diamonds' ..."

Elton John had met Lennon for the first time in October 1973, in the Los Angeles studio where Lennon was recording his *Rock 'n' Roll* album. The next year, Elton John was in a New York studio doing backup vocals for Lennon's *Walls and Bridges* album, and the result was the hit single "Whatever Gets You Through the Night."

As John recalled, "I said, 'Now, I really want to do one of your songs as a single. Which song would you like me to do?' He said, 'No one ever recorded "Lucy in the Sky" ' ..."

John suggested that Lennon stop in Colorado on his way back from a trip to California. The session took place at Caribou Ranch in July, with Lennon billed as "the reggae guitars of Dr. Winston O'Boogie."

John's smash "Philadelphia Freedom" was inspired by one of his bouts of fan worship. The World Tennis League was started in 1974, and he was an ardent supporter of Billie Jean King's team, the Philadelphia Freedoms.

"We had the playoffs in Denver," King said. "Elton came because he'd been recording up at Caribou ... He was all excited, saying, 'You've got to listen to this tape. This is it, the song I wrote for you ...' So he played me a rough mix of 'Philadelphia Freedom,' and ... it was great. And when he got to the chorus he said, 'Listen to this part. Hear the beat? That's when you get mad on the court.'"

"Philadelphia Freedom" had that good old Gamble-Huff style backbeat, just like the great O'Jays and MFSB records that came out of Philadelphia, and it took only five weeks to become John's fourth No. 1 single.

In August 1975, Elton John joined the Rolling Stones onstage in Fort Collins, dressed in a cowboy hat and an L.A. Dodgers windbreaker. He wanted to give a barbeque for the Stones at Caribou, but after the show, the Stones turned down his offer.

A veritable who's-who of rock music's elite passed through Caribou Ranch's gates—America, Jeff Beck, Rick Derringer, Earth, Wind & Fire, Dan Fogelberg, Michael Murphey, Souther, Hillman & Furay, Rod Stewart, Stephen Stills, Supertramp, War, Frank Zappa, the Nitty Gritty Dirt Band, Joe Walsh, Chicago, Eddie Rabbitt, Sheena Easton, Badfinger, and more.

Ultimately, other studios cropped up around the world that offered similarly exotic atmospheres—refurbished medieval castles in Europe, complexes in the middle of the Caribbean—and the "in" place to record among top bands shifted. Caribou stayed busy, but when the late-1970s recession turned the boom to bust, labels scaled back recording budgets and expensive destination studios fell out of favor.

Caribou finally shut down after a March 1985 fire destroyed the control room, causing about $3 million worth of damage. Guercio donated the remaining equipment to the University of Colorado–Denver in 1986.

MICHAEL MURPHEY

Michael Murphey was one of the cornerstones of Austin's so-called "cosmic cowboy" scene. In 1972, the Dallas native had "Geronimo's Cadillac" scrape into the Top 40.

But his Colorado journey began with the classy, heartfelt ballad "Wildfire"—"the song about the horse"—which shot to No. 3 in the summer of 1976.

Murphey had spent the mid-1960s in Los Angeles, putting in a brief stint with the Lewis & Clark Expedition. "Wildfire" was written after the group broke up.

"A friend and I took a cross-country trip to New York in a pickup truck with a camper on it. We wanted to see the heartland first and foremost, experience thunderstorms on the plains. I ran across a legend from Nebraska that I had heard of in my youth, one of the stories my grandfather would tell—that of the ghost horse of the plains, the mustang that could never be captured.

"I wrote it down in some notebooks and then forgot about it. Then I was writing songs with a guy named Larry Cansler. I went to sleep on the floor and dreamed this whole scenario of the Wildfire story. I woke up at three in the morning and wrote down the whole lyrics on a yellow legal pad. I went upstairs and woke up Larry and we worked on it until the sun came up.

"It took me many years to understand where it came from, going back to western ghost stories."

In 1971, Murphey moved back to Texas. He played "Wildfire" in concert and people kept requesting it. By late 1974, he was living in Colorado.

"I'd just gone through a divorce, and I was also disenchanted with the carpetbaggers from the record companies who were ruining the creativity in Austin, trying to turn it into a record business town. I just wanted to get away from all that …

"The first year I was in Colorado, I lived without a telephone. I would go down to Bailey and call from the gas station. Nobody could reach me. After I calmed down from the whole hype of the Austin scene, I began to realize that I could look back inside myself and create from that."

Murphey recorded his album *Blue Sky, Night Thunder* at Caribou Ranch, the recording complex five minutes outside of Nederland, and "Wildfire" ended up as the album's first track. He tipped his hand in favor of Hollywood-style Western music—Jack Murphy's piano gave the romantic, soft, hovering ballad a dreamlike quality.

"We were dealing with Western images and lifestyle, and we were using a big palette of musical colors to do that—from things that sounded country with steel guitars to very jazzy stuff and rock 'n' roll sounds and everything in between. It was a time of great jumbling and cross-pollination of styles that I haven't seen the likes of since.

"I was spending a lot of time in South Dakota with a medicine man … I was very caught up in the poetic way of speaking that comes from the Lakota people. In fact, *Blue Sky, Night Thunder* comes from a phrase that he used—'Life is blue sky, night thunder.' Their spiritual traditions are caught up in their imagery of the universe and American land …

"Per capita, 'Wildfire' and that album sold more copies in Colorado than any other state. Because of it, my association there continued, even after I left and went down to New Mexico."

As Michael Martin Murphey, he began directing his music more toward the country audience. He scored his first country No. 1 hit in 1982 with "What's Forever For" and became a major star.

Ever since the release of his best-selling *Cowboy Christmas* in 1991, Murphey made stops in Denver to celebrate via his annual "Cowboy Christmas" tour, a blend of campfire storytelling and reflecting with Western arrangements of carols. His fascination with the West also led him to start WestFest, an annual celebration in Colorado.

In May 1975, under Jim Guercio's direction, Chicago teamed up with the Beach Boys in one of the most successful tours in rock history. It was a twelve-city odyssey that grossed $7.5 million and played to a total of more than 700,000, despite a general recession that had hit the rest of the music business hard.

Guercio, who was best known as Chicago's producer, had gotten his start producing a string of hits for the Buckinghams, including "Kind of A Drag" and "Mercy, Mercy, Mercy," and he became a staff producer for Columbia Records. He left a year later for a brief stint as a lead guitarist for the Mothers of Invention, but in 1968 he returned to Columbia to produce Blood, Sweat & Tears and Chicago.

Guercio was also the owner of Caribou Ranch. He gathered up enough money producing Chicago through five albums.

"We were still recording in New York," keyboardist Robert Lamm said. "Guercio said, 'I think it would be a smart idea for us to find a place where we could go and make music, and we wouldn't have to deal with hotels and taxis and studio time, ideally in some place that would be inspiring. We could work any time we want as long as we want.'

"We looked at footage of properties; he had people looking for him. We made the move to Caribou. It was a big financial commitment on Jim's part."

"We must have done a third of our albums up there," Chicago trumpeter Lee Loughnane recalled. "It was a climate where you could get away from any influence or distraction that would take away from creativity. It would result in new fits of inspiration and make for better art, supposedly.

"And it worked for quite a while."

In 1974, Chicago met the Beach Boys at Denver's Stapleton Airport.

"They had come into town to do a show. We started talking at the luggage carousel and we wound up inviting them to the studio," Lamm said.

"Peter Cetera was putting down a track for *Wishing You Were Here*, and he had always envisioned having the Beach Boys' vocals on that record. Bang, there they were at the ranch. Three of them sang on that hit.

"I looked at Carl (Wilson) and said it would be nice to do something with the two bands in concert. It was like Mickey Rooney and Judy Garland saying, 'Let's put on a show! My dad's got a barn!'

"The light bulbs went off over everybody's heads. In that era, as today, everybody wanted to be a headliner. There weren't many times when a couple of superbands would get together to do something."

In the early 1970s, the Beach Boys battled over their live show, with Carl Wilson insisting that a constant updating was necessary and Mike Love fighting to give the people what they seemed to desire desperately—an in-concert jukebox. The conflict became academic. In June 1974, Capitol Records released *Endless Summer*, a two-record set of early hits, and *Spirit of America* followed the next year. The collections sold in the millions.

The Beach Boys were forced to admit that their only future was in their past, and Guercio played an important role in their careers. He quickly moved up the ranks into a full managerial position. His company, Caribou, was officially named as the Beach Boys management arm, and Caribou Records the band's label. He did double-duty, playing bass with them on the tour and whipping the road band into shape.

"That tour was our comeback," Wilson said.

The two bands appeared in a sold-out show at Fort Collins' Hughes Stadium.

Chicago keyboardist Robert Lamm at Caribou Ranch in 1974

that worked from the getaway. Then Elton jumped up, played a little piano, banged a lot of tambourine, did a lot of singing and smiling. It was one of those magical moments. Everybody who was there got their money's worth."

It seemed almost miraculous that within a year the Beach Boys were back on top, grossing as much money without any new recorded product as they had in their heyday. But Guercio and Caribou Management didn't stay with them for long. The following spring, he was relieved of his business responsibilities with the Beach Boys.

Chicago's situation with Guercio also had been deteriorating, and the band members eventually eliminated their dealings with him circa 1977.

"We had five years of incredible success. Along with success comes problems of adjusting to a crazy rock star lifestyle. I don't know that we did a very good job of it on a personal level," Lamm said.

"Some of us were too young and not ready to look inward to see what else was in there, as the Caribou situation should have encouraged—being out there thinking about what was important and having that come through the music. A number of us weren't ready for that—we wanted to party. We were in our mid to late twenties. We were interested in coming down to Boulder to chase girls."

"The ranch was the beginning of the end," Loughnane said. "Jimmy presented it to us as a band investment, and we said, 'Okay, we'll take a pass at it.' But I think he had it in mind that he'd buy it and control it.

"We had some successful albums out of there. There was nothing wrong until we wanted to square up with Jim.

"Well, there was one other thing. We discovered if you stayed too long at Caribou, you got a little buggy. You'd find yourself hiding out in the woods with an elk shirt on."

"We flew up to Colorado State University in our private plane," Loughnane said. "I was getting ready in the dressing room, and all of a sudden I hear this 'teabag' voice saying, 'I say, chaps, how are you?'"

And there was Elton John.

"He'd been at Caribou; he'd heard about the gig," Lamm said. "I told him to hop on stage during the encore. The show was one of those

In 1973, the year Caribou Ranch opened, Chicago filmed a network television special there, *Chicago: High in the Rockies*. A second TV special, *Meanwhile, Back at the Ranch*, aired in 1974.

THE DOOBIE BROTHERS

The Doobie Brothers' numerous hits collectively formed one of the most impressive repertoires of any American band. Their legendary shows of the 1970s were marked by the percussive thrust of dual drummers, the full arsenal of rock chops from the guitarists, and the patented Doobies harmonies. The Doobies cited a number of ties to Colorado, the only state where they headlined stadium shows twice, in 1975 and 1979, at Folsom Field in Boulder.

Marty Wolff, the group's longtime lighting director, was a Denver-Boulder concert promoter in the early 1970s. Through Wolff's Star Lighting, many Colorado denizens were part of the Doobies' heyday, including Chas Barbour (the graphic designer behind the *What Were Once Vices Are Now Habits* album), Dan Fong (the official Doobies' photographer/media coordinator), and former concert promoter Doug Brunkow.

And percussionist Bobby LaKind once lived in Boulder and managed the Tulagi nightclub (where the Doobies performed in 1971). LaKind, who originally signed on as a member of the Doobies' lighting crew, became a full-time member after the release of *One Step Closer*. His congas and percussion graced every Doobie album and tour from 1976 until the band broke up in 1982.

"He was bouncing around the local scene in Colorado and became one of the crew," drummer and founding member John Hartman said. "We had pyrotechnics when we were out on the road. He had a mishap setting up before a show, and it blew up in his face. We felt sorry for him, so we paid attention to the little guy and he edged in. He could play congas and sing a little bit, so we added another guy to the percussion team."

LaKind died of inoperable colon cancer on Christmas Eve 1992 at the age of forty-seven.

Working the arena circuit in the 1970s, Ted Nugent's act couldn't be ignored. The self-styled "wild man of rock" was a carnivorous and hysterical showman—a noble savage sporting a loincloth, shaking his torrents of dirty blonde hair, and wielding a massive, hollow-body Gibson like it was a shotgun.

His demeanor was not inspired by drugs, but, he said, by blood lust. His skills with rifle and bow and arrow became legendary. His first two solo albums, *Call of the Wild* and *Tooth, Fang and Claw*, were indicative of his highly publicized passion.

"There's no question that it was my experience in the Rocky Mountains that brought about those album titles and songs like 'Great White Buffalo.' They come from camps on Colorado's western slope, the Grand Mesa, and Uncompahgre," he recalled.

In 1975, Nugent bagged his first whitetail buck with the bow and arrow outside of Grand Junction.

"I'll never forget it. I was long overdue. So far as I could tell, my success rate was one deer per 1,000 hours of hunting. Something had to change.

"October 10. The conditions were my favorite—misty, wet, dark, and stalky, with a steady east wind. Deer hunting weather!

"In the fog I could see shapes in the field approaching. A larger deer brought up the rear. Now I could see antler.

"My arrow was nocked, and I was cocked, locked, and ready to rock, doc, as he moved perfectly broadside. Instinctively, I anchored and released. The aluminum arrow arched the forty yards—smack-o, whack-o, right behind the shoulder. He

went 100 yards and over he goes. Bingo! Still! Don't ask me why, but I immediately sat down and stared at him lying over there in a heap. Goofy. Then I picked up the blood trail and peeked at him, then the blood, then him, then the blood! I guess my psyche just wasn't accepting the scene yet. Halfway to him I figured, 'What the hell am I doin'? He's dead, Nuge, go get him!'

"I charged over, knowing only that I saw headgear when I shot. I grabbed his rack and counted twelve points and thought I was going to die. A twelve-pointer! Holy guacamole! Eight points with four-inchy kickers. A buck! Dead! Mine! Oh, the glory of it all. I be-bopped all the way home in nothing flat. I called my dad, uncle, brothers, buddies, and neighbors. They all thought I was nuts. It was wonderful. It's always wonderful. I strapped that beautiful animal to the top of my truck and showed him off to everybody.

"That was hundreds of deer ago, and that Colorado connection is still powerful today. I come back in the fall for hunting season and go just as nuts. I can hunt in the swamps of my native Michigan, but there's no comparison to mountain time. It's always a thrill …

"When you make that hard-earned clean kill, you should take it for all you can. I cherish those moments. Embrace those sensations and let it drive you. Tooth, fang, and claw! The call of the wild! Hear it. Do it. Whack 'em!"

C.W. McCALL

Americans were chattering away like mad on their CB radios when advertising agency director Bill Fries assumed the identity of C.W. McCall and recorded "Convoy." The tale of the "rubber duck" turned into the trucker national anthem and was a No. 1 pop and country hit.

Fries was working at the Bozell & Jacobs advertising agency in Omaha as an art director. In a short time, another of his talents emerged—songwriting. Putting music, writing, and art together, he won several major awards for innovative campaigns and in 1968 became creative director for the agency.

One of B&J's clients, the Metz Baking Company of Sioux City, Iowa, asked him for a new way to sell bread. He created the character of C.W. McCall for an ad campaign. The bread company won a Clio award and gained such regional popularity that Fries recorded the theme song ("The Old Home Filler-Up an' Keep-on-a-Truckin' Cafe") and released it on a label he owned with a partner. After they sold 30,000 copies in three weeks,

MGM Records signed C.W. McCall to a recording contract.

"Wolf Creek Pass," a song about hauling a load of chickens to Pagosa Springs on Colorado's scariest highway, peaked at No. 40 on *Billboard*'s pop singles chart. Fries was listening to his CB while driving his Jeep when a road sign inspired him to write the lyrics to "Convoy," a saga about truckers using their CB radios to outwit the cops who were trying to enforce the gas-saving fifty-five-mile-per-hour speed limit at the height of the oil shortage in 1975.

"Our music seems to have filled a gap between country and pop, a vacuum that's been waiting all along," Fries said. "With 'Convoy,' we hit a national nerve—everybody's interested in CB radios. Truckers have always used them. Now, truckers have become cowboys to the American public."

Citizen band radios, which are actually simpler versions of police two-way radios, were suddenly big business. *Forbes Magazine* reported CB sales of $350 million a year. But by 1980, the CB craze had gone the way of hula hoops, a passing fad that captured the attention of millions of people for a brief period of time.

Fries kept his job at the advertising agency, a clever move considering that after "Convoy" he only made the Hot 100 one more time. C.W.'s prize possession, a Jeep, took him when he had the time to the San Juan Mountains of southern Colorado, his favorite hideout.

In 1990, Fries was back in the business with *The Real McCall*, a McCall album produced and co-written with Chip Davis, the creator of Mannheim Steamroller. In fact, the crew of musicians who make up Steamroller toured in the 1970s as McCall's backup band, the Fort Calhoune Nuclear Power Plant Boys.

But the duties of office prevented Fries from taking to the road to promote his new material. Under his real name, Fries had just won his second four-year term as mayor of Ouray, Colorado, population 684.

SHAD O'SHEA & THE 18 WHEELERS

Shad O'Shea was a veteran of both the broadcast and the music businesses. His humor had delighted radio audiences, and his voice was heard on radio and television commercials.

O'Shea relates, "My first radio job of any consequence, I drove my 1954 Mercury Monterey convertible from Sacramento, California, to Pueblo, Colorado—KGHF radio. I was the morning man there. Ninety bucks a week. Then Topeka, Kansas. Then rock 'n' roll exploded. The first novelty record I made was in 1958, at WNOE in New Orleans. I was in radio until the late '60s."

In 1970, the native Californian built Counterpart Creative Studios in Cincinnati and recorded some goofy and bizarre novelty records. Phil Ochs, the late folk singer, listed "Good-Bye Sam" in his Top 10 songs that should have been hits.

"'Convoy' was one of the all-time monsters of novelty records. The CB craze was going crazy. I was in the shower one night. My boys, Scott and Stew, were four and seven. They said, 'Dad, you should write a record about the CBs!' Right there, I started singing, 'Breaker one-nine, breaker nineteen …' The idea was coming to me. I grabbed a legal pad. The scenario was that everyone thought it was a call girl luring a bunch of truck drivers to a brothel—'Breaker one-nine, how you guys doing out there, we can handle a whole football team,' all that.

"I called my good friend Ernie Phillips, the No. 1 promotion man in America. It was his idea that the ending be, instead of a bordello, which all the truckers thought it was, a cafe, restaurant—Ernie's Eat-Em-Up Joint! Remember, that was CB talk. So we decided to call it 'Colorado Call', because back in '75 'Colorado Call Girl' would have raised a few eyebrows. There were some names of little towns in Colorado—Cañon City.

"I was so excited, I called the musicians the next morning, it took us an hour to cut the track. It cost $265. My engineer was mixing it. I said, 'I know in my heart this is a hit record.' He said, 'Shad, I don't hear it.' In those days, that's all it took. It bummed me out completely. I gave up on it and put it in a room with some other tapes.

"Three months later, 'Convoy' had sold six million copies. I told someone about the record I made and never did anything with it. But I played it for someone, they got excited, and I pressed 1,000 singles. Within two weeks, we had sold over 6,000 records in Ohio and Illinois on our Fraternity Records and had orders for 6,000 more. It was No. 1 in this area. We licensed it to Private Stock Records.

"But the Chipmunks had done a CB song. The head of a major record said, 'You've got a hit … but I think you might be too late.' Mine would have been a No. 1 record, I know that in my heart."

"Colorado Call" bubbled under the *Billboard* Hot 100 in March 1976, charting at No. 110. As a collectors' item, the original single on Fraternity Records goes for fifteen to thirty dollars.

"I don't blame my engineer. I don't blame anybody. I've since gotten much thicker skin, and if I believe in something, I don't care if everybody throws rocks at me. I go in and I do it."

ELVIS PRESLEY

Elvis Presley's dietary needs made his other pursuits appear tame. He once flew from Memphis to Denver to fetch a concoction of the now-defunct Colorado Mine Company restaurant in Glendale, a house specialty he had sampled only once after a concert and apparently couldn't find anywhere else—the Fool's Gold Loaf, a particularly sumptuous feast.

The main ingredients? One loaf of Italian white bread, smeared with butter and tossed into an oven at 350 degrees, and one pound of lean bacon, fried until crisp and drained on paper towels. After fifteen minutes, the loaf is removed from the oven and sliced lengthwise. The interior of each half is hollowed out, and the insides are filled with one large jar of Skippy smooth peanut butter and one large jar of Smucker's grape jelly. The bacon slices are added, and the loaf is closed. The cost was $49.95 per sandwich—hence the name.

In December 1975, Presley decided to leave the lonely confines of Graceland, his mansion in Memphis, for the holidays and his forty-first birthday (January 8, 1976). He took Linda Thomson, his girlfriend, and several of his "boys" to Vail, Colorado, to celebrate.

"He flew in on his jet, and we rented a Trailways bus," Captain Jerry Kennedy, head of the Denver vice squad, said. "We sang Christmas carols on the way up. We took off work for ten days; we got him lodging and ski outfits. We got permission to use the ski slopes at night."

Elvis and his entourage rented snowmobiles for noisy 3 a.m. rides through the snowy woods.

Shortly after the holiday revelry, Presley went on a now-legendary car-buying spree. Wearing a white woolen ski mask and a bulky snowsuit, he visited a luxury automobile showroom in Denver, arriving three hours after closing time with a large party, telling three in the group to pick out the cars they wanted—Kennedy, Detective Ron Pietrofeso, who had been Elvis' police guard during concerts in Denver months before, and Dr. Gerald Starky, a police physician who had treated Elvis a day earlier for a scratch he said was caused by his ski mask. The $13,000 cars he bought the three men were his way of saying thank you.

"Elvis asked me what I was driving. I told him that I had an Audi, an economy car," Kennedy said. "He told me, 'I'm going to give you a car like mine.' "

Presley purchased a top-of-the-line Lincoln Mark IV from Kumpf Motors for Kennedy, and Cadillacs for Pietrofeso and Starky.

Kennedy had met the King in 1969.

"I was the off-duty work coordinator, and he had a concert at the Denver Coliseum," Kennedy said. "They wanted security at the Radisson Hotel, and he had the whole tenth floor. We had to keep the girls out.

"Elvis came out of his room, and he was very friendly. He liked policemen. Elvis and I struck up something of a friendship. He felt like he was part of the Denver Police."

And the force treated him accordingly. He owned an officer's uniform that he wore on visits to the Mile High City and was given an honorary Denver police captain's credential.

Before he left Colorado, while watching the television news morning update, Elvis saw Don Kinney, one of the local anchormen, report on the car buying Presley had done, then look into the camera and quip that he wouldn't mind getting a car, too. Elvis had a new Cadillac delivered to the station the following day and then went home to Graceland.

"He was generous to a fault," Kennedy said. "He ended up purchasing a dozen vehicles in Denver. If he gave it to one person, he had to give it to somebody else, too."

Most of the time, Kinney kept the Cadillac safe in his garage, but he occasionally used it to make the drive from Denver to a family farm in Montana. On one such occasion, on August 16, 1977, the car broke down. Later that day, Kinney learned that Presley had done so as well—he was dead at age forty-two, found unconscious in the bathroom off his bedroom at Graceland.

With "Piano Man," Billy Joel notched up his first chart hit in 1974. But, as he explained, "My career was neither here nor there at that time."

In 1976's *Turnstiles*, his third album, the piano man from Hicksville, Long Island, put together top-notch material, the major product of returning home to New York City from California ("Say Goodbye to Hollywood").

Yet it took a long time getting off the ground. Jim Guercio, a Chicago native who got his start in the 1960s as a producer for brass-rock bands such as Chicago, the Buckinghams, and Blood, Sweat & Tears, began working with Joel. He wanted to use drummer Nigel Olsson and bassist Dee Murray, both part of Elton John's band.

"Guercio, who I later became a good friend with, had an idea—'Aha, Billy Joel, piano player!'

"I didn't think it was a good idea. I said, 'No, no, I'm not Elton John, I'm Billy Joel.'"

Still, Joel tried that lineup for two months, without satisfactory results.

"I was not a big entity at Columbia Records. I'd had a modest hit with 'Piano Man.' That was it. So I said, 'I'll give it a shot.' I cut a couple of tracks and it was awful."

Joel introduced the novel idea of recording his regular band. Ultimately, he split to Long Island with his own guys and produced *Turnstiles* himself.

"I had played the Village, a few clubs here and there. With the *Turnstiles* album, I put my own band together," he explained. "They knew it cold."

The basic tracks were done in New York, but most of the vocals, the overdubs, the mixing, and the production were done in Colorado, at Guercio's Caribou Ranch.

"I flew in the face of the commercially successful machine at Caribou, because I ended up leaving Guercio and Caribou management and producing my own album," Joel said. "Which in a way sealed my fate corporately. I can't tell you that I produced it any better than it could have been produced, but it was the first time I got to work with my own road musicians."

The first ten days of April 1976, Joel played his first gig with the band, at the Good Earth, a club in Boulder.

"While we were at Caribou Ranch, it was time to start playing ... I remember a lot of Earth shoes and hippie hair.

"It was the first incarnation of the touring band that I would keep in place for seventeen years. That was the jelling of that particular group of musicians. I'd had Liberty (DeVitto, drums) in place for some time; Doug (Stegmeyer, bass) was fairly new; Richie Cannata on sax; and Russell Javors on guitar. It came together at the Good Earth ... We started making our bones there."

Joel's *Turnstiles* was released in June 1976, and the success of "Say Goodbye to Hollywood" proved Joel's decision to self-produce to be right. Suddenly everyone was paying attention. *Turnstiles* peaked at No. 122 on the *Billboard* album charts in June 1976.

"Guercio, being the gentleman that he is, came to me and said, 'You were right, I was wrong—good for you for sticking to your guns.'"

Then came a breakthrough with "The Stranger," and a string of multi-platinum successes followed. Joel found himself at the summit of the pop heap.

"And you can trace our success as a touring and performing band back to the training ground of the Good Earth in Colorado."

The Good Earth was a Boulder nightclub on the third floor of a building on what is now the Pearl Street Mall.

The GOOD EARTH
BOULDER'S FINEST NIGHTCLUB
LIVE ENTERTAINMENT

FIREFALL

The Boulder scene's biggest success story, Firefall's soft-rock blend of country and pop defined the "Colorado sound" of the 1970s. The group landed six singles on the Top 40 from 1976 through 1981, including the Top 10 "You Are the Woman."

Firefall was founded by singer-songwriter Rick Roberts and former Zephyr guitarist Jock Bartley in the summer of 1974.

Roberts was the itinerant young Florida folksinger-songwriter who'd served as the de facto spark of the "second edition" of the Flying Burrito Brothers from 1970 to 1972 (after Gram Parsons left the band) before undertaking his own career as a solo artist during 1972-1973, with a pair of albums under his own name.

For Bartley, the beginnings were another turning point in his career. He'd started as a student of Colorado Springs emigré jazz great Johnny Smith, after moving there from Kansas.

"From eight years old, I was taking lessons from a master," Bartley said of Smith, who wrote "Walk Don't Run." "I wanted a little Sears red guitar, but Johnny said no. My first guitar was a 3/4 size Gibson. By the time I was thirteen, I was already pretty good. I was always the young guy in bands until I went to college in Boulder in 1968."

With a few band stints under his belt around the Denver/Boulder area, Bartley moved into Zephyr, taking over the lead guitar post of Tommy Bolin. In 1972, after he switched over to Gram Parsons' band, the Fallen Angels (which

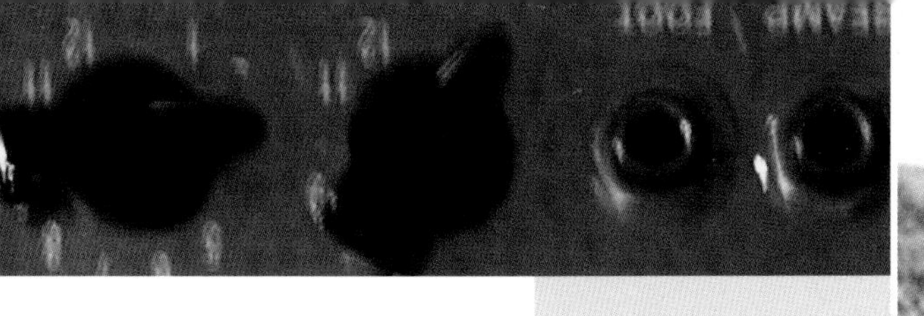

Firefall's heady time culminated with Fleetwood Mac's "Rumours" tour in 1978, which included a hometown Folsom Stadium gig before 60,000 Coloradans.

also featured Emmylou Harris), Bartley first met Roberts, whose touring schedule with the Burritos often overlapped Parsons'.

The third charter member of Firefall was another Colorado latecomer, Mark Andes. After four years as a founding member of Spirit, one of the most infamous psychedelic-era Los Angeles bands, he formed JoJo Gunne. When that hard-driving rock troop's first album was released in early 1972, the touring grind began, and Andes realized how far he'd strayed from his roots. By year's end he'd moved to Nederland, Colorado, and it wasn't long before he'd joined with Roberts and Bartley.

Roberts began an informal series of acoustic and electric jam sessions at his home in Boulder. As the jams became more productive, Roberts thought of a fourth to join, a singer-songwriter he'd met in Washington, D.C. named Larry Burnett, who was a taxi driver at the time. With his addition, the alliance made its initial appearances around the area in September 1974 with a repertoire that had swelled to more than thirty songs.

At Chris Hillman's suggestion, the drummer was soon added—Michael Clarke, original member of the Byrds (1964-1968) and later the Flying Burrito Brothers (with Roberts, through 1972). The five-man lineup took the stage of the Good Earth club shortly after Christmas 1974, and Firefall was born.

"We had all these pedigrees. With the core of the band, we had thirty original songs on the first day of practice."

Through 1975, the local gigs increased with frequency and then, in June, came the break. Roberts, Bartley, and Andes had been woodshedding on tour as Hillman's backup band when Hillman fell ill in New York during a date at the Other End. The club owner accepted a proposal to bring Burnett and Clarke into town, and Firefall finished out the engagement in Hillman's stead. The first night they played, an Atlantic Records A&R chief was sold on what he heard and saw.

By January 1976, they'd fully completed the recording sessions for the debut *Firefall* album with Jim Mason (of Poco renown). At the same time, they'd confirmed the addition of a sixth member, who'd joined them during the sessions—David Muse's work on keyboards, synthesizers, flute, tenor sax, and harmonica gave Firefall a depth that set them apart from other bands in their genre.

Firefall cemented a legend that had been brewing in the Colorado Rockies. The band's three singles—"You Are the Woman," "Livin' Ain't Livin," and "Cinderella"—sold in excess of one million copies together, and the album turned the magic platinum mark.

"With the players we had and the vocals on top, we sounded magical," Bartley said. "Rick and Larry wrote. Rick was this formula guy. 'You Are the Woman' was a three-minute song to get women between the ages of eighteen and thirty-five to call the radio stations. Larry was the junkie of the band, purging the soul with a song like 'Cinderella.'"

Firefall notched more hits—"Just Remember I Love You" and "Strange Way"—and two more gold records in the late 1970s. There was broad populist acceptance for a rock 'n' roll band that avoided the trappings of glitter or heavy metal flash, in favor of the eclectic, folk-rock/country-blues roots at the core of the music. Firefall's success with

Two Firefall songs—"You Are the Woman" and "Just Remember I Love You"—each have been played on radio more than two million times.

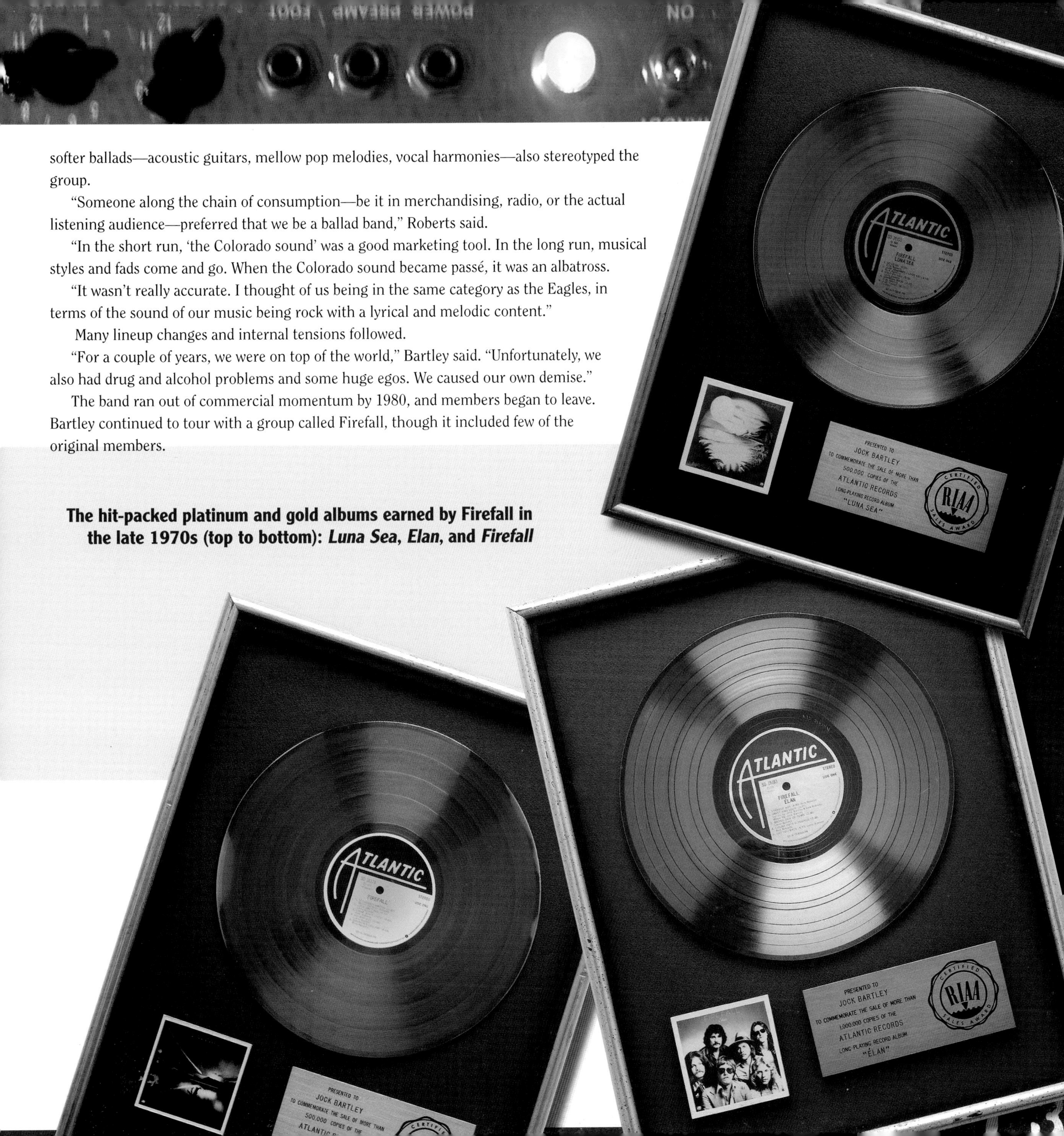

softer ballads—acoustic guitars, mellow pop melodies, vocal harmonies—also stereotyped the group.

"Someone along the chain of consumption—be it in merchandising, radio, or the actual listening audience—preferred that we be a ballad band," Roberts said.

"In the short run, 'the Colorado sound' was a good marketing tool. In the long run, musical styles and fads come and go. When the Colorado sound became passé, it was an albatross.

"It wasn't really accurate. I thought of us being in the same category as the Eagles, in terms of the sound of our music being rock with a lyrical and melodic content."

Many lineup changes and internal tensions followed.

"For a couple of years, we were on top of the world," Bartley said. "Unfortunately, we also had drug and alcohol problems and some huge egos. We caused our own demise."

The band ran out of commercial momentum by 1980, and members began to leave. Bartley continued to tour with a group called Firefall, though it included few of the original members.

The hit-packed platinum and gold albums earned by Firefall in the late 1970s (top to bottom): *Luna Sea*, *Elan*, and *Firefall*

CHRIS HILLMAN

Chris Hillman stayed with the Byrds for four years and six albums, then departed with Gram Parsons to develop acoustic country sounds in a new band dubbed the Flying Burrito Brothers. He remained with the band until its demise in 1971. At that time, he was the only remaining founding member.

In 1972, Stephen Stills offered Hillman a partnership in the formation of Manassas, and Hillman moved to Colorado. It seemed a comfortable solution to post-Burrito depression.

"Stills had showed up when the Burritos played at Tulagi in Boulder," Hillman said. "After the show, we went up to his real nice cabin in Gold Hill and hung out."

In Manassas, Hillman emerged as Stills' musical foil, collaborating in the writing and contributing vocals as well as instrumental versatility. When Manassas disbanded after two years of road work and two albums (which he co-produced), Hillman joined forces with J.D. Souther and Richie Furay in the Souther-Hillman-Furay band. The group recorded two albums, the first earning a gold record, and toured nationally before splitting up in the summer of 1975.

Back in Colorado, Hillman prepared his first solo album, *Slippin' Away*, a summation of his rock, bluegrass, and country roots, aided by old Burrito, Manassas, and Souther-Hillman-Furay pals. It peaked at No. 152 on the *Billboard* album chart in June 1976.

Amidst the recording of *Slippin' Away*, Hillman began to utilize his talents behind the board in the studio, producing the demo tapes that led to Firefall's contract, Rick Roberts' second solo album, *She's A Song*, and Dan McCorison's solo album, *Dan McCorison*.

"There were some good times in Boulder," said Hillman. On the plus side, there was a lot of interesting music coming up. There were a couple of clubs that were fun to play, and I had a lot of fun working with people.

"Unfortunately, there was a very heavy negative lifestyle prevalent. Drugs all over the place—a lot of cocaine. I think there was a dealer on every corner. It affected me; it affected everybody. And some people died. It was very excessive. I think the '70s were a very strange time in the history of this country, but, boy, there was some bad stuff going on in Boulder then."

GERARD

During the mid-1970s, one of the most popular rock bands in Colorado was an outfit called Gerard, a ten-piece aggregation known for melding sweet pop sensibilities with the roar of a big band. Whiz kid Gerard McMahon was the creative force behind the group—leader, chief writer, and arranger.

"Every review of our album compared us to Chicago," McMahon lamented. "And as much as I respect those guys, my music is not like Chicago's ..."

The British-born singer got his start playing bass in the clubs throughout the Midwest. That life held him back from creating his own music, and he found himself in Colorado, sitting in on orchestration and arranging classes at the University of Colorado. When he moved to New York in 1971, his midwestern apprenticeship served him well. He wrote, arranged, and performed commercials for major companies, then did scores for various Public Broadcasting System projects.

A year later, McMahon was in Los Angeles, where studio and production work established him in the city's music scene. Eventually, through an association with guitarist David Lindley, he was hired as a bassist in one of Jackson Browne's earliest touring bands.

McMahon decided that pursuing a solo career would be more rewarding. He left Browne's employ and soon found himself back in Colorado to do club dates and commercials. He met a number of people in the musical community, and he recorded and performed as Gerard.

After attending a concert one evening that showcased Tommy Bolin, Chicago producer Jim Guercio walked out, mesmerized by Gerard's opening set. The band's Guercio-produced album on his newly formed Caribou Records was titled Gerard. It did reasonably well in Cleveland, Des Moines, Oklahoma City, and Madison, but never broke nationally. The single "Hello Operator" bubbled under the *Billboard* Hot 100 in 1976, at No. 108.

"I listen to the music now from that period, and it's hard to believe that I did it," McMahon recalled. "It sounded very young and sappy, in a way. I'm not ashamed of it, but it's like reading old letters that you wrote: 'Did I say that to that girl? How corny could I be?'

"It's silly to be that way, because it was just part of a growth pattern. I look back at it as a way of going to school, actually. It was a beginning as far as record-making."

After Gerard, McMahon disbanded the outfit and headed to Los Angeles, continuing to build on the promise he showed as a young musician in Colorado. He released albums as a solo act in the 1980s and established himself in industry circles as a songwriter, making contributions to the movie soundtracks for *Fast Times at Ridgemont High* and *All the Right Moves*. He co-wrote Carly Simon's "Give Me All Night," which peaked at No. 5 on the adult contemporary charts in 1987.

In the summer of 1972, Mary Macgregor, a pop singer from St. Paul, moved to Steamboat Springs, Colorado, a small ski town in the Rockies that was populated with many local clubs and live music. For the next four years, she and her husband lived in a secluded ranch house with no running water and an outhouse, and she sang folk and soft rock music in the area's nightclubs.

In 1974, while still living in Steamboat, Macgregor began commuting to Minneapolis, Chicago, and Nashville, where she sang for commercial agencies. During that time, she was invited by Peter Yarrow of Peter, Paul & Mary to join his tour as a vocalist.

"My career didn't take up that much of my time. I was on the road for a couple of months out of the year. And maybe every other month, I would fly to do a couple commercials, and be gone for a week," Macgregor said.

In the spring of 1976, Yarrow took Macgregor into the studio to record, and the first song produced was "Torn Between Two Lovers," co-written by Phil Jarrell and Yarrow. Yarrow brought the record to the new Ariola America label, with Macgregor as part of the package. The record's success was so unexpected that Macgregor didn't even have a deal with Ariola when it was released.

In 1977, "Torn Between Two Lovers" topped the pop and easy listening charts simultaneously, resulting in her capturing the Top New Female Artist award in *Billboard*, *Record World*, and *Cashbox*. But Macgregor hated her No. 1 single.

"I think it's a real implausible situation," she explained. "A lady who wants to have her cake and eat it too. At the time I recorded the song, I was married, and people thought I'd written it and wanted to know if I was 'torn.' It was real aggravating for me, although the success that it had was definitely not."

The song had traumatic effects. Macgregor had been happily married for five years and had no intention of ever being unfaithful to her husband. Yet the record's appeal soon put a devastating crimp in their relationship.

"When 'Torn Between Two Lovers' happened, it was like getting on an already fast-moving train. My life changed drastically, and my husband just couldn't deal with it. I was gone a lot. It was just hard on both of us and we separated for a couple of years. During that time, I moved to L.A. and we eventually divorced."

76. MARY MACGREGOR

KATY MOFFATT

Katy Moffatt never stayed within a recognizable style long enough to become a star, but she's made a living and seen the world.

For most of the 1970s, Katy Moffatt was a fixture in the Denver folk music scene, playing folk clubs and small rock venues and spending countless hours at musicians' haunts like the Denver Folklore Center.

"I consider myself to have grown up in Colorado. I went through so many major life-changing experiences there," Moffatt said.

Moffatt grew up in Fort Worth, Texas. After college years in Santa Fe, her skills as a songwriter and performer brought her to Austin, where cowboy hippies first began to turn redneck heads around with their progressive outlaw brand of country music.

After her Austin act with another female singer split up, Moffatt headed for the Colorado mountains, hoping to find fame in Boulder. She took a wrong turn late one night and ended up in Denver, alone and broke.

"I was literally living on the streets, trying to get gigs. And there was no interest from anybody. But I was bound and determined to take care of myself. So I did odd jobs when there were no gigs. I was a window washer in the dead of winter, a waitress, a factory worker—just about everything.

"I think the only reason that people latch on to my briefer period in the Austin scene, for example, as a formative musical time, is that Denver wasn't as heralded or widely known. But to my way of thinking, what was going on in the streets of Denver at that time, concurrent with Austin, was easily as fertile.

"It wasn't as easily grasped because of its eclecticism. Remember Peter McCabe, Randy Handley, Mary Flower, the bluegrass band Monroe Doctrine? It just went on and on—so many great singers, songwriters, players, and arrangers who were all young and just coming up. We all knew each other and played together. It was a genuine scene."

After a year and a half of "scrounging in bars," Moffatt eventually met Chuck Morris, an area nightclub owner and concert promoter who secured a meeting with CBS Records A&R vice-president Billy Sherrill. Sherrill, who had produced over a hundred gold records, signed her to a multi-record deal in 1975.

"Katy Moffatt," he said, "has got the best pipes since Tammy Wynette."

Sherrill brought Katy Moffatt to Nashville to personally supervise the recording of her first album, entitled *Katy*. Moffatt was pushed into turning out product. Her first single, the self-penned ballad "I Can Almost See Houston from Here," climbed the country charts and sold well in the western states, but the album was a commercial flop. She completed three albums for Columbia, but only two were released. The commercially slanted albums won rave notices, but the ever eclectic Moffatt found herself caught in the cross fire between the country and pop divisions of a large corporate record company.

Labels, female stereotypes, marketing problems, and the pressures of the studio, coupled with Moffatt's confusion in finding her musical direction, all contributed to stunting her career.

"Boy, did I learn some lessons in a hurry," Moffatt said. "The timing was great—labels were signing everybody with a guitar and underground FM stations were breaking new talent every day. It should have been a perfect situation, but something went terribly wrong with the business."

After living in Los Angeles and learning in the music business wringer, Moffatt has since won a loyal fan base with her acoustic folk-country style and her pure, sparkling voice, in a career marked by consistent critical acclaim, industry appreciation, movie appearances, and songs being covered.

"My career has been sort of backwards," she admitted. "Early on I had the big label throwing money around, the heavily greased agents and lawyers. But it all had to break down so I could learn what I had to do to survive as an artist."

Bob Dylan's album *Hard Rain*, a live document of his 1976 tour with the Rolling Thunder Revue, went gold.

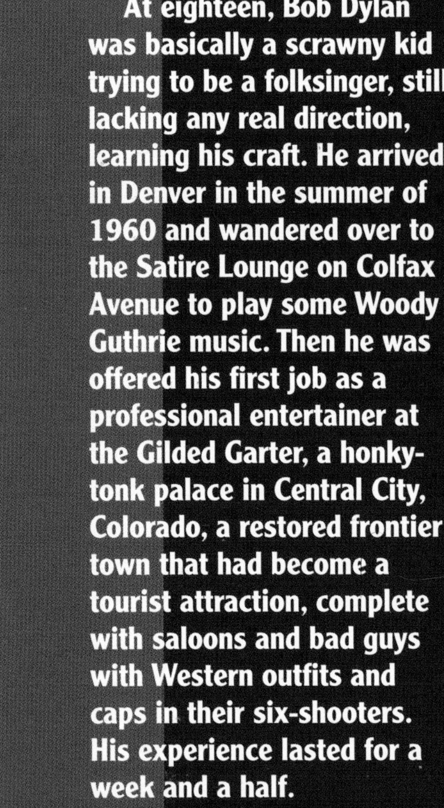

At eighteen, Bob Dylan was basically a scrawny kid trying to be a folksinger, still lacking any real direction, learning his craft. He arrived in Denver in the summer of 1960 and wandered over to the Satire Lounge on Colfax Avenue to play some Woody Guthrie music. Then he was offered his first job as a professional entertainer at the Gilded Garter, a honky-tonk palace in Central City, Colorado, a restored frontier town that had become a tourist attraction, complete with saloons and bad guys with Western outfits and caps in their six-shooters. His experience lasted for a week and a half.

By 1975, Dylan was once again ascending after spending the late 1960s and early 1970s refusing to behave like the counterculture hero that the previous decade had made him. The next logical step was to hit the road, but little about the ensuing tour followed any logic.

The Rolling Thunder Revue started out in October 1975 with the idea of a communal tour. Rather than playing formal concerts at large halls and coliseums, Dylan assembled a loosely knit merry group of old friends. The large, shifting entourage—including Joan Baez and such Greenwich Village regulars as Ramblin' Jack Elliott and Bobby Neuwirth with guests including Allen Ginsberg, Joni Mitchell, Mick Ronson, Roger McGuinn, and Arlo Guthrie—toured until spring 1976.

The Revue started out with surprise concerts at small halls and worked up to outdoor stadiums. Dylan and his Rolling Thunder Revue taped a show in Clearwater, Florida, and the program was auctioned off to NBC-TV after being offered to all three networks. A few weeks later, Dylan then rejected the tape. Instead, he gave his nod to a group of documentary makers who filmed the May 23 concert at Colorado State University in Fort Collins, Colorado, under cloudy skies. Rain drenched 25,000 fans.

The footage of the Colorado concert, appropriately titled *Hard Rain*, was broadcast on NBC in September. Most mainstream TV critics panned the show. That month also saw the release of the live *Hard Rain* album, which consisted of nine songs, four of which came from Dylan's TV special.

Dylanologists considered other concerts superior.

"I don't really talk about what I do," Dylan said to *TV Guide*. "I just try to be poetically and musically straight. I think of myself as more than a musician, more than a poet. The real self is something other than that. Writing and performing is what I do in this life and in this country. But I could be happy being a blacksmith. I would still write and sing. I can't imagine not doing that. You do what you're geared for."

TOMMY BOLIN

Tommy Bolin's fretwork was one of a kind. He was as adept at silky acoustic stylings and jazz improvisation as he was at hard-rock riffing. Going in to the last half of the 1970s, when the guitarist was fast on his way to becoming a rock music legend, some Coloradoans felt he could be the next Jimi Hendrix.

Before proving it, Bolin died at the age of twenty-five.

After being booted out of high school in Sioux City, Iowa, in 1967 for refusing to cut his long hair, Bolin drifted west to Denver. His earliest gig, with a group called American Standard, was forgettable. But he established a reputation with Zephyr. Colorado's premier boogie band brought Bolin his first album-making experience (he recorded on two of the group's early albums) and regularly attracted large audiences to its gigs.

There was a huge buzz about Bolin. The era of the guitar hero was dawning, and locals who saw him perform knew he was better than the fastest players and all over the neck besides.

Bolin blew off Zephyr for a largely unprofitable stint with Energy from 1971 to 1973. Members of Energy included Kenny Passarelli, who later joined up with Elton John, Stanley Sheldon, who went on with Peter Frampton, Joe Lala, who later played with Dan Fogelberg, and Max Carl, who established himself with Jack Mack & the Heart Attack and 38 Special.

But in 1973, Joe Walsh recommended Bolin for his old spot in the James Gang. Bolin penned most of the songs on the group's *Bang* and *Miami* albums, and "Must Be Love" was nearly a hit, peaking at No. 54 on *Billboard*'s pop singles charts and reaching the Top 20 in some markets.

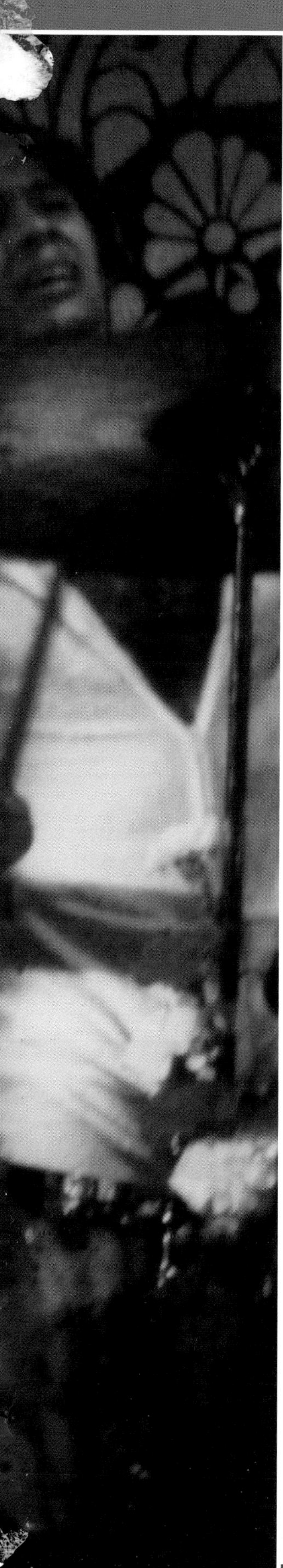

During that time, Bolin's prominence had risen to the point where he also played most of the churning guitar on master drummer Billy Cobham's *Spectrum*. The orientation of the jazz-fusion album, particularly a cut called "Quadrant 4," was monumental. Rock guitar legend Jeff Beck often credited it as a major influence in sparking his jazz pursuits.

At age twenty-four, Bolin had vaulted into the ranks of the electric guitar masters. Everybody believed in him, and he was always able to get what he wanted from people. He left the James Gang in August 1974 "when it was no longer a learning process" and lived off royalties until he signed a contract with hard-rock band Deep Purple, confronting devotees of the departing Ritchie Blackmore head-on.

"To be honest," Bolin said, "I'd never heard anything but 'Smoke on the Water.'"

He co-wrote seven of the tunes on Deep Purple's *Come Taste the Band* album (No. 43 in *Billboard*). Live, he mesmerized fans with the soft, melodic parts of "Owed To G," his solo spot.

During that year, he recorded *Teaser*, his masterpiece. The solo album featured Bolin ripping it up in the company of such diverse talents as saxophonist David Sanborn, drummer Michael Walden, and keyboardist Jan Hammer. *Teaser* explored Latin rhythms ("Savannah Woman") and reggae along with grinding rock, and it became a full-blown hit—one of the most requested records on the FM airwaves.

Bolin's year in Deep Purple was a hectic one. On a world-tour stop in Indonesia, his roadie was killed in a hotel elevator-shaft fall. Returning from the tour, he found himself named a co-respondent in Ritchie Blackmore's divorce suit (fifteen others were also named).

In the spring of 1976, Bolin returned to Denver triumphantly, raising the roof at Ebbets' Field. Happy and outgoing, he liked to talk about being a rock 'n' roll outlaw, and he spun tales about his appetite for revelry.

"I have the best of both worlds," he said. "I can make money with Purple and be as artsy as I want on my own."

After Purple disbanded that summer, Bolin returned to his solo career and launched a fall tour to support his second album, *Private Eyes*.

Shortly after his band played support at a Jeff Beck concert, Bolin collapsed and died in the bathroom of a Miami Beach hotel on December 4. His body was ravaged by alcohol, barbiturates, cocaine, and heroin. According to friends, Bolin had been having periodic problems with drugs and drinking for some time. The pressures that came from being constantly broke and his breakup with longtime girlfriend Karen Ulibarri appeared to have added up to a severe depression.

Another young rock star had made tragic headlines. Bolin was buried in the family plot in Sioux City. Ulibarri put a ring on his finger that Jimi Hendrix had been wearing the day he died (a gift to Bolin from Deep Purple's manager). She had been saving it for Bolin because he kept losing it.

Tommy Bolin was as adept at softer acoustic playing as he was at hard-rock riffing or jazz improvisation.

Stallion was five musicians who moved into Denver from the streets of Chicago, polishing elements of western music with an upbeat city-bred approach.

"I joined the group late, in '75," lead singer Buddy Stephens said. "They flew me out because they wanted a singer. In those days you needed a high singer—a baritone singer so you could get the harmonies."

Working with producer Dik Darnell of Pyramid Productions, the Denver-based quintet—Danny O'Neil (guitarist), Jorge Gonzales (bass), Stephens, Wally Damrick (keyboards), and Larry Thompson (drums)—signed with Casablanca Records. The band had a Top 40 record on the charts, "Old Fashioned Boy (You're the One)" in March 1977. Bubbling under the Hot 100, "Magic of the Music" reached No. 108 in July 1977.

"Casablanca was an image-conscious label—they had Kiss and disco," Stephens said. "We weren't the tall, skinny rock stars that everybody loved. We dressed out as a bunch of city guys gone out west—dudes. Three of us in the band were balding, so they made us wear hats. I wore a $900 suit, boots, and a multi-colored vest. I looked like Bat Masterson."

Stallion was their group identity and their symbol.

"Our logo was the Mile High Stadium horse," Stephens said. "They pushed us to be a little rockier."

While most of the band members were relative newcomers to Colorado, Stallion took an interest in a humanitarian issue, choosing to adopt the cause of the Wild Horse Organized Assistance program (WHOA), designed to preserve the endangered wild mustangs in the western states. "We were trying to be worthwhile," Stephens said. "We were like Chicago was when they first started out, a brotherhood thing …"

Stallion toured with Elvin Bishop and Styx, but the record company and management didn't quite see eye to eye. The band broke up in 1979.

"We got a lot of advertising, got a lot of airplay. I can honestly say we came about as close to making it as anybody could, without doing so."

The members of Stallion took on KIMN disc jockeys in a charity softball game at Mile High Stadium.

In the pantheon of rock-song sports anthems, Gary Glitter's "Rock and Roll Part 2" has joined the strains of Steam's "Na Na Hey Hey Kiss Him Goodbye" and Queen's "We Will Rock You."

It got its start in 1974, when Kevin O'Brien, then twenty-two, was the public relations and marketing director for the Kalamazoo Wings, Michigan's entry in the International Hockey League. "Back then, organ music was nearly synonymous with hockey games. But there was a movement to introduce some canned music during the games, so I started rummaging through my old 45 collection."

Tucked in a box in O'Brien's basement was Glitter's "Rock and Roll Part 2." "I tossed it on the stereo and immediately thought, 'This is the song we have to use to bring the team out onto the ice.'"

In 1976, O'Brien took a job as marketing director for the Colorado Rockies of the National Hockey League. His copy of "Rock and Roll Part 2" went to Denver with him. He persuaded franchise officials to play it as a rousing celebration after Rockies goals. It didn't blare through McNichols Arena that often because the team stunk, but soon local radio stations were playing the three-minute tune, referring to it as the "Rocky Hockey Theme Song."

In fact, it was solely identified with the Rockies until 1982, when the hockey team moved east to become the New Jersey Devils. Denver's other pro teams felt free to adopt the song. The Denver Broncos introduced "Rock and Roll Part 2" to the National Football League, admitting they took the song from the Rockies, while the Denver Nuggets did the same in the National Basketball Association.

Now "Rock and Roll Part 2" has been played incessantly on the public-address systems and by bands in every high school, college, and professional arena and stadium in America.

Fans get on their feet, clapping, some punching the air as they belt out the song's trademark, "Hey!"

"I can't believe that happened to my song," Glitter said.

Glitter began life in England as Paul Gadd, and he tried almost everything seeking to get off the chicken-in-a-basket circuit before aspiring svengali Mike Leander suggested a radical "image overview." Gadd adopted the name Gary Glitter and created an outlandish, outrageous persona. His costume was towering platforms and an appalling foil jumpsuit that opened shoulder-wide at the top and took a V-dive for the navel, drawing attention to his hairy chest and the wad of fat above his belt.

But somehow, his endearingly silly glam-rock struck a chord with the British public. Glitter and his Glitter Band sold millions with troglodytic variations on repetitious but engaging tunes. In 1972, "Rock and Roll Part 2" bulldozed its way onto the charts. The inspiration for it came from movies Glitter saw as a kid.

"When I went to cinema on Saturday mornings, I loved cowboys and Indians, and remember how the Indians used to run around the fire before the battle chanting, 'Hey, hey, hey, hey, hey.' Years later, I was trying to create a '50s kind of sound with a song. I wanted something totally different with a great beat, and I remembered the Indians chanting. I wanted it to sound like 50,000 chaps at Wembley," a soccer stadium outside London.

The guitar was put through a fuzz-box and played close enough to the speakers to cause feedback, and Leander provided a loud, thumping drumbeat. Glitter overdubbed the few words "Hey" and "Ugh" in various combinations to make it sound like a crowd.

"We didn't have sophisticated recording equipment, but the two of us came up with something unique, and I don't think I'd ever be able to re-create what we did."

Actually, "Rock and Roll Part 1" was the A-side. "'Part 2' was just a remix of the other song. But 'Part 2' caught on big, for some reason."

Gllitter soon faded from view in the United States. Yet all the stadium and arena airplay didn't make him rich. Venues buy a blanket license for the rights to use music, but the fees simply augment the royalties pool, regardless of which music is played most frequently in those places.

In 1999, several NHL arenas stopped playing Glitter's "Rock and Roll Part 2" in light of his arrest on child-pornography charges.

GARY GLITTER

Dan Fogelberg rose to prominence on the West Coast amidst Southern California's burgeoning folk-rock singer-songwriter scene of the 1970s. In 1974, he went up to Aspen with Glenn Frey and Don Henley of the Eagles, and J.D. Souther.

"The Eagles were putting their show together, rehearsing at the Gallery, a club under the Little Nell. A lot of L.A. bands went up and broke in their show before they went on the road. There was nothing there but waitresses and ski bums and bartenders. It was the first time I had hung for any length of time, my first real taste of Colorado, and I really liked it.

"But Aspen wasn't my place. Even then, the lifestyle was a little fast-paced for the likes of me. I was good for about two or three days, and I'd crawl out with my tongue dragging down to my legs. I didn't have the liver those guys had.

"When I was playing with my band Fool's Gold, we did a couple of nights at Ebbets' Field, an industry showcase for Colorado. My road manager at the time, Patrick Cullie, mentioned that Chris Hillman had his house for sale. I went up and looked at it, fell in love with the mountains, and just impulsively bought the house. When the tour was done in 1975, I moved to Nederland."

Perched 9,000 feet up on top of the Rocky Mountains, songs eventually spilled out of

Fogelberg. The *Nether Lands* album found him singing about "living on the edge"—vivid, emotional, personal, and ambitious, it found him emerging from his Colorado hideaway, an exchange of naiveté for the temptation of new experience.

"We called my road the Ho Chi Minh trail, because it was literally impassable most of the year," Fogelberg said. "The title cut was inspired by living a fairly solitary life high up in the mountains. There's a spirituality in those mountains that I love. The first year it hit me the hardest, and the grandeur that came out in *Nether Lands*, the symphonic atmosphere, I was trying to create a sonic atmosphere of the Rockies as well as singing about it."

Nether Lands peaked at No. 13 on the *Billboard* pop album charts in 1977 and was a platinum seller.

"Colorado was a very different place, very unpopulated. It was a very hip, new-age hideout in Boulder and Nederland. California had been exhausted, and a lot of the people that had started quests there ended up gravitating to the mountains—myself included," said Fogelberg.

"It was never a huge music scene as much as an inside family. For years, my nearest neighbor was Mark Andes. The Navarro boys were below me living in a communal setting. Richie Furay was over on Sugarloaf Mountain. Chris Hillman and Stephen Stills and Manassas were there. Everybody gravitated to Caribou Ranch—it was our boys club."

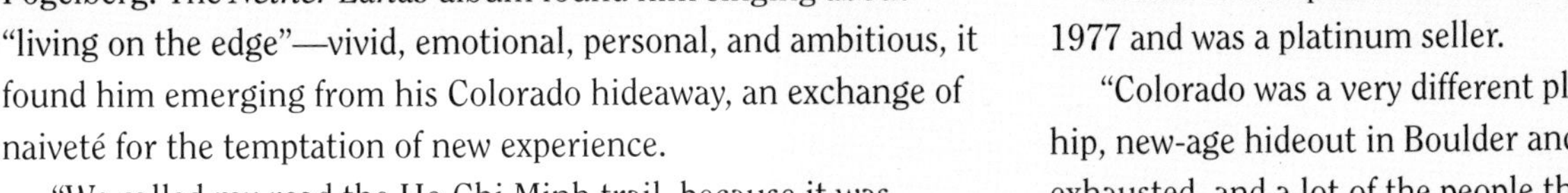

In 1980, Fogelberg found and bought land in Pagosa Springs on the western slope of Colorado. He built a house and barns, and since 1982 he has led a quiet life in the San Juan Mountains.

"I cherish my privacy. As an artist, to create, I've got to keep some anonymity."

During the many hours spent in his truck driving back and forth between Boulder and the ranch he was building on the western slope, Fogelberg listened to a lot of bluegrass tapes, feeding the desire to play some roots music. After sitting in with Chris Hillman's acoustic band at the 1984 Telluride Bluegrass Festival, he decided to make a record with his favorite acoustic pickers. The resulting album, *High Country Snows*, became one of the best-selling bluegrass albums of all time.

But his albums took longer to make when he maintained a near-reclusive lifestyle in Colorado—he was constantly shuttling back and forth to the record business in Los Angeles. The singer-songwriter built his own studio on his ranch so that he could stay home.

The Wild Places (1990), his twelfth release, was self-produced and mostly recorded at his spread. The album, about the sweetness of his solitude in Colorado, included a tender, soulful cover of the Cascades' 1963 hit "Rhythm of the Rain." The song, with a touch of the Beatles' "Rain" added to the coda, was a Top 10 adult contemporary hit.

"That song was a result of the freedom of having my own studio in Colorado to experiment," Fogelberg said. "I could ski during the day and work at night."

Recording at Caribou Ranch in 1977, Carole King was looking for a backup band. Dan Fogelberg, who lived in Nederland, suggested Boulder's Navarro.

King saw Navarro perform in the tier of a barn, the Stage Stop, in Rollinsville near Boulder. She went on to sign the band to her own label. King enlisted Navarro as her "side-by-side" band for her *Simple Things* album, which reached No. 17 on the *Billboard* pop album charts. The group also recorded several albums of its own brand of mellow rock music for Capitol Records in the late 1970s. The group's debut set, *Listen*, was released simultaneously with King's *Simple Things*.

What was a reclusive legend (seven years prior, King had recorded one of the most popular albums in music history, *Tapestry*) doing with a "positive-energy" band from Boulder?

"I have never been happier with a band," she said simply. She and the six young members of Navarro all clasped hands and meditated together in "the circle," as they called it, before every session and show. In concert, she opened solo, slowly introducing musicians until she had left her audience in Navarro's hands.

Right before King latched onto Navarro, the band had, in fact, broken up.

"We'd split up and re-formed so many times that it was a big joke around town," lead guitarist Robert McEntee said. "But this time was for good … we thought."

Local promoters used to joke around and call Navarro "granola rockers," and the image stuck nationally, too. A 1977 *Rolling Stone* story about the band was headlined "Carole King and Navarro Mellow Out," and was accompanied by a picture captioned, "Good Vibes in Boulder."

After parting ways with King, the band moved to Austin, Texas, for a time before drifting back to Colorado. McEntee and guitarist/songwriter/singer Mark Hallman played in Fogelberg's band.

Carole King's *Simple Things* album went gold.

MICHAEL JOHNSON

Pop singer and guitarist Michael Johnson's wide-ranging experience started with his natural attraction to music during his early childhood. Back in 1958, as a thirteen-year-old in his native Denver, he and his older brother Paul (then twenty) began teaching each other the basics of playing guitar. Their first professional gig was at the local VFW hall that year.

"We played for five bucks a night and all the screwdrivers we could drink," Johnson recalled.

"I played at high school dances in Denver as soon as I was able to. I played bars and clubs—the Exodus, another called the Green Spider. They're probably selling plumbing fixtures out of there now."

Johnson grew up in Denver in a Catholic family of six. He attended Denver's North High School and Holy Family High School, a Catholic school, but got kicked out of the latter. "I mooned a nun," Johnson said.

In 1963, Johnson went off to Colorado State University to study music education, but his college career was truncated. He left for Spain to study at the Conservatory of Liceo in Barcelona, then returned to the United States and signed on with Randy Sparks in the Back Porch Majority (a sort of training ground for the New Christy Minstrels). He was a member of the Chad Mitchell Trio from 1967 to 1968, spending some of that time co-writing with another member, John Denver.

Johnson returned to creating and performing his music, and his popularity increased with each new recording and his continued touring. It was time to pursue national recognition. From 1978 to 1980, he scored big pop and adult contemporary hits—"Bluer Than Blue" (No. 12 on the *Billboard* singles charts), "Almost Like Being in Love" (No. 32), "This Night Won't Last Forever" (No. 19), and "You Can Call Me Blue" (No. 86).

"I never lived anywhere longer than a year," Johnson said. "I lived out of a suitcase."

In the mid-1980s, Johnson moved into country music, conquering the charts with "Give Me Wings" and "The Moon Is Still Over Her Shoulder."

By then, Johnson had circled the world with his music.

"Denver's not where most of my clothes are anymore, but it's my home, where my heart is. Every time I come back, I ask, why don't I live here?"

Then in 1985, Springsteen played stadiums across the United States, ending his holdout against playing outdoors. But two shows at Denver's Mile High Stadium were scheduled late in the summer concert season—September 22 and 23—and Springsteen lost the gamble. An icy rain fell on the morning of Sunday the twenty-second, and the temperature fell into the low thirties with twenty-five-mile-per-hour winds. It was decided to delay the performance until Tuesday the twenty-fourth.

On stage both Monday and Tuesday, Springsteen was profuse in his apologies for Sunday's postponement—but the weather during those shows wasn't much better. By the time Monday's show ended, temperatures were back in the thirties. On Tuesday, the E Streeters played in a cold, drenching downpour that made everything slippery. At one point, Springsteen had to quit playing his acoustic guitar because he couldn't pick it up. It was a heck of a way for him to spend his thirty-sixth birthday.

If Bruce Springsteen learned anything during his visits to Colorado, it's that rock 'n' roll is an indoor sport.

On June 20, 1978, Springsteen and the E Street Band made their Colorado debut at Red Rocks Amphitheatre in support of *Darkness on the Edge of Town*, his then-current release and his first in almost three years. The interim had been spent battling his ex-manager, letting the *Born To Run* hype settle down, and recording several albums' worth of songs.

He had agreed to do his first-ever outdoor show only after weeks of cajoling by his manager and booking agents. A gig in the wide open spaces? He was apprehensive about a lack of intimacy, dubious about the havoc that it might wreak among his sound crew, and cautious of problems with audience communication.

But on that Tuesday night, Springsteen put on a legendary performance, one that he later claimed was the best of the entire "Darkness" tour. Springsteen and the band managed to keep their Jersey sensibilities intact—"Nice place you got here ... bunch of big rocks," Springsteen said with a laugh. His loyalty to his new friends out West was incredible. "The idea is to deliver what money can't buy," he said.

However, playing at Colorado's famed outdoor amphitheatre set a precedent. Springsteen returned to Red Rocks on July 16 and 17, 1981, his first outdoor shows since he played there in 1978. On the first night, a summer rainstorm drenched the audience. A few songs into the set, Springsteen tried to talk the crowd out of continuing. He thought it would be better to start all over another night when the weather was good. The proposal was shouted down in a spirited voice vote, and the show went on in an intermittent downpour.

EARTH, WIND & FIRE

In the annals of pop R&B, Earth, Wind & Fire's place is assured as a multi-platinum, multi-Grammy-winning supergroup. The band's hits ranked as some of the most joyous moments of the 1970s.

Earth, Wind & Fire featured the vocal acrobatics of Philip Bailey, who was born and raised in Denver—he graduated from East High School. With schoolmates Larry Dunn (on keyboard) and Andrew Woolfolk (on sax), he played with a local group, Friends & Love.

"We played all kinds of music—Blood, Sweat & Tears, Three Dog Night, Sly & the Family Stone, Carole King. Denver wasn't a heavy black urban area … I think once I joined EWF, I brought a certain pop sensibility to it," said Bailey.

Bailey had heard Earth, Wind & Fire's first album. "We opened the show when the group came to town in '71 to play a promotional gig at the Hilton. Then I hooked up with them in Los Angeles and joined."

Earth, Wind & Fire had first recorded as a brassy, jazz-like band. But founder Maurice White reworked the concept, and Bailey recommended Dunn and then Woolfolk, who had been busy in New York studying sax with jazz maestro Joe Henderson and who was on the verge of taking up a career in banking when Bailey called. The band began playing an exuberant dance music that had life-affirming, often metaphysical lyrics wrapped around an exciting rhythm.

Bailey's distinctive falsetto, pure and sweet, became as legendary as Barry White's basso. Earth, Wind & Fire had six Top 10 singles, including the Beatles' "Got To Get You into My Life" (No. 9 in September 1978), which it performed in the ill-fated movie, *Sgt. Pepper's Lonely Hearts Club Band*. The song was recorded in Boulder.

"We recorded the *That's the Way of the World* album and more at Caribou, but 'Got To Get You into My Life' was recorded at Northstar Studios, a little studio in Boulder. We were on a deadline. We were writing while we were on the road, and we rehearsed a song in another city on the way to Denver, then had a concert the next night. Then we went to Boulder and did the track," Bailey said. "We brought out George Massenberg, who was an innovator of engineering. He brought his outboard gear and hot-rodded the board.

"It was the single off the *Sgt. Pepper* record and it went pop for us. When we started reworking the original, I was wondering at the time, was the whole treatment that we had going to be too different from what the Beatles song always sounded like? But it ended up being a major smash for us."

Bailey had his own solo career—in 1982, he hit No. 2 with "Easy Lover," a duet with Phil Collins. And he had a dual identity as a singer—he also recorded Christian music. "The time spent away from one another was necessary for everybody in the band. I came in at age twenty, straight from a year of college and getting married. I literally grew up in Earth, Wind & Fire, so it was more than a band, it was a family, and a lot of multi-faceted relationships were established as a result."

Earth, Wind & Fire was long-lived, adding fresh chapters in the 1980s and 1990s. The band was inducted into the Rock and Roll Hall of Fame in 2000.

"Over the years, I've been exposed to things I could never dream of as a kid in Denver," Bailey said. "At the end of the day, I've been able to support my family and work for myself. I get paid for being the best me I can possibly be. How many of us get the chance to say that?"

Denver was home for Philip Bailey, Earth, Wind & Fire's lead singer.

POCO

Rusty Young played in Böenzee Cryque, a Colorado band whose odd name was inspired by the signing on the Benzie-Kricke Sporting Goods Company, which intrigued vocalist Sam Bush. Getting local airplay, a single got placed with Uni Records, and "Still in Love with You Baby" went to No. 1 on KIMN's hit list of April 1967.

Böenzee Cryque went to Los Angeles, where it broke up, and Young played pedal steel guitar on sessions for Buffalo Springfield's "Kind Woman." In 1968, with Springfield in disarray, two members, Richie Furay and Jim Messina, quickly set about assembling a band of their own. They recruited Young, who called in two buddies from Colorado—George Grantham, also from Böenzee Cryque, and Randy Meisner, who came from a rival Colorado band, the Poor—to play drums and bass, respectively.

Poco originally called itself Pogo, but Walt Kelly, the creator of the comic strip, sued, and the new band changed its name.

Poco started out with great commercial promise. Then Meisner left to co-found the Eagles, and guitarist Messina slipped into the Poco bass slot until Timothy B. Schmit signed on in February 1969. In November of that year, Messina split to form a prosperous duo with Kenny Loggins, and guitarist Paul Cotton stepped in to sing and play guitar. In 1973, Furay departed to form the Souther-Hillman-Furay band. It was a near-mortal jolt to the group.

Poco plugged on for the next three years, watching the Eagles emerge as the triumphant synthesis of L.A. country rock, and when Meisner left the Eagles and retired to his native Nebraska, Schmit quit Poco to take his place. Young alone remained of the original lineup. He, with Cotton, had had it with Poco—they were going to start the Cotton-Young Band and were writing songs for and auditioning female singers, "like a Fleetwood Mac situation."

But the band recruited keyboardist Kim Bullard and an English rhythm section, Steve Chapman on drums and Charlie Harrison on bass, to take on the road for a final tour, releasing one more record as Poco. The breakthrough, at last. In 1979, with its fourteenth album, Poco finally cracked the top of the album charts.

Legend resurrected the Poco spirits. Young, fittingly, wrote and sang on the gold album's surprise hit single, "Crazy Love." Cotton's "Heart of the Night" was a second Top 20 hit—not bad for a band that some had written off as a stale anachronism of the country-rock era.

"A lot of people helped and did us favors and went out on a limb for us over the years," Young said. "We couldn't let them down. We owed them something. We believed in the value of the future, not the past."

Poco disbanded five years later. Young moved to Nashville in 1985, hoping to follow such country-rockers-gone-country as the Nitty Gritty Dirt Band and Michael Murphey onto the charts, "a Colorado boy battling the bugs and humidity, staying out of the ballpark for a while, waiting to see what's going to happen in country and rock music."

Young orchestrated a Poco reunion in 1989, and the band's *Legacy* was certified gold.

"We had such a tremendous influence," Young said, citing how the group's sound was adopted by the best-selling early Eagles. "I thought it would be interesting to put it back together, and I missed my original partners. It was never as exciting as that first 1968-69 period."

Böenzee Cryque (left to right): Rusty Young, George Grantham, Joe Neddo, Sam Bush, Jim Jansen

In the creative scene of Los Angeles, Chuck E. Weiss is regarded as one of the coolest cats for his offbeat blend of Americana. What he describes as "twisted jungle music"—tastes that range from New Orleans dirge jazz to demented electric country-blues, brazenly mixed with boozy attitude and jive poetry—has a cultural and historical value.

The synthesis represents the breadth of experience Weiss gained growing up in northeast Denver in the 1950s and 1960s, where his aura (his idea of cool was gold, pointed-toe shoes and black cut-off t-shirts) gave him a reputation for being a little offbeat, but right on the beat.

"I was the only Jew for a hundred miles," he recalled with a laugh. "I felt like a Ubangi dropped in Times Square on New Year's Eve.

"Denver was more cosmopolitan then. When our parents were kids, it was a hub for the railroads. Hence you had that huge skid row downtown that's now yuppified, LoDo. The con was born there. All the grifters came in the early part of the century and they'd get their training and then they'd go to Chicago and other cities. That gave rise to all the bohemians coming to Denver …

"When Kerouac discovered the place, it was already wide open. As a kid, I caught the tail end of that. People were different. The place had a lot of soul. There was a jazz station. There were so many little coffeehouses and clubs down in the Capitol Hill area—the Sign of the Tarot, the Exodus.

"We used to take the bus down to Larimer Street to go find stuff in pawnshops. You could hear a million great Mexican rock 'n' roll bands. There was one I liked called Mando & the Chili Peppers. Of course, they never went national, but there were always little things like that happening.

"I don't think anyone was ever there to document it. I don't think anybody ever took it seriously. Of course, it molded me, so I took it seriously."

Weiss learned to drum, and circa 1970, Chuck Morris, a local manager and promoter, asked him to sit in during an appearance by Lightnin' Hopkins at Tulagi, a Boulder nightclub. The gig went well and Weiss persuaded Hopkins, one of the last great exponents of Texas blues, to take him on tour.

Weiss hit it off with Tom Waits at the now-defunct Denver club Ebbets' Field, where Waits was performing.

"We were both sitting at the counter of the little coffeeshop next door to the club. I was wearing a chinchilla coat and three-inch platforms and I thought he was just some bum folksinger. I remember braggin' to him about all the people I knew."

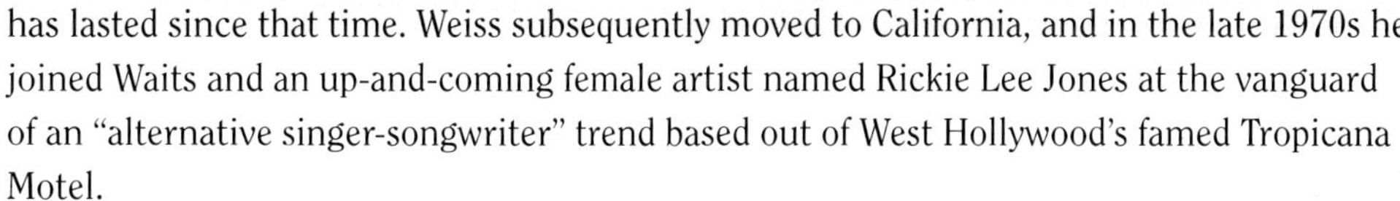

The pair cultivated a friendship that has lasted since that time. Weiss subsequently moved to California, and in the late 1970s he joined Waits and an up-and-coming female artist named Rickie Lee Jones at the vanguard of an "alternative singer-songwriter" trend based out of West Hollywood's famed Tropicana Motel.

Jones later immortalized Weiss in her Top 5 hit "Chuck E.'s in Love" and won the 1979 Best New Artist Grammy. Waits sprinkled Weiss' likeness around a lot of his music.

Perhaps that encouraged the perception of Weiss as some sort of hipster novelty artist, but his music retained a life-learned authenticity. He played with his band at the Central, an L.A. nightclub, and later partnered with friend Johnny Depp to convert the space into the trendy Viper Room.

"I always wanted to sing like a black man and do business like a Jew. Instead, I sing like a Jew and do business like a black man," Weiss said.

These days, L.A.'s club-crawling night owl has settled down.

"The only bohemian thing that happens now is the music, when I'm rehearsing and gigging with hepcat musicians. Other than that, I lead a pretty normal middle-class life. I got a routine. I go to the barbershop, I got my cats at home, I watch sports on TV …"

CHUCK E. WEISS

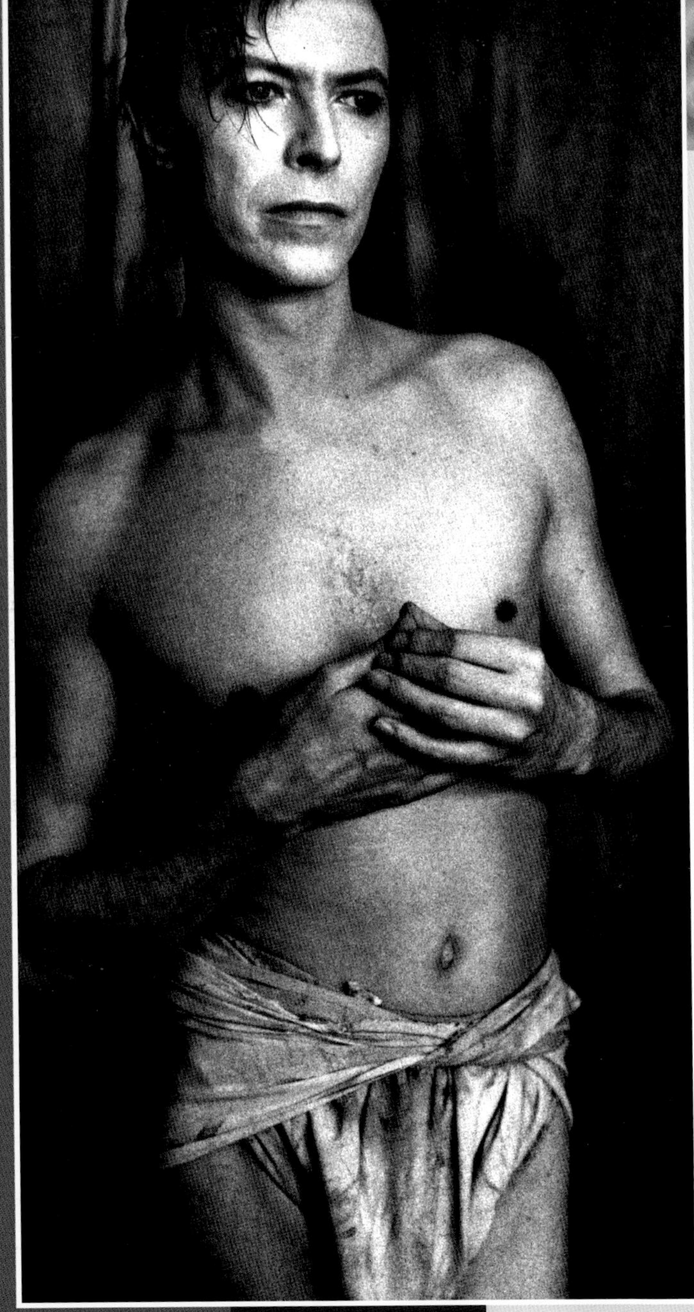

On July 19, 1980, Bowie showed he had another surprise up his sleeve. He made his theatrical debut playing the title role in Bernard Pomerance's play *The Elephant Man*. The Tony Award–winning hit opened its run in Denver, as the producers wanted to work out the kinks in a smaller market.

"The first moment on that Denver stage was probably the most scary moment of my life," Bowie recalled.

"Around music, with something I've written, a piece that I've designed and all that, I've got a fair amount of faith in what I'm doing. But I didn't really know what was going to happen that first night. It was great just to be allowed to continue the performance."

Bowie had lived in Berlin the last few years as "a frame of reference," avoiding the United States unless he was working. But an appearance on the popular *Saturday Night Live* television show brought him to New York City during Christmas of 1979. There he saw *The Elephant Man* and met its director, the voluble Jack Hoffiss.

"It was nuts, it made no sense at all," Bowie admitted. "I'd never been offered a play before, and because of that, I accepted! Jack really convinced me that if I was going to fall on my face, he'd fall with me.

"I thought it was a wonderful performance piece, strange enough to keep my interest. So I jumped at the chance—I just wanted to do it."

Bowie always had more than a passing fancy in wedding theatrics and rock. He worked with Lindsay Kemp's mime troupe circa 1966 as David Jones, and his past experience helped him to prepare for his role as *The Elephant Man*. In the drama, set in early-nineteenth-century England, Bowie played John Merrick, a young man horribly deformed from birth who was gradually transformed from a sideshow freak into a darling of aristocratic British society.

"I'd run out of good books to read," Bowie smiled after opening night.

"But really, I've wanted to direct from the word go. One of the many reasons I became involved in rock 'n' roll was that it gave me the opportunity to assemble shows completely and direct them—give myself some free practice and get paid for it. It was a good way to make a living.

"It's the idea of putting over various points of view which intrigues me—seeming illusions creating environments that aren't there. Rock productions and the theater stage are both very similar. You have to employ the same methods of vision to create a microcosm or a macrocosm.

"It's your yin and yang, ain't it?"

In *The Elephant Man*, Bowie performed sans makeup or padding, letting his body illustrate the contortion—his twisted torso slumped to one side, his head arched at an uncomfortable angle, his right leg dragged. "I get headaches, I take aspirin," he allowed.

Bowie shortly took over the lead role in the New York production and won rave notices.

In the 1970s, David Bowie was rock's ultimate chameleon. From the hard rock of his persona Ziggy Stardust to the R&B of his persona Thin White Duke, it was said he went through musical styles faster than clothes, always moving on to another role, or even films.

VAN HALEN

When Van Halen was a bar band, the boys looked up to bands that defined the rock 'n' roll party lifestyle. Perhaps intoxicated with their recent rise to more-or-less stardom in 1980, they were ready to do their best impersonation of hopelessly spoiled rock stars, too.

Van Halen's concert rider—the part of a performing contract that lists a band's concert-hall requirements (from food and stage size to clean towels and a heated dressing room)—required that meals always included servings of M&M candies, with the brown ones removed. It read, "There will be no brown M&Ms anywhere in the backstage area, upon pain of forfeiture of the show with full compensation."

At the start of the tour in support of the *Van Halen II* album, at a college show at the University of Southern Colorado in Pueblo, the band decided that the proviso was not being met. They trashed their facilities—and did $10,000 worth of damage.

"We were taking a gi-normous production out on the road that was built for 20,000-seat arenas into a 3,500-seat exhibition hall in Park Bench, Utah," singer David Lee Roth explained in his usual overdrive, hyper-jive way. "Nobody was used to the kind of manpower and logistics it took to wrench that around. Our teardown time was something like nine and one-half hours.

"Every back stage looks identical—you have a bowl of Pringles and soda pop. An idea was tossed around—'How do we prevent technical errors in this monster production? We'll write something about M&Ms in the middle of the contract rider!'"

Ten thousand dollars was a lot of money even for Van Halen, but the result was national publicity for the tour—even *Time* magazine ran a piece on the band. It helped catapult *Van Halen II* into the major-act world.

In the 1970s, Heart found immediate success delivering acoustic serenades and tomboy rock 'n' roll with equal aplomb, racking up a string of hits—"Crazy On You," "Magic Man," "Barracuda," "Straight On," and others.

The two-record *Greatest Hits/Live* (1980) pulled together the obvious highpoints, fleshed out with six spirited live tracks—including a warmly elegant cover of "Unchained Melody," recorded at McNichols Arena in September 1980.

"It's one of those songs they used to write a long time ago—beautiful, no effects," singer Ann Wilson said.

"Unchained Melody" was a 1965 hit by the Righteous Brothers that, recycled, got Demi Moore and Patrick Swayze all hot and bothered in the movie *Ghost*. Wilson incurred oxygen debt singing it in the Mile High City.

"When you sing rock 'n' roll or do something athletic, you use up more oxygen. We went up to check out Caribou Studios, and they had oxygen bottles on the wall like a cigarette machine. We did a casual track and my voice sounded thin.

"So I kept a tank of oxygen stage left when I played Denver."

"Unchained Melody" was left off the CD reissue of Heart's *Greatest Hits/Live*, but the version was included on 2002's *The Essential Heart*.

WARREN ZEVON

Singer-songwriter Zevon's ironic tales of physical and psychological mayhem had earned him a cult following, and he was dubbed "the Sam Peckinpah of rock" after the director who opened the door for graphic violence in movies. In 1978, Zevon had a Top 10 single with "Werewolves of London." But his career was temporarily set back by his alcoholism.

After a year in the studio and "in training," Zevon's 1980 release, *Bad Luck Streak in Dancing School*, represented something of a comeback for him, and he was eager to tour. First, he enlisted the aid of East Coast guitar ace David Landau. Then he met the group called Boulder.

In the early 1970s, Warren Zevon spent a couple of years touring as the Everly Brothers' pianist/bandleader. After their breakup, he worked alternately with Phil and Don and sojourned to Aspen long enough to be appointed honorary coroner of Pitkin County, Colorado.

"My ex-wife grew up in Aspen, which is a sort of rarity, I presume. So we ended up there. A friend of mine was running for councilman, and late one night in the Hotel Jerome bar, I said that if he won, I wanted to be appointed coroner. He said, 'Well, it is an appointment.' He won, and I was. I like to think of it like a perpetuity."

Boulder was seven players, most of them writers and five of them singers. The nucleus formed in Florida in 1972, and the other members, all veterans of club bands throughout the United States, joined in installments. The band was complete, however, by 1976, when they relocated to Colorado and acquired their name.

Boulder did college and club dates, but the members were wary of becoming a copy band and burning out on the road. They finally built their own studio in a two-car garage in the vicinity of Denver. "One of our roadies was a carpenter, and we went all out with hammer and nails and plasterboard," drummer Marty Stinger recalled.

Boulder began recording material for their debut album in Florida in January 1978 and did additional work at Caribou Ranch. In November 1978 they signed with Elektra/Asylum and moved to Los Angeles.

"The producer from Elektra scammed the whole deal and screwed the band—which is not an uncommon situation, but we had our turn at it," lead singer Bob Harris said.

However, Boulder's debut album included a harrowing and intelligent version of Zevon's "Join Me in L.A."

"We liked the theme of the song, and we were moving to L.A., where we'd never been before," Harris said.

Zevon took to the road, not with the L.A. session guys from his albums, but rather with a little-known Colorado group. The "audition" consisted of a spirited version of "Johnny B. Goode." His somewhat sudden decision to record the few-months-new touring band in concert spoke volumes about the guy's essential rock 'n' roll attitude.

"The idea always appeals to me to find a self-contained band, or at least find musicians who are accustomed to playing with each other," he said.

The difference was apparent on the live recording *Stand in the Fire*, cut at the Roxy in Los Angeles. One of Zevon's best albums, *Rolling Stone* called it a portrait of the artist defiantly walking the line between emotional exorcism and mass entertainment.

Throughout, Boulder anchored the star's feisty roar with a tight, tenacious beat. Zevon struck up the band for *Stand in the Fire*, a vigorous, guitar-driven celebration of the rock 'n' roll spirit: "Our lead guitar player's scalding hot/And Zeke's going at it, giving it every thing he's got," he shouted proudly in a lusty, Elvis Presley–like baritone.

Zevon performed shirtless on the summer tour.

"That was the culmination of a two-year physical fitness period in my life. I think I was celebrating the Chuck Norris–like physique of that era," Zevon said.

"It was a real turning point for Warren, because he had just gotten out of rehabilitation, and kicked the bottle. He had this incredible amount of energy. All of a sudden he knew where to put it, and he could turn it into being good," Harris said.

"He went to some tailor in Beverly Hills and bought these $1,200 suits and was going to play in them. He'd been doing dancing and karate and was going to come across really classy. And about two or three weeks into the tour, he'd ripped the pants and the coats just dancing around on stage. So after that, he went out in blue jeans and t-shirt.

"Seeing him onstage every night, he's probably the most consistent performer I've ever seen. On the bus one night, he said, 'Man, I had to realize that these people out here are my friends.' It went from being good to phenomenal."

The success wasn't enough to keep Boulder going. Meanwhile, Zevon continued his solo career.

Time magazine's reviewers gave Song Title of the Year to Warren Zevon's rollicking "Things To Do in Denver When You're Dead," from his eleventh album, *Mr. Bad Example*. *People* magazine called it "a hoot."

"Um, it had to be a two-syllable town—Indianapolis wouldn't work," Zevon explained. "It had to start with a 'D.' It had to have a Rattlesnake Cafe. Those were kind of the parameters. Everyone seemed to enjoy it the last time I played Colorado."

In 2003, Zevon died of mesothelioma, a form of lung cancer, at age fifty-six.

Warren Zevon's tour, including a group called Boulder, was titled "The Dog Ate the Part We Didn't Like," a line borrowed from Zevon's friend, novelist Thomas McGuane.

TIM GOODMAN

Tim Goodman's debut album was the first release on Feyline Records, a custom label headed by Colorado promoter Barry Fey.

Fey got the go-ahead from CBS Records (Columbia) to assemble talent for his own label. Under the arrangement, Feyline handled all of the basic record company functions but got to use the corporate muscle of CBS for distribution.

Feyline Records got off to a slow start. Fey recorded a band called the Flyers, but the band sounded like a watered-down Firefall. CBS heard the final tapes and raised a corporate eyebrow.

The next signing was Tim Goodman, another artist with a Colorado past whose *Footsteps* was a more suitable debut for Feyline Records.

Goodman had spent years honing his craft in a wide variety of locales. His travels as a working musician literally spanned the entire country, including the mountains of Colorado. The singer-songwriter-guitarist had greatly improved since his days at the Utah Moon in Boulder. He was managed by Marty Wollf, who, ironically, was Barry Fey's arch-rival as they both tried to promote shows in the Denver area in the mid-1970s.

Footsteps was produced by Doobie Brothers lead guitarist John McFee. "New Romeo" was bubbling under the *Billboard* Hot 100 in September 1981, at No. 107.

"A guy named Alex Call wrote it. He was an original member of Clover with John McFee. He sent me a cassette and, on the flip side, there were some titles scratched out. The first tune was 'New Romeo.' I called Alex and asked him about this tune. He said, 'Oh, I'm holding onto that for myself.' I worked on him for a year before he let me cut the song."

Feyline Records went under. Goodman formed Southern Pacific in mid-1983.

MOJO NIXON

Rock eccentric Mojo Nixon parlayed an irrepressible personality, a roguish sense of humor, and a fondness for lusty rockabilly into swaggering punk originals like "Elvis Is Everywhere," "Debbie Gibson Is Pregnant With My Two-Headed Love Child," "Don Henley Must Die," "Stuffin' Martha's Muffin," and "Moanin' With Your Momma," achieving a measure of national fame

Nixon had always been gonzo. The singer lived in Denver circa 1980-1981 when he was still appearing under his birth name Kirby McMillan. He and his punk band Zebra 123 were questioned by the U.S. Secret Service for their part in the Assassination Ball at the notorious Malfunction Junction.

"It took place November 22, 1980, which happened to be the anniversary of Kennedy being caught in the triangulation there at the grassy knoll. Zebra 123 had been banned from everywhere. We weren't skinny-tie new-wave cute, we were pissed off—three chords and a cloud of dust.

"We got together with two other bands and decided to put on our own show. This girlfriend of mine took a picture of Carter and Reagan—the election was going on then—and made it look as if they'd been shot from below and their heads were exploding, not unlike JFK's.

"That got the Secret Service all over us. They came and gave us a big lecture, and they didn't like our show. So there's a file on me somewhere."

McMillan didn't become Mojo Nixon until he moved to San Diego and joined up with Skid Roper.

GARY MORRIS

Gary Morris sustained a string of smash country records in the 1980s. He credited Colorado as the place where he gained his most valuable experience.

The Texas native intended to enroll in college and play football, but he went to Colorado for the summer with two buddies.

"That was the beginning of my singing career," Morris said. "We stopped at a bar in Colorado Springs called the Golden Bee. We asked the bartender if we could do a few songs. We stood up on some tables and did 'Gentle on My Mind,' 'Early Morning Rain,' and 'Visions of Sugar Plums.' The audience just went crazy. We collected thirty-five dollars in tips and quickly translated that figure into what we could make singing twenty songs. We thought, 'This is it!'"

The trio traveled on to Boulder, where Morris rented an apartment and got a job as a construction worker. They also sang at a bar called the Three Kings "for beer and cheeseburgers." As summer's end drew near, Morris opted to forego college and turn his attention to singing and performing. For several years, Morris fronted a trio that entertained regularly at Taylor's Supper Club in Denver. He also gained valuable studio experience singing and writing jingles for accounts such as Coors Beer and Frontier Airlines.

From 1976 to 1979, Denver was a full-time address for Gary Morris when he fronted Breakaway, a seven-piece country-rock band, with his writing and vocals as the driving force.

"The band was conceived to support my singing," Morris recalled. "In time, though, it became a 'personality' band with everyone involved using a nickname and so on. As I became more serious musically, I saw the need to make some drastic personnel changes. We were vying to get signed as a pre-Alabama, pre–Charlie Daniels Band type of group, but it wasn't in the cards at that time."

Morris eventually made the decision to go solo, even though Breakaway "was as good a band as you'll ever hear." He made the trek to Nashville to take a shot at the real music business. "Headed For A Heartache" and "The Love She Found in Me" were the records that established him as a Nashville brand name. *Why Lady Why* peaked at No. 174 on *Billboard*'s pop album charts in 1983.

"Hey, Denver's the place I call home," the country singer said. "I'm forced to spend at least half of the year in Nashville because of my career, but every spare moment I get, I'm back in Colorado."

THE NAILS

'98

The Nails began their musical life in country bars in the Boulder, Colorado, area as the Ravers, the state's punk rock forefathers, led by punk poet/Patti Smith look-alike Mark Campbell (vocals, guitar).

In 1976, Campbell arrived in Boulder from San Francisco, where he'd been turning out 16mm films and performing "sexually explicit" songs in small clubs with another guitarist/poet in a duo they called the Pits of Passion. One day Campbell was reading the University of Colorado bulletin board and noticed a card hung out by student David Kaufman, who sought to form a reggae band.

"My interests were moving in that direction anyhow, so I called him," said Campbell, and the Ravers' nucleus was formed.

The five-piece band developed quite a cult following. Its combination of reggae, ska, mid-1960s rock, and high-volume tone poems set the Rocky Mountain music scene on its edge. This was in 1976, at the very beginning of the New York/London punk/new wave explosion—and in Colorado, Firefall and the like still ruled the bar band scene.

The Ravers recorded "Cops Are Punks" at Boulder's Mountain Ears Studio, and the single received national press from the magazine *Trouser Press*. One fateful day in 1976, the Colorado police raided the band's basement rehearsal hall, mistakenly thinking it was a bomb factory. Shortly thereafter, Campbell and Kaufman elected to seach out wider vistas and moved the entire band to New York City. Years of steady gigging in the Manhattan clubs followed.

"We had a friend in real estate who let us use an empty five-story house on the Upper East Side. The bad was that it had no furniture, so we all slept on the floor," Campbell said.

Once transplanted, the group slowly began its transition to the Nails, mining the rich "American poetic tradition" also worked by Lou Reed, the Doors, and Bruce Springsteen.

Campbell explained that Nails music emanated from "a mystical and sexual area. I write in a cinematic way, trying to create through language and music, texture and atmosphere, a specific mood. Each song—little fictions, I call 'em—tells a story to explore those moods."

Released in 1981 and distributed nationally on RCA in 1984, the sardonic "88 Lines About 44 Women" made people everywhere sit up and take notice. Certainly many members of the male species knew at least a few of the archetypal females in the song. And a lot of women recognized themselves in the tightly compacted two-line life stories. The Nails had constructed a song that took an unflinching look at real life, in the New York tradition of Lou Reed's "Walk on the Wild Side," the New York Dolls' "Personality Crisis," and Jim Carroll's "People Who Died."

Los Angeles progressive radio giant KROQ-FM put the song in heavy rotation and "88 Lines" zoomed up the dance floor charts of the Western Association of Rock Disk Jockeys. The Nails subsequently played their first U.S. tour, concentrating on Southern California and Colorado.

DAVE GRUSIN

Player, conductor, arranger, composer, producer—Dave Grusin covered a lot of musical ground.

"But I'm not keen on the idea of competition in my area. If they want competition, they should have eight guys sit down and write the same thing and see who does it the fastest," Grusin mused. "It's not really important to pit different types of work against each other. So I've tried to take a low profile. I'd rather just do the work."

Born in June 1934 and raised in Littleton, Colorado, Grusin was exposed to music right away. His father, Henri, a watchmaker and violinist, had thirty years before played chamber music in hotels throughout the East Coast. It rubbed off on Grusin, who picked up piano at the age of four.

As a teenager, Grusin was taken to hear jazz at the Philharmonic concerts, where he heard Lester Young, Ella Fitzgerald, Ray Brown, and Oscar Peterson. Enrolled in the University of Colorado's music school, Grusin played with some jazz groups, working the usual frat parties and clubs. He wanted to play jazz more than dance music, however, and that attitude got him fired. He had begun enjoying true jazz artists like Art Tatum and Count Basie.

Grusin credited his father with instilling in him and his brother Don an understanding of classical music and "the literature of great orchestration." While still a piano major at the University of Colorado at Boulder, he found time to play with visiting artists like Art Pepper, Terry Gibbs, and singer Anita O'Day.

But film composers became Grusin's real heroes. In 1959, Grusin moved to New York. He moved up to become the music director of *The Andy Williams Show*, a job that eventually brought him to Hollywood. At that time, he also did his first record dates.

In 1964, he left Williams to score television sitcoms, hoping they would buy his ticket into films. Once he broke into film with *Divorce American Style*, more assignments followed quickly. Records created the next challenge. Sergio Mendez & Brazil '66 called upon Grusin to arrange hits such as "Fool on the Hill" and "The Look of Love." Quincy Jones called upon him as a player and arranger on many of his albums as well as the Brothers Johnson albums.

In the 1980s, the Colorado native brought his talents into focus. As a producer and businessman, he ran GRP Records, a classy mainstream jazz label with popular artists like the Rippingtons, Spyro Gyra, David Benoit, Lee Ritenour, and Tom Scott.

As an artist, the jazz pianist played select sessions and recorded his own records. Four cracked the *Billboard* album charts, and 1981's *Mountain Dance* was the most successful, peaking at No. 74.

As a film composer/producer, Grusin worked on the soundtracks for such notable pictures as *On Golden Pond* and *Tootsie*, and his tunes were nominated for Oscars. "Theme from St. Elsewhere" hit No. 15 on *Billboard*'s easy-listening charts.

CARL WILSON

Dennis Wilson offered the first solo album from the Beach Boys, 1977's *Pacific Ocean Blue*. Carl Wilson's self-titled solo debut for Caribou Records came second.

But Carl, guitarist of the Beach Boys, was the man who many people credited with keeping the group together all those years.

"I never pushed to do a solo record because my first responsibility had always been to the Beach Boys," he explained. "But the group can't really provide me with an outlet for the other music I love to play—good, straight-ahead rock 'n' roll."

That funkier, rocking side of Wilson dominated *Carl Wilson*. Myrna Smith, formerly of the Sweet Inspirations, co-wrote all of the songs with Wilson and supplied vocals on the tracks.

When it came time to choose a producer, Wilson gravitated to Jim Guercio, who ended a three-year absence from the studio to undertake the project at his home base, Colorado's Caribou Ranch. He also played bass and percussion on several tracks.

Carl Wilson charted for two weeks on the *Billboard* Top 200 in May 1981. In support of his album, Wilson embarked on the first ever solo tour by a Beach Boy.

Wilson died in February 1998 from complications of lung cancer at the age of fifty-one.

RANDY BELL

In 1984, Randy Bell, a twenty-four-year-old resident of Denver, struck a deal with a major label—Epic Records released the single "Don't Do Me." The power-pop ode made a brief appearance on the *Billboard* singles chart, peaking at No. 93 in July 1984.

Bell, who resided in Thornton, hadn't played many concerts in his burgeoning career, even in the Colorado region.

"I never played the bars," he said. "I put my money into good-quality home-recording equipment. I started doing that when I was eighteen or so. I'd go down to the basement and listen to what was popular on the radio, then write my own material based on that and try to record it."

One of Bell's first homemade efforts, an original tune called "More Than Alive," was voted No. 1 by the listeners of Denver's KTLK in the station's *Colorado Music* album contest. Bell entered it under the name "Randy Rock" but ditched the moniker soon after. The local showing led him to the finals of Miller High Life's Rock To Riches talent search. At the finals, held in New York's Palladium in April 1982, he wound up with second place.

"Don't Do Me" was the first product to come out of Bell's "long term, multi-album" contract with Epic. He quit his day job at Rocky Flats in his continuing search for a smash. But Epic marketed him to teenyboppers—his bare-chested visage appeared in such fan magazines as *Teen Beat*. It didn't work.

When U2 came through Denver on a maiden American tour, promoter Chuck Morris drove the Irish quartet up to Morrison to show off Red Rocks Amphitheatre. The band immediately fell in love with Colorado's classy outdoor venue, and manager Paul McGuinness vowed that one day they would film a performance there.

Three years later, U2 fulfilled the promise. The college-radio underdogs had made a mark on the rock scene by dint of honest, emotional performances, and Red Rocks was booked for June 5, 1983.

From day one, the logistics proved to be formidable. No one had ever attempted such a project before, and it was a costly proposition. For the full effect of the mountain scenery to be caught on camera, the huge rocks had to be lit up at a cost of $40,000, according to McGuinness.

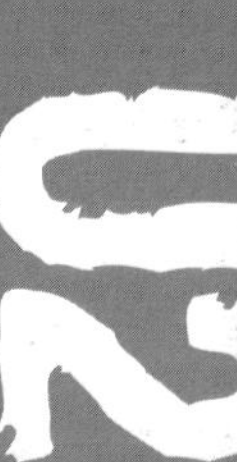

However, the band proceeded with the lofty plans. Gavin Taylor, the director of *The Tube* (an avant-garde English video program), was flown over to oversee the filming. Steve Lillywhite, the producer of U2's albums, was also transported from Europe to mix the live audio on location. Special effects including backdrops and two bonfires on the rocks were generated.

Despite the sheets of rain that sliced through Red Rocks for days beforehand, U2 delivered its typical punch.

But on the day of the show, the weather threatened to ruin the entire scenario. Temperatures dropped to forty degrees at showtime, and a day's worth of drizzle evolved into a deluge. It was no place to be holding a concert.

Yet 4,400 kids showed up to brave the nightmarish elements at Red Rocks, even after the promise was given of another show to be held the following night at an indoor venue. U2 took the stage, and the drama made its way to the wonderful *U2 at Red Rocks* (a rock documentary aired on the Showtime national cable television service) and *Under A Blood Red Sky* (a video and live album).

The swirling fog that rolled in over the mountains gave the setting an eerie quality, something akin to a Scottish moor. The segments in which the band was delivered to the site via helicopter appeared to be from the movie *Apocalypse Now*. And the concert pieces were exceptionally striking. In the video of *Sunday Bloody Sunday*, lead singer Bono immortalized his holy gladiator profile, unfurling and waving a huge white flag in the crowd against the hellish glow of the flaming torches high on the cliffs.

It's doubtful that any other band could have turned the adversity at Red Rocks into its favor so convincingly. The subtle peace-and-brotherhood appeal was attributed to the Christian beliefs that three of the four members shared.

"We're not just sentimental Irish lads—I think there's more depth to us than that," Bono insisted.

"But I detest the way religion is turned into an industry in America. I want to kick in the television in disgust when I see people begging for funds. We'll never do that.

"We just want to share a message. John Lennon, Bob Dylan—those people were artists who wrote about what was happening in their lives."

The mystic, against-all-odds performance was a spiritual and commercial breakthrough, and it turned U2 into A-list rock heroes.

"I'd like to thank the man who invented the wide-angle lens—he made the 4,000 people there look like millions," Bono said.

"In Europe, nobody knew who we were. They saw the video and said, 'Who are these guys?'"

U2 fans who attended the Red Rocks concert were praised for their incredible devotion amid the soggy conditions that night.

U2's motion picture *Rattle and Hum*, a documentary of the Irish superband's 1987 world tour, featured live recordings from concerts at Denver's McNichols Arena on November 7 and 8. During the first show, the band battled the distracting presence of cameramen on stage. Bono evenually dropped his microphone in disgust and muttered, "I feel like a book that shouldn't have been made into a movie." But three songs from the second night made the *Rattle and Hum* soundtrack – "Pride (In The Name of Love)," "Silver and Gold," and a cover of the Beatles' "Helter Skelter."

JELLO BIAFRA

The most spectacular censorship attack on an individual artist took place in 1986. It was directed at Jello Biafra, leader of the punk band Dead Kennedys.

California authorities charged him based on a parent's complaint about the inclusion of artwork by Swiss surrealist H.R. Giger titled "Penis Landscape" (a poster depicting sexual organs) in the Dead Kennedys' *Frankenchrist* album. Biafra was held on the grounds of distribution of harmful material to minors. Although Biafra was eventually acquitted, the obscenity trial left him head over ears in debt, without a group, and unable to record for years.

Born Eric Boucher in 1959, Biafra grew up in hippie-happy Boulder and, like a lot of disillusioned punk rockers, left town after high school.

"In some ways it was a great place to grow up, but then turned into a miserable place. The hippies discovered Colorado and came in droves. That's when they were considered very dangerous: 'Don't go down on the Hill, Eric, you might run into some hippies!' Of course, that was where I went.

"By the time I was coming of age in junior high and high school, where I could really start to immerse myself in this culture, the culture was gone. It wasn't the '60's anymore, and people were just beginning to realize how stupid and boring it was to be eighteen in 1975.

"The music was much more salable, respectable, and had been slowed down and watered down. They had figured out how to take the rebellion of everybody from Bob Dylan to Steppenwolf—yes, Steppenwolf scared people at one time—and water it down into Bad Company, Lynyrd Skynyrd, and worst of all, country-rock and disco.

"Country-rock ruled in Boulder. That, and jazz-fusion, were pushed to the gills by media and record stores. Some L.A. country-rock mafia had moved to Colorado and lived around Boulder, so you'd also have these pre-yuppie monied hippies swaggering into town: 'Hi, I'm Rick Roberts (Firefall)—give me a free meal!' 'Hi, I'm Stephen Stills—get the fuck away from that pool table!'

"But one thing saved me. Starting in the ninth grade, I got so fed up with radio that I began buying records just on the basis of which covers looked the most interesting. I discovered the used record stores. I scoured the twenty-five-cent bins and especially the free box, where they'd throw in anything they didn't think they could sell. Looking back, this was the advantage of living in a country-rock town—Stooges for a dime, MC5 for a quarter, 13th Floor Elevators, Nazz, and Les Baxter for free …

"I went to see the Ramones live at the Rainbow Music Hall in Denver, and my whole life changed. They were so powerful, yet so simple—'Yeah, I could do that, too. Why not? I think I will!' And the rest, as they say, is sordid history. Myself, Wax Trax Records, Ministry, the Nails—we all grew out of that show."

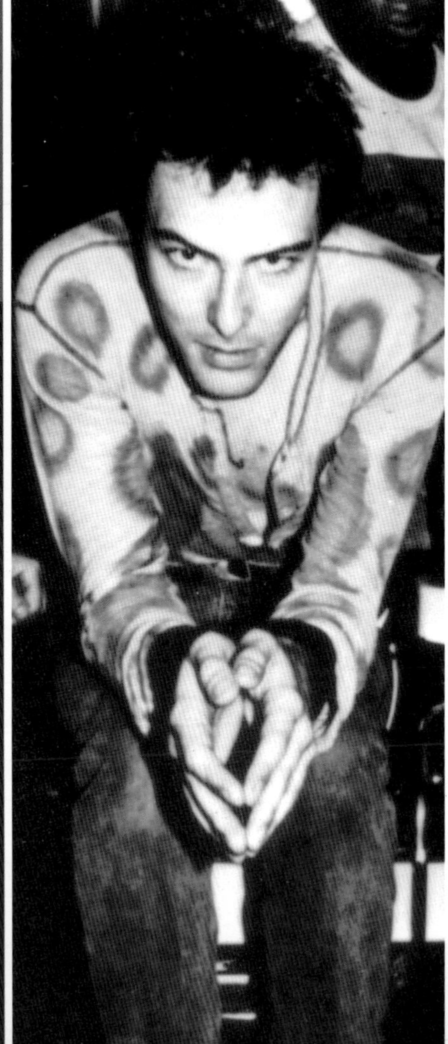

A self-described "cultural terrorist" and born provocateur, Biafra went to San Francisco and decided to form a band. He made bad as lead singer for the Dead Kennedys, upholding an aggressive anti-capitalist style that featured smart but harsh political lyrics with furious music.

Biafra constantly challenged the status quo. He even ran for mayor of San Francisco on a dare. He cut his hair, circulated petitions, and made the talk-show rounds, and with zero political clout he still managed to finish fourth in the race.

The Dead Kennedys always refused to sign with a major label (the band could have, but Biafra wouldn't change the name).

The prolonged legal confrontation left a powerful anti-censorship legacy, but the ordeal strained morale, and the group broke up soon after.

Biafra's controversial spirit raged on. He harnessed his sharp observations about American politics and culture, doing spoken-word tours and releasing spoken-word albums on Alternative Tentacles, the record label he created in 1981 for the Kennedys.

DAVID CROSBY

The 1950s "establishment" told drug horror stories—notably, that marijuana leads to harder stuff. David Crosby didn't believe them, but they were right in his case.

The musician, a pivotal member of two seminal groups, the Byrds and Crosby, Stills, Nash & Young, smoked his first joint in Boulder.

"It was nineteen-hundred-and-frozen-to-death," the singer reminisced. "I spent a winter playing in a basement coffeehouse on the Hill called the Attic. A fellow musician gave me my first joint and I loved it. I was driving a car at the time, thought I was going eighty-five, but the speedometer read forty."

In the 1960s and 1970s, Crosby managed to out-drug Stills, Nash, and Young combined. But the 1980s were rough on him. His well-documented drug-abuse problem and the resultant paranoia left him a shell of a performer. He got busted so often he should have installed a drive-through window. The arrests piled up: cocaine, heroin, guns, assault, and battery. By 1985, he was lucky to be alive.

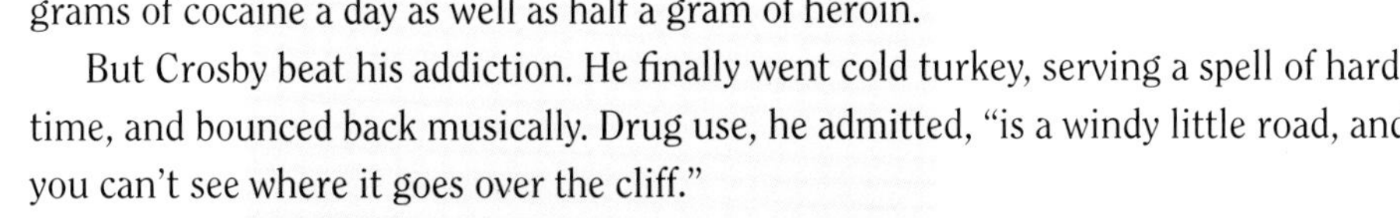

A one-year jail sentence stemming from drug and possession charges in Texas caught up with Crosby before death did. When he finally surrendered to authorities, by his own admission, he and girlfriend Jan Dance were consuming approximately seven grams of cocaine a day as well as half a gram of heroin.

But Crosby beat his addiction. He finally went cold turkey, serving a spell of hard time, and bounced back musically. Drug use, he admitted, "is a windy little road, and you can't see where it goes over the cliff."

Stevie Nicks: "I feel like Colorado is mine. My ancestors immigrated there from Cologne, Germany. My late great-aunt lived up in Cripple Creek—she ran a brothel. I have a lot of relatives in Colorado Springs. I remember being in Aspen writing 'Landslide' and 'Rhiannon.' And I have real bad asthma, and Denver has the best doctors in the world."

On August 20, 1986, Nicks filmed the final concert on her "Give A Little" tour at Red Rocks Amphitheatre—just eight weeks after she had played two sold-out shows at the venue.

"They told me, 'You can't go back so soon and film there, nobody's going to come.' I said, 'I can—you don't understand. This is a sacred thing to me and everybody who will be there.'

"And it sold out. I knew in my heart where I should do my movie, where my feet are planted. Every year or two I need to go to Red Rocks and spend some time, whether I'm performing or not.

"If I ever have children or grandchildren, if I want to explain my legacy to anybody, I'll just put on 'Red Rocks.'"

The results were broadcast on the Showtime cable network and made commercially available on the hour-long *Stevie: Live at Red Rocks* concert video, which featured her Top 10 hits ("Dreams," "Stand Back," and a fifteen-minute version of "Edge of Seventeen") and guest performers Peter Frampton and Mick Fleetwood.

Nicks' Red Rocks show ended when twenty-five doves were released into the crowd. One of them refused to leave her hand—and fifteen minutes later she was still clutching the bird backstage and demanding that a separate cage be found.

"I want to find a good home for him," she explained. "I want to visit him when I come back next time."

But Nicks kept him—only it was a her, named Rhiannon, of course.

"She wouldn't leave. I couldn't get her away, so I said, 'I guess this is my dove' …"

"I was one of the first troublemakers in the world of bluegrass, bringing electric bass on stage in the '70s," Forster said. "We'd play traditional festivals, and I'd walk out on stage with my electric bass and get boos and catcalls from the audience."

At the beginning of their career, the musicians traveled in a '69 Cadillac, their equipment behind them in an old U-Haul trailer they'd painted black. Tapes recorded by Sawtelle for the band's road trips provided an education in what Forster calls "the soul of music."

"(These) tapes had traditional bluegrass, then Freddie King, then a Jimi Hendrix cut. We learned early on that the soul of the material was important, and we agreed on certain qualities that songs either had or didn't have."

Hot Rize took those special song traits and infused them into a unique and exciting style of bluegrass, reaching the upper echelons of the bluegrass world. The band recorded numerous albums for the independent Flying Fish, Sugar Hill, and Rounder labels, including the Grammy-nominated "Take It Home" in 1990. The group performed at the top bluegrass festivals, touring Europe, Japan, Australia, and the United States, and also appeared on *Austin City Limits*, the Nashville Network, and at the Grand Ole' Opry.

As part of their stage act, Hot Rize became Red Knuckles & the Trail Blazers and, in good fun, parodied hardcore 1950s country music.

In 1990 Hot Rize parted ways amiably to pursue other musical ventures. The group's members performed together occasionally until Sawtelle died of leukemia in 1999. Forster is still a Boulder mainstay who, together with his wife Helen, hosts the national weekly radio program *E-Town*, recorded live at the Boulder Theater. Wernick still performs, and O'Brien, now based in Nashville, is a respected singer, songwriter, and multi-instrumentalist.

Hot Rize, based in Boulder, Colorado, was an innovative band capable of playing straight bluegrass with the best of the traditional bands, as well as mixing in elements of folk, jazz, and rock. The talented quartet not only inspired artists within the progressive-bluegrass genre, but also fueled the rise of the jam-band scene in Colorado.

Hot Rize formed in 1978, named after the secret ingredient of Martha White Self-Rising Flour, a sponsor of Flatt & Scruggs early in their careers. Four stellar musicians made up the band—Tim O'Brien on lead and harmony vocals, mandolin, and fiddle; "Dr Banjo" Pete Wernick on banjo and harmony vocals; Charles Sawtelle on bass guitar, guitar, harmonies, and lead vocals; and bass player, guitarist, and vocalist Nick Forster, who also became their emcee. All of them sang and played a quirky mix of traditional and contemporary standards and originals.

HOT RIZE

To commemorate the 227-date "Hysteria" world tour, Def Leppard filmed a concert video at Denver's McNichols Arena on February 12 and 13, 1988, *In the Round—In Your Face.*

Initially, the superstar British quintet had planned to film a performance video for the hit single "Pour Some Sugar on Me."

"But then we said to hang on a minute—we'd be daft to shoot just one song," singer Joe Elliott recalled. "So we decided to do the whole show and see what we got.

"We wanted to do it in the best possible place. On that leg of the tour, the *Hysteria* album hadn't really taken off nationwide. Denver was the first place we were doing two nights, and they were both sold out. It was obvious, we were kings in Denver.

"And we wound up with a hell of a lot of good footage. The audience was beyond belief."

The band members financed the filming themselves. "We couldn't get the record company to pay for that one," Elliott said. And the project served as a memorial to their massive high-tech, circular-stage construction.

"We wanted to make an event, so we put the stage in the middle. I described it as a sixty-by-forty-foot boxing ring without the ropes. It was a lot of fun—the director (Wayne Isham) auditioning girls that you wanted to shove down against the fence at the front, all the usual rock 'n' roll trappings.

"For us Englishmen, the only drawback with doing it in Denver was the altitude. When you listen to the tape, you can hear me getting out of breath big-time. It's a good thing we were in our mid twenties, because we would have been in cardiac arrest after five songs."

The ninety-minute *In the Round—In Your Face* video contained thirty seconds of additional footage from a trio of shows in Atlanta "because the director decided he needed more audience shots," according to Elliott.

The "Pour Some Sugar on Me" clip became a finalist for both Best Stage Performance and Best Heavy Metal Video in the MTV Music Awards. *In the Round—In Your Face* showcased thirteen more pop-metal hits, including "Foolin'," "Rock of Ages," "Photograph," "Animal," "Armageddon It," "Bringin' On the Heartbreak," "Rock! Rock! (Till You Drop)," "Women," "Too Late For Love," and "Hysteria."

The most riveting aspect of *In the Round—In Your Face* was the effort put forth by drummer Rick Allen. In a much publicized incident, he lost his left arm in an automobile accident during the recording of the *Hysteria* album. But Allen was determined to continue playing with one arm, and onstage, he unveiled his new drumming style for everyone to see. He fostered a technique where his left foot substituted for his missing limb to go along with a specifically designed Simmons electronic drum kit.

WINGER

In 1988, Winger's self-titled debut album was certified platinum for one million sales.

Ten years earlier, Denver native Kip Winger was holding court—underage—at the Godfather and other Denver-area 3.2 beer emporiums for teens. Prior to his sophomore year at Golden High School, Winger, then sixteen, took the GED and went on the road.

"Winger (at the time a band with his brothers) was getting a lot of gigs, and school was getting in the way," he recalled. "We linked up with producer Beau Hill, who was working out of Denver's Applewood Studios. He drove up in his Porsche, and we rode up on our ten-speed bikes."

Winger spent 1980 in New York opening in bars for the likes of Zebra and Twisted Sister. When the city's scene lost its momentum, he returned to Colorado to study acting, music, and voice at the University of Denver. But he was always sending tapes to Hill, who stayed in New York. Winger eventually rejoined Hill, sleeping on the floor of Hill's apartment.

"I had never done anything but play music, and I had an ego. I had always made money at it. But when I got to New York, there was a thousand of me, waiting tables and getting treated disrespectfully. It was overwhelming and intimidating, but it was the best thing that ever happened to my songwriting."

Hill finally cracked the big time by producing Ratt's breakthough hit "Round and Round," and he allowed Winger to play bass on some sessions. Winger got some equipment together and his hopes up—prematurely—for a record deal.

"When you grow up in the Rockies or Midwest, you don't have any connections. You think if you had some, you'd be happenin'. But they don't mean shit. You've got to have the goods as a songwriter or you don't make it."

Winger's demos were repeatedly turned down by record companies. He considers April 1986 the start of his career because he finally made some money writing horn and background vocal parts as Hill's production assistant for the *Hearts on Fire* soundtrack, featuring Bob Dylan. Alice Cooper then asked him to play on two albums and a tour.

"I remember the 1987 concert at McNichols Arena in Denver. When I was a kid, I used to rid my bike down to McNichols and stare

Kip Winger: "It was Christmas 1968 when I got my first bass. I was seven, and I wanted to be Paul McCartney. I had fiddled around with piano lessons the year before, but my other two brothers and I wanted to do a band, so our parents got me a Panoramic and my brothers a guitar and drum set."

at it and say, 'I'm going to play there someday.' And when I finally did, I couldn't move. I dislocated my knee the week before. I had to be carried on and off the stage."

The Cooper gig was good-paying, guaranteed work, but Winger decided to pursue his goal of leading his own band. He went into Boulder's Mountain Ears studio and didn't emerge until his contacts and experience landed him a recording contract.

Winger's chiseled good looks were seen on MTV, where videos for "Seventeen" and "Headed For A Heartbreak" received heavy exposure.

"It's weird—I was accustomed to hanging out wherever I wanted, but now people are waiting at the hotel for autographs and pictures," he said. "But I dig it. I waited for years for this to happen, and then it was all of a sudden."

Although he based himself in New York, Winger maintained that "Denver is the best place to be. It gave me a perspective on life.

"In Denver, you get a chance to nurture yourself and grow spiritually. It doesn't cost a million dollars to rent space, and the players are in close proximity, so you get a vibe, a sound, a longevity. That's much more preferable."

The musicianship in Winger was stronger than in any other pop-metal hair band. But a backlash overtook the group. On *Beavis & Butthead,* MTV's top-rated animated series of the mid-1990s, the heavy-metal-loving adolescents used to torture the neighborhood kid Stewart for wearing a Winger t-shirt.

Kip Winger's first gig was at Walnut Hills Elementary School in 1970. He was nine years old.

Magic Music, featuring a young Chris Daniels (second from right), played acoustic-based music in the 1970s.

"We did the hippie thing—Leftover Salmon before there was a Leftover Salmon," said Daniels. "We lived in school buses and a donut truck in Eldorado Canyon. We had two acoustic guitars, a flute, bass and percussion, usually tablas. The songs had a lot of elves, druids, and fairies in them. We had all kinds of brushes with fame."

Magic Music performed at the first two Telluride bluegrass festivals in 1973 and 1974, and at the first Earth Day festival in 1970. It also held its own in local clubs and was often booked at the Good Earth, with the funky Freddi-Henchi & the Soulsetters.

"Back then it worked," Daniels said. "The hippies would get all blissed out and mellow with Magic Music, then Freddi-Henchi would take the stage and everyone would get the soul shakes.

"In the early '70s, there were a whole series of communes and 'families' living in little mountain towns above Boulder, stretching from Nederland, Gold Hill, Ward, Allenspark, Estes Park, and even down to Horsetooth Reservoir.

"Some were pretty insulated, like Stephen Stills and the whole Caribou crew. Unless you were part of a chosen few, you did not enter. Others, like Magic Music, were porous and seemed to attract both camp followers and satellites. Magic Music set up headquarters in Allenspark, and the Hummingbird Cafe was the focal point. Bands like Rosewood Canyon and performers like Michael Covington (of Joni Mitchell's 'Michael from Mountains' fame) either lived nearby or played the cafe with Magic Music."

Daniels left the area to earn a B.A. in music theory at the University of California, Berkeley, then returned as a member of Spoons, an influential Boulder country-rock band. In the early 1980s, he toured with former Amazing Rhythm Aces front man Russell Smith, who lived in Boulder at the time.

In May 1984, Daniels formed a rhythm & blues horn band as a one-night joke at the old Blue Note in Boulder. Two decades later, Chris Daniels & the Kings have produced nine albums, toured worldwide, and remained a top local concert draw.

"We wanted to do anything with horns," said Daniels of the Kings' post-new-wave genesis. "Everybody thought it was real cool, and they'd say, 'What's that stuff?' But it's really a love affair with what happens with horns.

For twenty years, Chris Daniels & the Kings have entertained Colorado music fans with a souped-up mix of jump blues, blue-eyed soul, and horn-infused rock. The Kings have also earned something of a worldwide fan base, especially in the Netherlands, where they've even coaxed the nation's queen to shake her royal booty.

In addition to making great music, Daniels has played a hefty role in shaping the Front Range music scene. The Mile High mainstay spent five years as executive director of the Swallow Hill Music Association, which promotes folk and acoustic music in Denver.

Originally from Minneapolis, Daniels moved to New York City as a teenager, where he worked as a backing musician for David Johansen, later a founder of the glam-rock band the New York Dolls. He relocated to Colorado in 1971 and served a stint in Magic Music.

One of the things we did was push the hard rock 'n' roll sound with horns, which no one had ever done before.

"In the days of the fabled downtown Boulder music scene, there were six or seven clubs in a five-block radius. Sonny Landreth would be at JJ McCabes, the Kings at the Walrus, Steve Conn at the Boulderado, Woody & the Too High Band at the Blue Note, and everybody going back and forth on the breaks, even timing our breaks so we could sit in with each other's bands. It was like New York's 52nd Street in the '40s."

After building a following on the local circuit, the Kings hit the road and built loyal regional followings in Nashville, Minneapolis, and New York, and even in parts of Europe.

The band made a dent on the new "adult-album" format in larger markets. In 1987, their debut album, *When You're Cool*, hit No. 1 in Minneapolis, Denver-Boulder, and Detroit, and broke the Top 20 in San Francisco, Washington, D.C., and Montana. The video for the title track, Daniels said, gained a significant amount of play on VH1. *That's What I Like About the South* (1989) was produced by Al Kooper—famed for playing with Bob Dylan, starting Blood, Sweat & Tears, and producing Lynyrd Skynyrd and the Tubes. "Depot Street" made the Top 40 in Radio & Records, and "I Like Shoes" became a KBCO favorite. *That's What I Like About the South* was released in Holland—a cover of Chuck Berry's "Roll Over Beethoven" went to No. 1.

"It's real roots music, which is why we've had such success over there," Daniels said. "The basis of this music is blues, R&B, funk, swing—all very American stuff. I think what they like is that when we come over we're not bringing them what they get when they hire a real traditional Stevie Ray Vaughan clone. With us it's something much, much more, and it flips them out."

Landreth and Hazel Miller, a Denver blues-soul singer, recorded with the Kings on *Is My Love Enough* in 1993.

"Hazel Miller and I sang together for the first time at the first Boulder Blues Festival. I saw Hazel in the wings and pulled her onstage. She blew the doors off the place. She's probably my best buddy as far as 'band leaders' go. We talk about the trials and tribulations of keeping it going. We've sung the national anthem together at sports events and done a zillion shows together."

Louie Louie (1998), the Kings' collection of jump blues and swing, was done in tribute to Louis Jordan and Louis Armstrong. On 2003's *The Spark*, Daniels traded his trademark Stratocaster for an acoustic guitar and his horn-based music for intelligent singer-songwriter material with hints of blues, bluegrass, and funk.

Daniels deserves credit for keeping a big band together and for pursuing horn-based music.

"We've tried to give something new to an old form," Daniels said. "You've got three guys in a band, you can womp the other two on the side of the head. I've got nine, and they can gang up on you real good," Daniels laughed.

"In their hearts, they all love something slightly different than what you're doing. But instead of saying, 'Play it like this,' I say, 'Interpret this your way, pull those elements in.' That's been the trick—and the magic.

"Since the beginning, the backbone of the band has been the solos—the music's instrumental sections are journeys. There's a direct line between Louis Armstrong, who took soloing from where it was, to Carlos Santana's and Jerry Garcia's long, extended solos. We picked up on a lot of that. When we're playing, you'll see a guy take a leap into space—and we follow him. It's made for a few train wrecks, but most of the time it's magic."

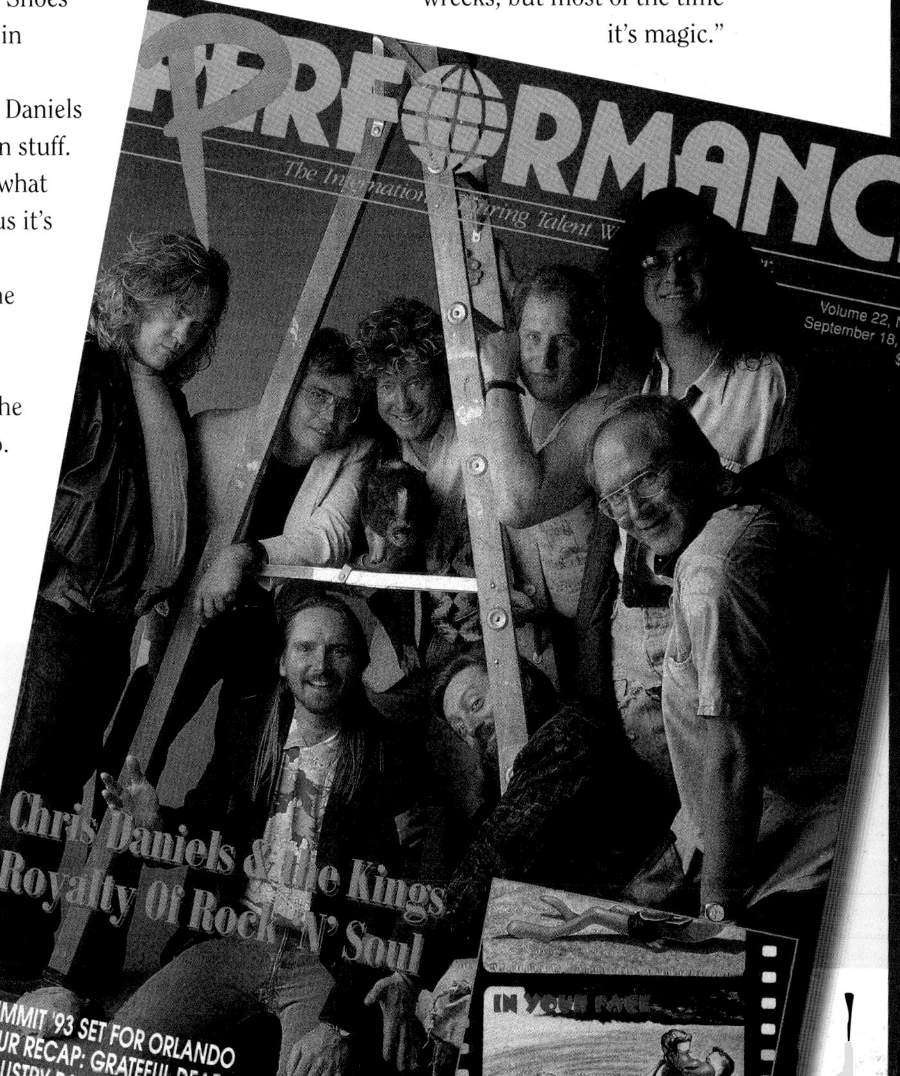

THE SUBDUDES

During the Subdudes' decade-long stint in Colorado, the group enjoyed favored status as a magical, marvelous musical treasure. The critically acclaimed band's rich, soulful harmonies, insightful lyrics, and rootsy grooves kicked off the Americana genre before the term became clichéd, winning over listeners across the country.

Front man Tommy Malone, bassist Johnny Ray Allen, and percussionist Steve Amadee grew up together in Edgard, Louisiana. They formed their first band in high school, inspired by Malone's older brother, guitarist Dave Malone of the legendary Radiators.

Keyboardist John Magnie, a Denver native, was then introduced to the trio in 1984.

"I thought he was from Louisiana," Allen admitted. "He played that Professor Longhair style of piano that you have to be from New Orleans to understand."

The four friends performed in various combinations with other local musicians for several years. They had a lot of strange names and played a lot of strange dives. But as players came and went, frustration grew.

And so the Subdudes were born one spontaneous night in April 1987. Magnie was playing piano at Tipitina's bar in the Crescent City, and the three other musicians came down and started jamming. Amadee, a drummer who liked to travel light, used a tambourine—"It was ripped off from my landlady"—and the scaled-down acoustic sound worked. They wound up playing every Monday night.

Later that year, the Subdudes—the group's name was a pun on the subdued sound of the music—and their families decided to leave the Bayou State. New Orleans had a high reputation for being a great music town, but only a few bands were able to make a living there. They were sometimes working day jobs as housepainters and roofers.

Magnie suggested moving, en masse, to Fort Collins, Colorado, where it was quiet and inexpensive.

"Most of the New Orleans bands that go to New York or Los Angeles try to be like other bands," Magnie said.

"The music in New Orleans is underrated, but the scene is overrated," Allen added. "We'd never done anything like leave home, so we decided to get halfway to L.A. and go to Denver for six months."

Magnie scouted out some gigs. The band quit their day jobs and refined the Subdudes' sound. The chance paid off. The Subdudes' reputation spread throughout Colorado almost immediately as they were being booked three and four nights a week. They became a fixture at Herman's Hideaway on South Broadway in Denver, where they continuously packed the place with a loyal following.

Anyone who ever saw the quartet live likely will always remember them, as Amadee worked a tambourine as if it were a full drum kit. That and Magnie's wheezing accordion began imbuing Malone and Allen's concise three- or four-minute songs with the ethnic R&B associated with the varied styles of the New Orleans region. Their funky, danceable performances garnered them rave reviews from the local media.

The band soon attracted the attention of entertainment attorney Ed Pierson and manager Patrick Cullie, and a demo of the song "On His Mind" won *Musician* magazine's Best Unsigned Band contest. It sounded like a timeless classic, something Ben E. King might have considered recording in his heyday. By the fall of 1988, the Subdudes had acquired a recording deal with Atlantic Records. The label signed the foursome in an official ceremony in Governor Roy Romer's office.

The Subdudes didn't light up the charts—it sold nearly 30,000 copies—but the national music community really loved the band's mastery of American music styles. They had good word-of-mouth from peers. Bonnie Raitt, Linda Ronstadt, Huey Lewis, John Hiatt, and especially Bruce Hornsby were zealous fans. The band built a reputation for session work, accompanying Shawn Colvin, Roseanne Cash, Joni Mitchell, and others, and toured frequently.

"We learned a lot," Magnie said. "Before we moved to Colorado (from New Orleans), we weren't in road bands—we gigged in and around town because we weren't well known enough to travel."

On record, they always delivered both charm and first-rate chops, masterfully mixing elements of New Orleans R&B, roots rock, gospel, and country. *Lucky* (1991) featured a cover of Al Green's "Tired of Being Alone."

But two more albums didn't set the charts on fire, and by then, the rigors of the road and the burden of being a unique band had taken a toll. The members decided to call it quits in November 1996.

“The Subdudes had a real intricate balance that involved songwriting, especially,” Magnie said. “We just ran it out of gas, used up what we had there—the process fell apart.”

Spinoff projects ensued—Tiny Town, 3 Twins, the Dudes. Sans Allen, the Subdudes reformed in 2003, added Tim Cook (vocals, bass, percussion) and Jimmy Messa (bass, guitar) to the mix and secured a recording contact with Back Porch Records. The band released *Miracle Mule* in April 2004.

STEVE TAYLOR

Steve Taylor, a Northglenn High School graduate (class of 1976), emerged in the 1980s as an intriguing artist in the contemporary Christian genre.

Taylor's demos were recorded during his last year at the University of Colorado in Boulder. In the summer of 1982, he got a slot at the annual Christian Music Conference in Estes Park, Colorado. It was his first live set. The crowd's reaction impressed the head of Sparrow Records, and a deal quickly followed.

Songs like Taylor's quirky "I Want To Be A Clone" debut, "I Blew Up the Clinic Real Good" (about violence at abortion clinics), and "This Disco (Used To Be A Nice Cathedral)" (a No. 1 hit on Christian radio) outlined Taylor's perspective without sounding preachy or self-righteous. *Newsweek* called him "evangelical rock's court jester."

But Taylor's tendency toward satire, black humor, and witty metaphors didn't endear him to gospel-weaned members of the church. He couldn't conform, so he formed a secular alternative-rock band called Chagall Guevara. The song "Murder in the Big House" could have been a hit, but the band worked for MCA (the industry joke was that it stood for Music Cemetery of America).

So Taylor returned to the contemporary Christian fold in 1994.

"It's a little different now, having had the chance to do the other side. The blinders came off," he said.

"In gospel music, I felt constrained by expectations, people assuming things about me that weren't true. But the same thing happens in pop music on another level. There are just as many regulations you're not supposed to cross. I traded in one set of rules for another."

Taylor has produced two gold-certified albums for Newsboys and the platinum-certified self-titled album for Sixpence None the Richer. All three albums earned Grammy nominations. His work as a director has earned him two *Billboard* Video Music Awards.

Once a Nashville renegade, later a favorite son of Texas, Willie Nelson boasted a popularity that elevated him to a stature approaching that of a contemporary national folk hero.

In the 1980s, the venerable country singer maintained residences in Texas, Malibu Beach—and a mountain home in Evergreen, Colorado, described as a two-story, 4,700-square-foot Swiss chalet on a 116-acre estate. It included a large teepee.

He found the Little Bear, a bar that gave him a place for his music.

"I had wanted to get away from Texas for a little while just to check out the rest of the world. I had lived down there for a long time. My nephew, Freddy Fletcher, was coming up to Colorado a lot. He had a little band, and they were traveling around. So I took my daughter Suzie one day and we drove from Austin up to Evergreen, up where Freddy had a little cabin. I thought, 'Well, this is a spot to come to.'

"The first place I had was up on Turtle Creek. Then we bought a place over in Evergreen, up on upper Bear Creek …

"I only had a few days to spend at either Colorado or Texas because I was touring so much. I had a place in Austin with a recording studio and a lot of other different things—a golf course, for one—that were calling me back there. I had a run of bad luck with the weather in Colorado—every time I'd fly back home, it would be snowing! So about the second time back, I got to thinking, 'Wait a minute, it's snowing here, there's a golf course over there. What do I really want to do?'

"So mid '80s, I decided to head back and spend most of my time off down in Texas."

Nelson owned the house in the Colorado mountains until November 1990, when it was seized by IRS agents who robbed Nelson for $16.7 million in "unpaid back taxes" for the years 1975 through 1982.

"I wrote a lot of songs while I was living in Colorado, had a lot of fun, did a lot of nice things that you can only do there. It affected me in a lot of ways. I sure hated to leave, I know that."

WIND MACHINE

Steve Mesple is proud to live in Louisville, Colorado, yet the guitarist found the "local musician" stigma uninspiring.

"Heck," he said, "even I wouldn't go to see a band from Louisville."

But Mesple's music with his band Wind Machine got attention from the entire country.

Wind Machine never met a style it didn't like. The band played guitar-based, mostly instrumental music, which could only accurately be described as "mass fusion," since the band dabbled in sounds that ranged from blues to bluegrass to jazz to new age. They utilized a vast arsenal of instruments, ranging from the guitar to the mandolin to the dobro, from the trombone to the electric fretless bass, to their own invention, the "guitjo," a six-, seven-, or eight-string guitar with the bass strings restrung with higher-pitched treble strings.

"We're never bored in this band," Mesple said. "We've played at jazz festivals and folk festivals, bluegrass festivals and blues festivals. I have friends who say, 'Don't spread yourself too thin—you need to specialize in one style.' I tried to, but I was unhappy."

The sincerity and honesty of Wind Machine's music could be sensed in the atmosphere of family and friendship that surrounded the band.

The core group since Wind Machine's inception in 1986 was Mesple on guitars, mandolin, harmonica, banjo, and vocals; Joe Scott on guitars, guitjo, and banjo; and Blake Eberhard on fretted and fretless bass and trombones. They started as the house band at the Bratskellar in Larimer Square.

"We knew there was something different happening," Mesple said. "Joe and I would play four-minute songs of rapid-fire sixteenth notes, and our timing was right together."

The predominantly electric first album, *Wind Machine Featuring Steve Mesple*, and the second, *Unplugged*, were released independently.

But after *Unplugged*, Mesple was in a car accident during a blizzard near Berthoud. "I was lucky I wasn't killed. I was smashed by a delivery truck going sixty miles an hour, climbed out the window of my car, and got hit by another car. My hands were messed up, and for quite a while I couldn't hold a pick. My finger would swell up like a pickle.

"But interestingly, I could fingerpick—that didn't bother my hand. So for four months of rehabilitation, all I did was sit around and write acoustic stuff. And that's where the *Rain Maiden* album came from."

Released in 1989, *Rain Maiden* put Wind Machine's signature acoustic style in the national spotlight, with Boulder's Silver Wave Records offering the band distribution and promotion.

For *Road To Freedom*, the personnel then included the teenage sons of Mesple, Taylor (keyboards) and Ethan (percussion). Mesple harbored reservations about his boys joining the band, but they shared their bandmates' dedication.

"They are two of the finest musicians I've ever met," Mesple stated. "They are adult musicians temporarily trapped in the bodies of thirteen- and fifteen-year-old boys.

"We insist that they be good human beings. We'll love and support them no matter what they go into, but they have to be responsible. It's just frightening that they've already made career decisions."

Road To Freedom reached the Top 4 in the major NAC (new adult contemporary) and related radio airplay charts. The title track reached the No. 1 spot in *Radio & Records*' Hottest Tracks chart. More than 250 stations played cuts from the record.

Wind Machine rehearsed obsessively. "If you want to be a world-class act, you have to make a world-class effort," Mesple said. But Wind Machine was also a fun group. The members often ended concerts with "Eat Your Heart Out, Stanley Jordan," a tune where everybody played one guitar at the same time.

The roots of Dotsero can be traced back to a garage band in Denver. Performing together was nothing more than a whim to Stephen Watts (tenor and soprano saxophones, wind synthesizers) and his brother David on guitar when they were attending the University of Colorado. The band moved to gigs in local music rooms and broke onto the national music scene with its 1990 release, *Off the Beaten Path*, combining jazz, pop, R&B, and rock.

One of contemporary jazz's hottest ensembles, Dotsero followed up with *Jubilee* in 1991. That album spent five weeks at No. 1 on the *Radio and Records* charts, was No. 1 on the Gavin Report's Adult Alternative chart, and spent ten weeks on the *Billboard* Contemporary Jazz chart. In 1994, Dotsero released *Out of Hand*, which cracked the charts again.

"It was a time when the radio stations all picked their own music," David Watts said. "You could hear anything from Pat Metheny to Kenny G to David Sanborn to Yellowjackets any given day, depending on which disc jockey was playing which music.

"Five tunes from *Jubilee* charted—stations from The Wave in Los Angeles, WOR in Chicago, QUD in New York, the Oasis in Texas, all had their own favorite. If they liked you and your tunes, they were very accessible. You could call them up and say, 'Thanks for playing our record,' and they'd record an interview and say 'How can we get you out here?'

"Today, it's a whole different bag. Stations hire an outside company that does a demographic study as to what will sell the most advertising for them. They're the ones that say what records get on the air, and it's all based on a format to sell the most advertising per hour. Your songs have to be no longer than four minutes so that they can get eleven songs in an hour and then ship in enough advertising. The jocks don't pick any of the music; there's hardly any interviews.

"It's money. The stations have to keep their ratings up. But there's nowhere near the creativity that there used to be."

Dotsero recorded at Colorado Sound Studios with producer Kevin Clock. Core members have included Michael Friedman on bass, longtime cohorts Tom Capek (on keyboards), and Kip Kuepper, Larry Thompson, and Mike Marlier on drums.

The name Dotsero, taken from the Ute Indians, means "something unique." It's also, as explained by the Watts brothers, the site of one of their favorite fishing spots—Dotsero, a little western slope town on the banks of the Colorado River.

DOTSERO

JINX JONES/EN VOGUE

Jinx Jones grew up in Colorado and spent his teen years playing Christian youth dances around Denver. He moved on to perform at long-departed 3.2 beer clubs such as My Sweet Lass, Dirty John's, and Sam's. It was the 1970s, and his bands had names like MacBeth, Waves, and Emerald City.

By the early 1980s, an original music scene began to brew, and for more than a decade, Jones was ubiquitous. If he wasn't fronting one of a half-dozen bands—from Jinx Jones & Friends to the Tel Rays to the Blue Jets—he was backing Chuck Berry at a local gig or tending to his own guitar store, Cadillac Guitars.

Jones was partial to a pink Stratocaster and a retro wardrobe pulled from the racks at Value Village, but he had a handful of varying musical allegiances. After bouncing between rockabilly, funk, and everything in between, Jones had done all that one musician could do in Colorado. As the 1980s came to an end, he packed up his guitars and moved to San Francisco.

"One day, I just impulsively decided to pull up stakes and move out of town," he said. "My intention was to get into a different musical environment—get into the record industry in a bigger way."

Jones fulfilled a lifelong dream when producers Denny Foster and Thomas McElroy recruited him to tackle both guitar and bass duties on En Vogue's 1992 breakthrough album, *Funky Divas*. One day in the studio, Foster and McElroy had Jones piece together a heavy funk track inspired by Funkadelic's "Free Your Mind and Your Ass Will Follow." Jones played everything but the drum machine on the song, but the label worried that it was too aggressive and balked at putting it on the album.

The label relented, and the tune—"Free Your Mind"—became one of En Vogue's biggest smashes.

"Then they were getting ready to take it out on the road. My wife was pregnant, and she basically told me that if I went out with those four good-looking black women, she was going to leave me," Jones said with a laugh.

"Spending years and years playing music, it's a wonderful journey. You get to sample a lot of different great experiences. One thing that I really wanted to do was participate in a recording that would be on everyone's radio. And I was very lucky to do that."

En Vogue's "Free Your Mind" made No. 8 on *Billboard*'s Hot 100 in 1992.

SPINAL TAP

The funniest movie ever made about rock 'n' roll was 1984's *This Is Spinal Tap*, a fictional and admirably accurate spoof of heavy-metal stereotypes and the music business (penned by actors Christopher Guest, Michael McKean, and Harry Shearer, and director Rob Reiner).

The "rockumentary" introduced a gracelessly aging British band. The music was passable fare with bright, imaginative lyrics ("Sex Farm," "Big Bottom"), so metal's adherents didn't get it. But *This Is Spinal Tap* became an inside joke for anyone who had spent a few minutes backstage at a rock concert. The people laughing hardest were the very folks the band lampooned—musicians like Ozzy Osbourne and Aerosmith's Steven Tyler claimed to be the inspiration for the film.

In 1992, Spinal Tap re-emerged. The new conceit? The band members turned their collective backs on rock stardom after the disastrous "Smell the Glove" tour documented on *This Is Spinal Tap* (the group had a history of constant personality clashes and musical differences). But Spinal Tap had decided to reunite, claiming that the movie was "a gross distortion."

"It was a double-edged gun—it made us infamous, but it made us look pathetic," guitarist Nigel Tufnel said. "The director, Martin Di Bergi, chose to show us not finding the stage. But you saw us performing. We must have found the stage on those occasions."

A tour celebrated Spinal Tap's twenty-five-year reunion, and it opened at the Air Force Academy's Arnold Hall in Colorado Springs. (In *This Is Spinal Tap*, the band was mistakenly booked at an air force base—Tufnel stormed off during the gig when his radio-miked guitar picked up air-traffic-control messages.) Spinal Tap amplified the absurd pomp of metal music, and the devastating parody earned sustained laughter, not scattered giggles.

Prior to the concert, Tufnel explained his latest invention.

"Guitarists are always saying, 'Could you make the tone a bit warmer?' I've designed something. It's made of wool and goes over the knobs of the guitar—it's a 'tone cozy.'"

Spinal Tap assaulted the media. The poker-faced band cropped up giving comical interviews to every magazine and talk show in sight. People commented that the single "Bitch School" was sexist. "It's about dog obedience," Nigel Tufnel said. "The three of us love dogs. Read the lyrics—'You're so fetching when you're on all fours.' How can you misconstrue that?"

DIZZY REED/GUNS N' ROSES

Many locals remembered Dizzy Reed from his performances in Colorado with bands like Bootleg and Gauntlet, when the keyboardist achieved more success than most regional musicians ever dream of—Guns N' Roses recruited him in 1990 to give some additional color to their sound. Reed provided support on the two *Use Your Illusion* albums, and he toured with the controversial band.

"I was born in Chicago, but my family moved to Colorado when I was six years old or so. I grew up in Boulder and attended, and graduated from, Fairview High School," Reed said.

"Pat Gill (of the Feds) and I started our first band together in the sixth grade. We were called the Hairy Bananas. We went through a few names and finally settled on Bootleg. We played together for ten years, until we were twenty, and finally went our separate ways."

Dizzy Reed slept on floors with the guys in Guns N' Roses before they hired him years later.

Reed went to Los Angeles in 1983—"I goofed off and ran out of money"—and came back to Colorado, hooking up with a band called Gauntlet.

"Every time I would meet a girl at a club, she would say, 'Do you know the guys in Gauntlet?' They opened for Ratt at the Rainbow Music Hall. I walked in and saw the girls screaming and the guys sitting down and booing because their girlfriends were into it.

"Immediately I knew, 'I have to join this band.'"

After recording a demo at Colorado Sound Studios, Gauntlet split to Hollywood. Gauntlet changed its name to the Wild and lived in a studio apartment behind Sunset Boulevard for two years. Guns N' Roses moved in next door when they were the biggest band in Hollywood, and Reed got to know Axl Rose and Slash. Eight years later, he ended up with Guns N' Roses.

"I didn't really audition, because I was a friend from their early club days. They called up when it was time to get a keyboard player, and I said, 'Let me think about it … OK!' If you audition a bunch of people, you don't get someone who fits in. There's more to it than music."

THE MOODY BLUES

During their initial heyday from 1967 to 1972, the Moody Blues had some sensationally successful recordings in their "cosmic" symphonic rock style.

In the mid- and late 1990s, the Moodies enjoyed another period of great success. The band ranked as one of the decade's top concert draws, playing around the world augmented with symphony orchestras.

The concept started with a summer show in Colorado on September 9, 1992, when the band recorded the live album and television special, *A Night at Red Rocks With the Colorado Symphony Orchestra.*

"We wanted to celebrate the twenty-fifth anniversary of our *Days of Future Passed* album," singer-guitarist Justin Hayward revealed. "In the absence of a record company revitalizing it, we figured we'd do it ourselves.

"We thought we'd work with an orchestra live—we'd never done it. And Red Rocks had been a favorite venue of ours—it's a stunning, beautiful setting."

In 1967, *Days of Future Passed* was one of the earliest collaborations between a rock band and an orchestra. The Moody Blues were a trifle ahead of their time. "Everyone thought we were crazy," Hayward laughed.

Uniting the group with the London Symphony Orchestra, *Days of Future Passed* was a landmark in rock recording, establishing a wave of progressive concept albums characterized by classical overtones. The album spawned the massive hits "Nights in White Satin" and "Tuesday Afternoon," and the Moody Blues' following increased to messianic proportions.

Red Rocks marked the first time they had performed with an orchestra before a live audience. On that special night, paired with the eighty-four-member-strong Colorado Symphony Orchestra, the Moody Blues were able to recreate their majestic studio sound as originally envisioned. The symphonic sumptuousness of the Moodies' early hits were discovered by a new generation of young fans.

"We thought it would be just a one-off thing," Hayward said. "It was really the brainchild of our late manager, Tom Hulett. He had a desire to see us with an orchestra, and he went about putting it together. We did one night at Red Rocks for a PBS special.

"And the response came from all over—orchestra directors, even mayors of towns—'Can you come and do this show with our orchestra?' That's when we realized that most decent-sized cities and towns in America have their own professional-quality orchestra. That doesn't exist in Europe, so we didn't know about it. I thought the logistics would be impossible.

"But of course they're not. Our manager toured with Elvis Presley. Hey, Elvis used to pick up forty-seven musicians every night and it sounded great. So we thought we'd try it. The stage is ours, the seats are ours, the microphones are ours—the only thing that changes is the player. I'm not sure a lot of people in these towns know they've got an orchestra until they come and see the Moodies. I hope I'm not offending anyone there, but that's often the way."

Denver-based travelling conductor Larry Baird, a rock 'n' classical buff who studied theory and composition in college, arranged and orchestrated the music. According to Justin Hayward, "There's more validity than there is for other bands. We have pieces of music that are recognizable, so the orchestra has its own hits to play. If it was just a backing situation, I would view it differently. But the orchestras are featured in their own right."

A deluxe-edition, two-CD set of the Moody Blues' classic *A Night at Red Rocks With the Colorado Symphony Orchestra*, released November 2002, presented the entire two-hour concert on album for the first time.

OZZY OSBOURNE

Both 1993 releases were jump-started when "Changes," a version of the Black Sabbath song from the 1972 *Vol. 4* album, was issued. A live-performance clip culled from the *Live & Loud* home video hit MTV. Osbourne had performed the ballad at Red Rocks Amphitheatre in Colorado, backed by Zakk Wylde on piano.

"I'm going through a different change," Osbourne explained. "I had a hard time on this farewell tour." The releases marked the final performances of Osbourne with the lineup of guitarist Wylde, bassist Michael Inez, and drummer Randy Castillo.

Castillo, a Denver native, was a familiar face around town back in the 1970s. The muscular drummer played with the Wumbleys before forming the Offenders, a band on the edge of the local punk scene (they used to spray-paint their hair instead of springing for dye). Castillo had joined Motley Crüe when he lost his battle with cancer in March 2002.

An in-concert home video and double-live disc—both titled *Live & Loud*—documented Ozzy Osbourne's "Theatre of Madness" and "No More Tours" treks in 1991-1992.

PAUL McCARTNEY

In 1993, Paul McCartney's U.S. "New World Tour" served up Fab-tinged family fun for nearly two million fans at seventy-eight concerts, including a performance at Folsom Field in Boulder on May 26. He put eight live songs from that show on his twenty-four-track album, *Paul Is Live*, including "Live and Let Die" and "Let Me Roll It."

McCartney, fifty, was happy to be playing.

"I always thought you had to finish in rock 'n' roll at twenty-four or so. But it just keeps on going. When you're thirty, then you think you'd better finish at forty. When you're forty, you think you'd definitely finish at fifty. At fifty—I don't know. I suppose you just stop thinking about it. I'm still enjoying it, and as long as audiences keep coming and I keep seeing smiling faces out there, I'll keep showing up."

The *Paul Is Live* video was intended to complement the live album, but there were differences between the two. In the video, there was an obvious lack of continuity within each sequence to underline the breadth of the tour. For example, the color footage of "Let Me Roll It" was shot in Boulder, the black-and-white in Paris, and the audience bits were Milanese.

JAMES BROWN

Steamboat Springs had a contest to name an otherwise unnoticeable highway bridge north of town in 1993. Locals were sharply split. After much public debate and two elections that pitted factions such as longtime area ranchers against ski-bum newcomers, the residents voted and overwhelmingly selected "The James Brown Soul Center of the Universe Bridge" in honor of the Godfather of Soul over one of the region's historic names.

Brown himself showed up in a stretch limousine for the official dedication, leading the crowd in an a cappella version of "I Feel Good." The span had already been defaced by racist graffiti, but Brown said he wasn't bothered by the vandalism: "I hope they use the writing to teach the kids how to spell."

Town officials wouldn't put up a dedication plaque, saying it would only wind up on someone's college dorm-room wall.

TAG TEAM

Tag Team's "Whoomp! (There It Is)" was every B-boy and B-girl's jeep-ready anthem in the summer of 1993. The slammin' slang caught fire nationwide after Chicago Bulls fans shouted it during the NBA playoffs.

Partners Cecil "DC" Glenn and Steve "Roll'n" Gibson—two "old fools from the old school that are so cool"—were Denver natives. They met while attending Manual High School during the early 1980s. The local hip-hop scene was in its infancy at the time, and they relocated to Atlanta.

Glenn claimed to have coined the phrase while spinning records at Atlanta's Magic City club—"America's number-one adult entertainment complex," he intoned.

"People had been saying 'There it is' forever. Everybody in Arsenio Hall's television audience used to do the 'Wooof' chant. We put that together with the 'There it is' dance-floor chant we were hearing at the club."

Gibson recalled that DC said, "Oh, man, we need to do a song called, 'Whoomp, there it is.'

"All I said was, 'How do you spell it'?"

Chanted on street corners, in clubs, and at concerts, the exuberant, double-edged street phrase spawned not one but two hit singles, Tag Team's "Whoomp! (There It Is)" and 95 South's funkier "Whoot, There It Is." Arsenio Hall pitted the two groups on his *Arsenio* show. Viewers prefered "Whoot," but record buyers judged "Whoomp!" the best. It lasted forty-five consecutive weeks on the *Billboard* Hot 100. A No. 2 pop hit and a No. 1 R&B hit, it became a pop-culture phenomenon.

But Tag Team didn't come close to matching that initial level of commercial success.

In the 1990s, it was Pearl Jam's turn as rock's hottest new band. The Seattle quintet's debut album *Ten* sold more than five million copies in the United States. In late 1993, the *Vs.* album debuted at No. 1 on *Billboard*'s chart and sold nearly a million copies in the first week of release.

The burden of Pearl Jam's popularity fell hardest on singer Eddie Vedder. "These shows are a difficult situation," the reluctant messiah said. "I want fans to be able to see the show like it should be. But instead of making 2,000 people happy, you end up upsetting 20,000 people who can't get in. The letters I get—'They don't care about their fans or they'd play bigger places.' It's the opposite. I'm really surprised how all this happened. You just become this huge band."

Controversy struck in the form of an abruptly cancelled late-November gig at the University of Colorado in Boulder. Pearl Jam had been booked for a three-night stand, and the first show, on a Friday night, went without a hitch. A crowd-control plan that had worked well in Europe was implemented. Fans in front were packed into where their surging energy could only be released upward. "Surfing"—passing people overhead—was directed toward the stage barricade, where security personnel fished out the bodies and funneled them to the outskirts.

When Pearl Jam took the stage on Saturday, though, the band members were angered to see teams of headset-wearing policemen wandering through the crowd of about 4,000 people. For seemingly no reason, the campus had augmented the venue's normal peer-group security force with dozens of stern-looking uniformed officers. The disagreement focused on a university concern over security brought by "moshing," in which participants in the crowd slam into each other.

At the end of Saturday night's show, the popular Seattle quintet, which was "pro-mosh," started criticizing the stage security, complaining that the fans were being treated too roughly. Vedder took the opportunity to vent his displeasure over the unnecessary police presence during the last few minutes of the show, confronting a few of the cops present and reportedly grabbing one officer's headset.

On the morning of the Sunday show, during a meeting with campus officials and the promoter, the band insisted that the venue ease its security. When the school wouldn't budge, alleging that Vedder's actions the previous night had "created some tension," Pearl Jam canceled the gig, promising to return in the spring at a different venue to honor the tickets held by disappointed fans.

The third Pearl Jam show was rescheduled for March at the Paramount Theatre in Denver. The Paramount's reserved seating didn't allow moshing. Midway through the performance, after a false start on a song, Vedder alluded to the Boulder controversy.

"It's an interesting situation … this is a nice theater, really, and we don't want to damage it … There were problems at the last show—I won't say anything until the lawsuit's over … but it seems like you're bored, and we've been so excited to come here …"

After the frenzy, Vedder milled about backstage.

"My lawyer has advised me not to talk about it," Vedder said. "But I won't just pay the fine and be done with it. I didn't do anything. I don't want (a charge of obstructing government operations) on my record."

THE FLUID/SPELL

The Fluid had its roots in Denver's early 1980s punk scene. Rick Kulwicki (guitar, vocals) and Matt Bischoff (bass, vocals) were in the Frantix and gained a measure of national notoriety with "My Dad's A Fuckin' Alcoholic," a single that radio wouldn't even consider playing, let alone say the title over the air. James Clower (guitar, vocals), Garrett Shavlik (drums, vocals), and Bischoff were in White Trash. In 1985, rookie vocalist John Robinson joined the band, and the Fluid debuted.

The Denver band started raising hell in the indie-rock world and acquired a substantial following and significant success on college radio. The group was the first non-Northwest signing for Sub Pop Records, the tiny record label that launched Nirvana and other Seattle acts, but the Fluid's appeal was more punk than grunge.

The sound was captured on *Purplemetalflakemusic* (1993), a wonderful, ugly roar of a debut on Hollywood Records featuring big, threatening guitars and Garrett Shavlik's careening, driving beats.

The Fluid's records charted high in *Rockpool* (an industry trade magazine), *CMJ* (a college-music-trade magazine), and the British weeklies. But the Fluid's career on a major label was brief. Weak sales and a tour from hell killed the band, and Shavlik quit.

"I didn't have my heart in it anymore," Shavlik explained. "I would have rather had a page-turner than a roadie—I could have read Tolstoy while I was on stage. I still played my ass off, but I was bored. And I think everybody else in the band kinda felt that way, too. We weren't progressing.

"What we did was amazing, and I'm really proud to have been a part of that. But I was so lucky and fortunate to have this link with Spell."

The drummer had penned much of the music and lyrics on early Fluid albums, but when singer John Robinson started contributing songs, Shavlik lost his creative responsibility. Out of boredom, Shavlik (who went to Boulder High) wrote some songs with Tim Beckman (of Rope, who went to Westminster High School) and Chanin Floyd (Beckman's wife, who was in 57 Lesbian and went to Littleton High).

Spell became Shavlik's new project. The band's tape circulated among friends in the music underground, and it landed the trio on the cover of *CMJ* as Best Unsigned Artist of the day. The phone started ringing.

The decision was hard on Shavlik, who had put in six years with the Fluid. But he realized that Spell offered him the opportunity to test some new ideas with Beckman and Floyd.

"When I got back off the first jaunt of the 'Purplemetalflakemusic' tour—which turned out to be the last tour—I called up Tim and said, 'I'm gonna have to quit the band.'

"'Aw, bummer, are you going out on another tour?'

"'No, I'm quitting the Fluid!'"

Spell signed to Island Records (home of U2 and Melissa Etheridge) and recorded *Mississippi* in Denver with a local producer.

"Basically, the record is our demos from four different sessions over three years. We just released the whole recording process. The hardest thing to get was the continuity."

The official bio called Spell's sound "sexually charged noise pop energy." Beckman called it "three chords and the truth."

"Superstar" was one of the first songs the fast and loud Denver-based trio wrote. The boisterous, cynical take on fitting in led off with a hard power-pop guitar riff and a vocal sound similar to X and Sonic Youth. It had the elements of a punk-rock hit: a scrappy guitar riff, a vocal that was alternately spunky and phlegmatic, and a wordless hook ("A E YA EE YAEER YA EEYA," according to the lyric sheet).

The song was added in eight markets, including Detroit and Boston, when it was sent to alternative radio stations. KTCL-FM played it in the Denver area.

"It's very polarized. In some circles, we're the little darling bastards of Denver," Shavlik said. "It was special for the people who were there from the beginning. To them, we were a cool noise band with hooks. But the day the news broke that we signed on the dotted line, all of a sudden we were arrogant sellout rock stars."

"Superstar" didn't find an audience. It was disappointing.

"I wish they could have made a better video. The video was lame, just a performance shoot. MTV liked the song—they play it as a theme for their sport shows—but they wouldn't show the clip," Beckman said.

"That's okay—everybody makes mistakes."

The members of Spell (left to right): Tim Beckman, Garrett Shavlik, Chanin Floyd

MICHAEL JACKSON

In February 1995, Denver songwriter Crystal Cartier thought she had a rock-solid case against the planet's most famous music man. The local crooner had filed a lawsuit in federal court in Denver, claiming that she wrote "Dangerous" in 1985, and that she produced and recorded it five years later for her album *Love Story: Act One*—a long time before Michael Jackson released his *Dangerous* album in 1991. The lawsuit sought $40 million, claiming a violation of copyright and trademark laws.

The trial's crescendo came on the seventh and final day of testimony. Cartier—the "Queen Size Lover," as she once billed herself—was booted out by the judge for wearing fishnet stockings and a skin-tight black leather miniskirt to court.

Jackson captured the attention of courtroom spectators and possibly boosted his defense by singing in the courtroom.

A string of questions gave Jackson all the prompting he needed to burst into abbreviated a cappella renditions of his hits, ostensibly to explain how the vocal melodies were conceived on the spur of the moment "like a gift that's put in my head." During his forty-nine minutes on the witness stand, Jackson sang portions of "Billie Jean" and "Dangerous" into the court microphone. Eyes closed, head bobbing, fingers snapping, he immersed himself in brief segments of bass line and melody.

The pop superstar adamantly denied Cartier's claim. "I wrote the words to 'Dangerous,'" Jackson testified between samples of his songs. "No one at all" assisted with the writing, he said.

"The first time I sang the lyrics, it was kind of a funny day (in September 1990). Well, not really a funny day. I usually sing in the dark because I don't like people looking at me unless I'm on stage …

"Then (while singing 'Dangerous' for the first time), this huge wall, maybe seven feet tall, fell on me."

Jackson wore black pants and a black shirt with red and yellow epaulettes and red and yellow collar tabs. He wore his hair pulled back in a ponytail. One strand trailed down the right side of his face.

He said he doesn't read music because "you don't have to." He also said he never heard of Cartier before she filed her lawsuit against him.

It took the four-man, four-woman jury less than four hours to rule that Jackson hadn't swiped Cartier's tune. Cartier retreated to her Capitol Hill apartment, refusing to leave except for special occasions like a TV appearance on *Geraldo*.

A cappella passages of Jackson singing "Billie Jean" and "Dangerous" on the witness stand became available via mail order through U.S. District Court at fifteen dollars a copy.

Denver songwriter Crystal Cartier dragged Michael Jackson into a Denver courtroom to sing in his own defense.

The Samples' emergence out of the burgeoning Colorado music scene was no fluke.

In 1986, vocalist and lead guitarist Sean Kelly and bassist Andy Sheldon moved out from Vermont to the University of Colorado and put a drummer-wanted ad on a campus bulletin board. It was answered by student Jeep MacNichol, and they met keyboardist Al Laughlin (a Boston transplant) at a party. The Samples took the name from their survival technique of making meals from free food samples at local supermarkets.

The Samples played their first show in front of a handful of people at Tulagi nightclub on Easter Sunday 1987. Then, the band's incessant touring built a solid grassroots following, especially in college towns.

"Most bands set out for a recording contract, but we didn't set out to do anything but play in Colorado," Kelly explained.

"We just kind of happened by ourselves. Our fans were supportive students. They would buy our tapes, and during summer vacation they'd spread out across the country to go home.

THE SAMPLES

"And we created a big base. We got letters from Texas and California, and we knew that there was an audience that liked the music, that we were on to something fresh."

The Samples played atmospheric pop, mixing American rock melodies and reggae rhythms. Most of the band's songs were written by Kelly, who frequently referenced rain, oceans, and other environmental aspects.

In four years, the Samples rose from a free-thinking Boulder band to a group with national impact, opening for UB40, the Wailers, and Johnny Clegg & Savuka. The quintet signed a major label deal with Arista Records. *The Samples* sold more than 50,000 copies nationally, but the band opted to be dropped from the label.

The Samples managed success without the backing of a big-time record company. They found new ways to distribute product to their audience, and a 7,000-person fan club gave them the means to spread the word. W.A.R.? Records, the Boulder-based label, issued eight Samples releases in a decade.

Through constant touring and such beguiling tunes as "Underwater People," "Did You Ever Look So Nice," and "We All Move On," the Samples grew to become one of Colorado's best-known bands through the 1990s, appearing on the H.O.R.D.E. tour and *The Tonight Show*.

Already popular in concert, the Colorado quartet's fourth CD, *Autopilot*, debuted at No. 1 on *Billboard*'s national Heatseekers chart, listing the best-selling titles by new and developing artists.

The Samples had a brief stint at major-label MCA Records, but their *Outpost* CD did poorly.

"You have to be a very committed individual for a career in music, because you have to put up with a lot of heartache," Kelly said. "The joys are unbelievable—like the very heartfelt letters we get from people. But you have to be really tough."

The Samples made it through independent record releases and an endless touring schedule.

BIG HEAD TODD & THE MONSTERS

Colorado never had local rock heroes take their buzz to a national level like Big Head Todd & the Monsters. They did it through hard work, representing a truly organic success story.

"I've always searched for what makes it exciting to be in a band—looking back on our career, remembering when we were first beginning," guitarist and lead vocalist Todd Park Mohr said.

The young, not-so-big-headed trio—Mohr, bassist Rob Squires, and drummer Brian Nevin—formed in 1987, graduates of

Columbine High School. The band's slightly jazzy, neo-'70s rock 'n' blues sound, fronted by Mohr's strong writing, powerful vocals, and charisma, started gaining steam.

The guys demonstrated the ability to tour relentlessly and get people to shows. They filled area clubs, and they grabbed attention in other towns such as San Francisco, Los Angeles, Chicago, Austin, Minneapolis, and Boston, where they would sell out venues with capacities of 1,000 or more. The band had a built-in crowd of University of Colorado alumni or people who'd seen them in Boulder.

And Big Head Todd got people into record stores. *Another Mayberry* and *Midnight Radio,* two albums recorded and released on the band's own Big Records label, moved about 40,000 copies independently and garnered response from publications like *Rolling Stone* and the *Washington Post*.

Clearly, Big Head Todd & the Monsters were ready for the national limelight. In January 1991, the band finally signed with Denver management company Morris, Bliesener & Associates. And a month later, the band caught the attention of music mogul Irving Azoff's Giant Records, a label distributed internationally by the mega WEA Corporation.

Big Head Todd recorded their debut for Giant Records at Paisley Park studios in Minneapolis. *Sister Sweetly* was the killer album that served to define the band. Listeners across the nation caught onto what Colorado already knew, and "Broken Hearted Savior" was a Top 10 track on the album-rock charts. Follow-up hits like "Circle" and "Bittersweet" made Big Head Todd & the Monsters' *Sister Sweetly* the eighth most played album on rock radio in 1992, according to the trade journal *Radio & Records*.

There were performances on the *Today* and David Letterman shows, and a tour supporting former lead singer of Led Zeppelin, Robert Plant. The album's steady development, on the back of word-of-mouth and constant gigs, took it to platinum status (one million in sales) three years after its release.

The band recorded the follow-up, 1994's *Strategem,* by themselves, setting up shop at home and at the Boulder Theater with two inexpensive eight-track digital tape machines. Big Head Todd joined Blues Traveler's H.O.R.D.E. tour and embarked on a maiden trek across Europe.

A musical unit since their high school days, Big Head Todd & the Monsters built their career with a do-it-yourself spirit.

The band worked with producer Jerry Harrison on 1997's *Beautiful World*, an energetic, honest batch of songs that blended gritty blues, easy funk, and acoustic charm. A dream came true for Mohr when blues legend John Lee Hooker agreed to perform his boogie classic "Boom Boom" with the band (he happened to be working in the studio down the hall).

But *Strategem* and *Beautiful World* didn't expand the band's audience like the consistent, satisfying *Sister Sweetly*. There was rarely a mention on MTV or in music magazines. Big Head Todd & the Monsters were content to continue their touring schedule.

"There's nothing that prevents us from communicating our music to people," Mohr said. "In our minds, our live show has become central to who we are as a band."

After three records on a big label, the trio was back to rebuilding its career with the same do-it-yourself spirit it had at the beginning. *Riviera* (2002) was released on Big Head Todd's own Big Records. In 2004, the band licensed *Crimes of Passion* to Sanctuary Records, which issued the album on the Big/Sanctuary imprint.

The three guys had accomplished a feat that precious few local acts had ever matched. Their friendship had endured, and their shared maturity and experience are evident.

"We got into it because we were buddies who played music together. It sounded good and we enjoyed it," Squires said. "And that's still the case, fortunately."

"Rock 'n' roll used to be about having an individual voice—a band had a sound, it did its thing," Nevin added. "Like anything else, it's become commercialized now. It's hard to fight to do something you think is creative and cool."

"And it's cool to be committed to the idea of a band," Mohr said. "I like Sting's solo career and records, but when he left the Police, he sacrificed the idea of a band. It doesn't sound like three people that argue and conflict and have an equal platform for ideas anymore. That democracy is what a band is about. It has an energy and human quality you can't get any other way."

Big Head Todd & the Monsters were content to continue their touring schedule, grabbing a fiercely loyal fan base.

DAVE MATTHEWS BAND

Dave Matthews Band was hailed as one of the few emerging rock superstars of the late 1990s. Since the band came out of Charlottesville, Virginia, in 1991, its success was fired by a tenacious do-it-yourself approach.

Because their sound—jazz-rock fusion grooves and improvisations; melodies carried by violin, saxophone, and acoustic guitar; and Matthews' earnestly delivered, world-weary, impressionistic lyrics—was so mutable, and no two gigs were ever alike, the Dave Matthews Band, like the Grateful Dead and other rootsy jam bands such as Phish and Blues Traveler, encouraged an army of fans to record shows and trade the bootleg tapes among themselves.

By playing nearly 200 gigs a year and releasing their own CDs, they built up a zealous following. Before long, new fans were telling their friends about the Dave Matthews Band, and the band was venturing farther afield, first to resorts in Colorado, an area of the country that had a history of supporting acts from outside the mainstream.

"All of Colorado was huge," Matthews said.

In 1994, the Dave Matthews Band chose to film the video for "What Would You Say," the band's first smash, at the Fox Theatre in Boulder. The marketing of the band was intentionally low-key—the band didn't shoot the clip until three months after the release of the *Under the Table and Dreaming* album, the group's major label debut.

"It was a way of saying thanks. Everything fell together there—the synchronicity, the fact that we'd always had a vibe there. And I think that's because it was Boulder," Matthews said.

The video for "What Would You Say" went Top 20 on MTV, sales of *Under the Table and Dreaming* took off, and Matthews became a star.

Live at Red Rocks 8.15.95, released in the fall of 1997, was the first in a series of live albums the band issued to give fans an alternative to the many bootlegs on the market. It landed in the Top 10 and sold a million copies with barely a flicker of marketing and promotion.

"We just felt it was a good way to give something back to the people who care about the live shows, including the improvisational elements," Matthews said. "It's not that we have a problem with bootlegs, because nothing could be further from the truth. We have no intention of stopping people from bootlegging our shows. The trouble comes with the idea of some guy who doesn't really give a crap about the band or the music, just simply trying to cash in on an easy buck."

The double live album was an unedited sound-board recording. Perhaps as a nod to the fact that the band was performing in Colorado, snippets of John Denver's "Sunshine on My Shoulders" cropped up in both "Proudest Monkey" and "Recently."

Live at Folsom Field … (2002) was recorded and filmed in July 2001 in Boulder at the University of Colorado's Folsom Field.

GRETCHEN PETERS

Acclaimed as one of country music's top songwriters, Gretchen Peters has written hits for Faith Hill, Martina McBride, George Strait, and many others.

She spent her formative years in Boulder, honing her singer-songwriter chops before heading to Nashville in 1988 and growing into one of the most successful creative minds in that competitive town.

When Peters was eight, her parents divorced. Her mother eventually moved to Colorado seeking a new life.

"Boulder was a whole other universe," Peters said. "But it reinforced the notion you didn't have to have a house in the suburbs, a husband, the four kids ..."

Peters fell in love with music and developed an appreciation for the music of Jackson Browne, James Taylor, John David Souther, and Gram Parsons. She played anywhere she could—solo, duo, or band—in the town's thriving live music scene.

"There was a spriritual, hopeful quality about the music that was coming out of the West that I really liked and that really affected me. On its worst day it could be perceived as sort of loopy, fruity, California flaky, but the wonderful thing was that it was a very open place, spiritually and physically, and I definitely felt I was lucky to be a part of that," Peters said.

"I did everything wrong—playing five and six nights a week, living in shacks, playing whatever I liked. It was two electric guitars, no fiddle, and a rock 'n' roll drummer. We didn't have a guy singer who could do all those Waylon Jennings and Alabama hits. We didn't do 'Orange Blossom Special.' Instead, it was whatever we liked—Rodney Crowell songs, Bonnie Raitt, Emmylou Harris. We had a ball.

"But by midnight, all the drugstore cowboys and real honky-tonkers would be liquored up enough. We could play a Dire Straits song and they'd love it! That's the thing about music. It all basically comes from the same place, so if you give it a chance, it'll lift you up."

The former Boulder resident's "Independence Day," an anthem in the fight against spousal abuse, won 1995 honors as the Country Music Association's Song of the Year. She wrote the title cut of Randy Travis' *High Lonesome* album, and Patty Loveless topped the charts with Peters' second Grammy-nominated song, "You Don't Even Know Who I Am." Her songs have been recorded by such non-country artists as Bonnie Raitt, Bryan Adams, and Etta James.

JILL SOBULE

Jill Sobule's self-titled album of 1995 garnered a lot of publicity, thanks to "I Kissed A Girl."

In the Denver native's innocent yet seditious ode to sexual experimentation, two ladies compare notes about what jerks their boyfriends are and end up dabbling in the love that dares not speak its name. The singer described the act as "just like kissing me, only better."

Sobule didn't understand why her song caused such an uproar—WYHY, a radio station in Nashville, broadcast parental advisories before playing it—but she refused to fuel the fire by confirming whether it was as autobiographical as it appeared. Sobule never intended it to be a definitive statement on her own sexuality.

"The thing is, it's a pretty innocent comedy song. I mean, it reminds me of a bad '90s 'Love American Style.' It certainly isn't a Melissa Etheridge, 'Yes I Am,' you know?

"I had one guy ask me in an interview, 'So, is it, you know, fact or fiction, heh-heh.' It was right after that Connie Chung 'just between us' thing. I said, 'It's over, and I'm ashamed of it, and I don't want people to know—but it was an affair I had with the wife of a very important Republican congressman with a new high position in government.'

"That's what I'm going to do each time—make up someone famous I had an affair with."

The alternative folk singer grew up in Denver in the 1960s. Despite her Jewish upbringing, she was enrolled in St. Mary's Catholic School for the strict discipline. She played and quit the electric guitar as a child, then, in college, started singing and playing acoustic.

In her third year at the University of Colorado, she went to Seville, Spain, and, after landing her first paying gig, dropped out of college. She headed back to the United States after her year abroad and started doing her own material, playing around in various bands. She migrated between Denver, New York City, and Los Angeles before getting discovered.

Her 1990 debut, produced by Todd Rundgren, was all but unheard in the States. She opened Joe Jackson's tour and completed a follow-up album with him, but it got turned down by her record company, and she was released from her contract.

"Then my management dropped the ball; I couldn't get arrested. It was a complete disaster, really bleak," Sobule said. "It was at that point when I said, 'What am I, crazy? I'm not getting any younger. Who needs this?' I was going to go back to school in Colorado.

"And then it just happened out of nowhere, as a fluke."

By way of a lawyer acquaintance, Sobule, a clever songwriter with an anectodal approach to lyrics, came to the attention of Atlantic Records. Her self-titled album was permeated with her melodic instincts and wry whimsy. With "I Kissed A Girl," she breezed past social taboos to ponder the notion of attraction to a member of the same sex.

"I Kissed A Girl" took on a novelty-song stigma, thanks to a wacky yet provocative video featuring supermodel Fabio playing a sometime boyfriend described as "dumb as a box of hammers." The video got heavy airplay on MTV and VH-1.

"I wish I'd never had to do two years of being completely disillusioned and in poverty, but it made me a better person. I just feel like I'm in a different place—older, kinda healthier, 'hopefully jaded.'

"This is actually the first thing that I've really been proud of, to tell you the truth. Not many people get one chance. I feel pretty amazed that I get another chance to do this."

But when sales were stagnant, it hit the Denver native hard.

"It isn't how I wanted to leave.

"It was a double-edged sword. At the time my record company had tons of artists out and they just threw stuff at the ceiling to see what would stick. So 'I Kissed A Girl,' novelty or not, stuck. That was great.

"But of all the songs on the record, that was kind of the dumbest, musically, and they never followed it up with anything. So I can see where people would think I'm kind of one-dimensional—'Hey, aren't you the "I Kissed A Girl" girl?'"

JOHN TESH

When he was co-host on the nightly *Entertainment Tonight* show, television made John Tesh a household name. But it sidetracked him from his true love—music.

His breakthrough came when he first appeared on PBS with *Live at Red Rocks.* Broadcast in 1995, it was hugely successful and was repeated endlessly by stations nationwide during pledge drives. The attendant album went gold and the video reached double-platinum sales.

The next year, Tesh daringly left the security of *E.T.* and its seven-figure salary to concentrate on writing and recording music. Most pop-music critics would run screaming from his over-the-top pop instrumentals, but Tesh was feted as a new-age icon, a star whose mix of styles sold more than five million albums.

"Denver is, in my mind, the reason I was able to do that," Tesh said. "Certain people are defined by certain things. Steve Martin is defined by, 'Ex-cu-u-u-se me!' I'm defined by, 'Hey, Red Rocks!' I love that. I really didn't want to be known as a talking head my whole life."

Ironically, the man most associated with Red Rocks didn't want to do the show there.

"I knew the Moody Blues had already done something there," Tesh said. "I didn't think we could afford to light the place. The budget increased to $1.5 million. I financed it myself—took loans from three banks."

Pianist Tesh and his eight-piece ensemble battled inclement weather. His wife, actress Connie Sellecca, came to town, got altitude sickness, and ended up in the hospital.

"It would be difficult for me to play there again, let's put it that way," Tesh said. "But it was magical, and I made my money back."

Throughout Asia and other parts of the world, Kitaro is widely recognized. He's released dozens of albums internationally. When he launched his career in America around 1986, his tour visited Boulder and the Japanese composer, producer, and multi-instrumentalist was smitten. He bought mountain property, and since 1993 he has lived on a 180-acre spread in Ward, nearly 10,000 feet above sea level.

Because Kitaro is a new-age guru who wishes to "instill harmony and a peaceful co-existence, building a balance between nature and humanity," he's deemed a spiritual leader by his devotees.

"Living in the mountains is nice for thinking about music," he said. "I like to be quiet and peaceful and feel the energy from nature. I spend many hours outside, walking, and then I go back to the studio and create."

There's no denying the serene beauty of the wildlife and pond and wind-damaged trees. The Grammy-nominated artist records his projects in his Moochi House studio. It's big enough to hold a seventy-piece orchestra, and it's where he rehearses with his touring band.

A visitor might expect "Camp Kitaro" to be crammed with candles, wind chimes, crystals, and jewelry. But Kitaro has that "Ward zen." There's a Humvee parked next to a snowmobile in the driveway, and a few golf balls litter a makeshift driving range. "It's a party house," he explained.

KITARO

PHISH

Phish was one of the biggest concert draws in America, the left-field success story of the 1990s. In concert, the determinedly eccentric Vermont quartet —guitarist Trey Anastasio, keyboardist Page McConnell, bass player Mike Gordon, and drummer Jon Fishman—was beloved by an army of noodle-dancing, sandal-wearing, tie-dyed nomads for its musical and social environment. Since the demise of the Grateful Dead, it couldn't be found anywhere else.

But there were growing pains. When Phish played the first of four sold-out gigs at Red Rocks Amphitheatre in August 1996, hundreds of itinerant fans from across the nation flooded the town of Morrison, looking for a "miracle"—a free ticket to the show of their dreams. Few had more than a car or campground to stay in, and the overflow packed the streets.

Despite months of planning—Phish had its own security expert—things deteriorated when a truck accidentally hit and injured a twenty-one-year-old Phishhead. A mob formed, dancing to the beat of bongo drums and chanting at heavily armed police, who shut down the main road into town for a time as they tried to move the gathering, estimated at more than 400, out of downtown. Bottles were thrown and a melee broke out. Several people were injured. Authorities reported ten arrests.

McConnell looked back at the Red Rocks affair with displeasure, sorrow, and acceptance.

"We didn't hear about it until well after we got offstage," he explained.

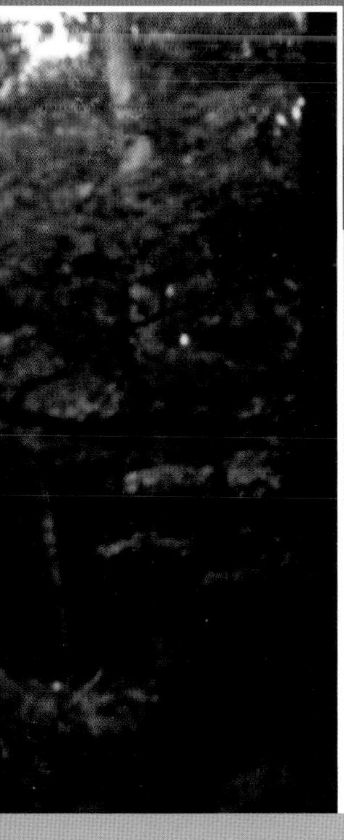

"From our perspective, we understand that the nature of our crowd creates certain idiosyncracies that most concert promoters and local authorities don't have to deal with. We do everything we can to prepare for the numbers of people who might show up for a show with no tickets.

"In preparing for Red Rocks, we knew there was a potential situation there, and we met with all these people to make sure we were doing everything we could to make everything as smooth as possible, where our fans would be as low-impact as possible on the community. We pledged money and support to make it go as well as we could. And nobody bothered to accept it, I guess. Unfortunately, none of the preparation that we put into it was followed through.

"We can't prevent everything all the time. And when a situation does happen, it's a shame that it gets blown out of proportion—I saw it on CNN—because more often than not our fans are really peaceful, nice people and not troublemakers."

In 2003, Phish led the trend of offering online access to live shows via the Live Phish Downloads. In addition, the band made several shows from its archives available for purchase, including *10/31/ 90 Armstrong Hall, Colorado Springs*, an early Halloween gig.

With singles like "All Mixed Up," "Don't Stay Home," and their biggest hit, "Down," the guys of 311 won 1996's alternative-rock lottery.

The group had been on a steady climb toward success since 1992, when the funk-rap-rock group conquered the Omaha, Nebraska, rock scene and moved the base of operations to Los Angeles. Rather than rely on radio, 311 built on the early buzz that surrounded the frenetic, charged, live performances.

Thanks to radio station KBPI's support, 311 headlined a 1996 sold-out show at Red Rocks.

"We played in California during the day, and then we hopped on a private jet, flew to Denver, and played our Red Rocks show," drummer Chad Sexton said. "We played two shows that day. That was kinda cool."

The band then released a long-form home video of live performances, *Enlarged To Show Detail*, including the truimphant Red Rocks gig. The video was certified platinum.

"Denver always supported us. It's one of the biggest and best markets where people were excited to see us," vocalist/guitarist Nick Hexum said.

"We tell a story in the video," Hexum said. "When we were moving to L.A., we had some friends in Denver. We stopped there and hung out for a day. Then we drove by Red Rocks, actually made it up there, stood on the stage, and said, 'Yep, someday we're going to play here.'

"That was before we were signed, in 1992. You get really ecstatic when your dreams are coming true. That's one of the best outside venues ever made."

SIXTEEN HORSEPOWER

When Sixteen Horsepower formed in Denver circa 1992, fans labeled the gripping, atmospheric music "prairie-goth," "roots-gloom," and "spooky campfire." Whatever the band was doing, it wasn't a take on post-grunge alternative music.

The haunting, lingering sound is a mix of rustic blues wailings, old-time country tunes, and modern-rock dramaticism. Colorado native David Eugene Edwards' mournful voice and the edgy, emotional content of his lyrics are driven by vintage acoustic instruments—bandoneon (a turn-of-the-century button accordion), violin, cello, hurdy-gurdy, and banjo.

The vibe reflects Edwards' love of traditional music. He grew up in Englewood and Littleton and attended Arapahoe High School.

"I played electric guitar in punk-rock bands in high school, but I've always played the acoustic guitar. I started getting into other types of music—not necessarily quiet, folky music, just 'rootsy' music from all over—Russia, Hungary, Czechoslovakia. That's my family's heritage.

"My grandfather and father are Nazarene preachers, which is a real old, southern-style sect. I always like the music around church. I think that's my main influence.

"Somebody found a banjo in the trash and gave it to me, and I started playing it. I went looking for an accordion and saw the used bandoneon in the window of a Boulder music store."

Married at age seventeen, Edwards left his grandfather's church to seek a more individualistic Christian path. He's the foundation of Sixteen Horsepower. Other members have included bassist Keven Soll and drummer Jean-Yves Tola, then Pascal Humbert on bass and Jeffrey Paul Norlander (a co-founder of Edwards' original band, the Denver Gentlemen) on strings and guitar.

"I sing about the things that are important to me, plain and simple," Edwards said. "They don't change. Things that are lasting and worthwhile. There are a million bands out there to listen to, but there's a certain amount of responsibility that comes along with making music. I refuse to take the attitude of 'I'm an artist; I can do what I want.' Your work affects people, and you have to be conscious of it."

Sixteen Horsepower's attitude was determinedly antique, and Edwards unleashed his doubts about sin and redemption with a religious fervor that echoed kindred spirits Nick Cave and the Gun Club. Two fine major-label albums, 1995's *Sackcloth 'n' Ashes* and 1998's *Low Estate*, built up the band's following in Europe. In the annual best-of list in *OOR*, the Dutch equivalent of *Rolling Stone* magazine, as voted for by Dutch critics, *Sackcloth 'n' Ashes* reached No. 4. *Low Estate* reached No. 9 in the *OOR* list.

The irony? The Denver-based band's rugged American music made bigger inroads internationally than at home.

"To me, it seems like they listen to this music because they're not associated with it in the way that we are," Edwards said.

"The reasons most Americans don't take it to heart like they do other types of music is because it makes them think of an earlier time that is depressing to them, of slaughtering Indians and slavery—a time of cruelty. America is trying to go into the future as fast as possible to escape that. But you can't."

MEDESKI MARTIN & WOOD

Chris Wood is one-third of Medeski Martin & Wood, one of America's hottest instrumental groove bands and a surprising pop-music phenomenon—an organ-bass-and-drums trio that had neither a guitar nor a vocalist. He's the youngest kid in the band and the most humble, perhaps the lingering effects of a Rocky Mountain high.

When he was six years old, Wood's family moved to Boulder, where he studied composition and classical bass. Before graduating from Boulder High School in 1988, he used to play bar mitzvahs, weddings, and corporate events in Denver. A musicians' service would mix and match random professional musicians (many of them much older and experienced) with a huge songbook that included country, pop, ethnic, and jazz standards, providing Wood with fantastic practical experience.

Wood left for the East Coast in 1988. "I expected to spend years as an obscure sideman for some famous jazz musician," Wood said, toiling most nights in New York nightclubs or on tour in Europe and Japan, where there's more money and greater appreciation for the genre.

Instead, he met organist John Medeski and drummer Billy Martin in 1990 while gigging around New York's innovative and energetic downtown scene. Playing loose, groove-based jazz with a touch of hip-hop and a flair for long, '70s-style jams, the threesome found a following in the New York clubs.

Then Medeski Martin & Wood did the unthinkable—"We attacked our career more like a rock band than a jazz group," Wood said. They loaded up the van and took to the road, crisscrossing the country on a mission of groove. The three-piece instrumental outfit began building a considerable cult fan base nationwide, much the same way Dave Matthews Band, Phish, and Blues Traveler had. They played to a storm of interest among college-age crowds.

It exploded with the help of Phish, which played Medeski Martin & Wood tapes before its concerts. Medeski Martin & Wood's fourth album, *Shack-Man*, debuted at No. 7 on *Billboard*'s jazz chart and No. 34 on the Heatseekers chart. It was No. 19 on *Billboard*'s Top 25 contemporary jazz albums of 1997.

Chris Wood, a Boulder High School graduate, class of 1988, was voted "most musical."

LOTHAR & THE HAND PEO

In 1997, Britain's Chemical Brothers were the kings of electronica—pulsing dance music with frenetic beats, lots of computer- or synthesizer-treated sound effects, minimal vocals, and a generally ecstatic ambience.

Unlike many of their electronica brethren, the Chemical Brothers, the bespectacled Tom Rowlands and Ed Simons, understood the potentially psychedelic nature of electronic music since they started out. The song "It Doesn't Matter" from their album *Dig Your Own Hole* was a high-tech adaptation of a thirty-year-old Lothar & the Hand People song, "It Comes On Anyhow."

Lothar & the Hand People were the first rockers to tour and record using synthesizers, thereby remaining a touchstone for many contemporary electro-warriors. They were pleased with the recognition.

"This piece was our most advanced and free-form one," singer John Emelin said. "We're really happy that thirty years later, someone is using our music on a record. That's a long time span."

The musicians who became Lothar & the Hand People came together in Denver in 1965. Emelin, a student at Denver University, decided to form a group.

"We played our first professional gig on New Year's Eve in Aspen. We all called our parents on New Year's Day of 1966 and told them we were dropping out of school."

Lothar was not a person but a theremin—an electronic wand that uses an oscillator to translate nearby physical movement into woozy, high-pitched sounds. The electronic space-age sounds heard in so many horror movies were produced by a theremin, and it also formed the basis for the eerie whistling in the Beach Boys' "Good Vibrations."

"We were just looking for a freaky name, and it got hung on our theremin, the first electronic performance instrument, invented in the '20s," Emelin said. "It's a wood box with a metal aerial protruding from one end. As you move your hand to the aerial, the frequency goes up. Move farther away from the aerial and the frequency goes down. You could control the circumference of this field, and if you got real good at it you could make it sound like a violin or a human voice.

"We had the idea that it would be possible at some point to have whole bands with synthetic sound rather than instruments. In 1966, that was a relatively weird idea."

LE

Lothar & the Hand People mugged for photographer Richard Avedon in 1967.

For the next year, Lothar & the Hand People played exclusively in and around Denver, but they eventually found themselves rather restricted. For what proved to be their last gig at "home," they were support act to the Lovin' Spoonful, and it was the headliners who suggested a move to New York. The band won a respectable following there in the fall of 1966, becoming part of a fascinating subculture.

But hopes were sadly slow in being realized. The band did two albums for Capitol Records—1968's *Presenting Lothar & the Hand People* and 1969's *Space Hymn*. The material was atonal and staccato. In Denver, KMYR played "Machines" and "Sex and Violence" from the first album, but there was no other chart action. Singles failed to sell outside New York.

"They gave us every chance in the world, I must say. Those were the days when record companies would sign people with the idea that it would take them two or three albums to get used to the process, and they'd see what happens. It was a time when anyone who had an idea, no matter how wild, could probably get the backing to do it."

Someone at Capitol must have carried a soft spot for the band, as *Presenting* was repackaged as a budget album in the mid-1970s. By then, it was too late for Lothar & the Hand People, who had gone their separate ways circa 1971.

For the song "It Doesn't Matter," the Chemical Brothers "sampled" a passage from Lothar & the Hand People's early and strange experiment with electronics—a sound-effect-laden tape loop on which singer John Emelin repeatedly chanted, "It doesn't matter"—and added a whopping, thumping dance track to it. As a result, Tom Rowlands and Ed Simons shared the songwriting credit with two Lothar members, Emelin and Paul Conly.

"We were a little too far ahead of our time," Emelin opined, and it's hard to disagree.

The Chemical Brothers are big Lothar & the Hand People fans.

GINGER BAKER

In June 1966, Ginger Baker recruited guitarist Eric Clapton and bassist Jack Bruce to form Cream. The group's success catapulted them to stardom. In the second half of the decade, Cream set the pattern for the power-trio format, and Baker virtually created a new lexicon of rock drumming, elevating his instrument to co-lead status.

After leaving Cream, Baker never attained as high a profile. He resurfaced with Clapton in 1969 as half of another short-lived supergroup, Blind Faith. He formed Ginger Baker's Air Force and, later, the Baker-Gurvitz Army, before retreating from the scene to found a studio in Nigeria. He re-emerged with a solo career, moving to Los Angeles from Italy in 1988. In 1992, he joined the metal group Masters of Reality, and in 1993,

Cream reformed for a performance at the trio's induction into the Rock and Roll Hall of Fame.

That same year, Baker moved to Colorado. He hadn't been encountering any problems getting his visa, but he had three counts against him that were never going to go away—two drug busts (in 1970 and 1971) and fraudulently obtaining a visa (when he toured in 1972 and failed to mention the busts on his visa permit). Under no circumstances was he ever going to get a green card.

"I could … live here permanently as long as I behaved myself or didn't leave the country. But I can't not leave the country," Baker said.

Baker did a lot of work on his ranch in Elbert County, near Parker, building two barns, a guest house, and a home. His son Kofi, a drummer, played on the club scene.

Baker had secured a spot on the jazz scene by releasing two acclaimed albums with Charlie Haden and Bill Frisell. Then he hooked up with his own group, the DJQ2O—the Denver Jazz Quintet To Octet, a unit of local jazz musicians known to play following Baker's games at the Denver Polo Club, which he organized. *Coward of the County*, with special guest James Carter, featured Ron Miles on trumpet and Artie Moore on acoustic bass, plus Fred Hess (tenor sax), Eric Gunnison (piano), and Shamie Royston (organ).

Then, in 1997, the Department of Justice showed up.

"It was after the first polo game. Somebody made a phone call. My groom was English, and we were still working on getting her green card. She'd been with me for two and a half years. I trusted her with my horses," Baker said.

The groom was handcuffed, jailed, and eventually deported. Two weeks later, the Department of Justice showed up again to deliver a subpoena stating that Baker's status in the country was under investigation. Baker spent nine months waiting for the other shoe to drop.

His lawyers said Baker was only going to be fined, but then he appeared on KRFX radio and dissed the Immigration and Naturalization Service on the air. The Department of Justice reopened the investigation, saying Baker didn't live in America—he lived in the United Kingdom.

At the same time, the Internal Revenue Service considered Baker a U.S. resident for tax purposes. Baker, in turn, refused to pay taxes for two years—and he used the money to move to South Africa in 1999.

"They'll never let me back in? Big deal. I'm heartbroken. America is not the world, although they seem to think so."

JOE COCKER

Ever since he reinvented the Beatles' "With A Little Help from My Friends" and Traffic's "Feelin' Alright" in the late 1960s, Joe Cocker often seemed like one of rock's saddest casualties. Still, he survived in the music business. In the 1990s, he seemed more focused and confident than in any period in his life. He was immensely popular in Europe.

Since 1991, Cocker has lived in Colorado.

"My wife, Pam, and I had been living in Santa Barbara for going on ten years. I did a gig in Telluride, and we met a lot of old friends who had strangely enough all ended up in the North Fork Valley. We thought we'd buy a bit of land and go up there in the summertime. But once we got a feel for the place ..."

The Cockers hurried back to Santa Barbara and put their home on the market, then packed their belongings and moved to Crawford, a self-described cowtown of 250. They opened the Mad Dog Ranch Fountain Cafe and Trading Post for a few years.

Around there, Cocker's just an average Joe.

"I go in total reverse when I'm home," he said. "I love to walk with the dogs up there and be out in the open. I relish those days when I rarely see a soul. It sounds a bit strange, but it's such an opposite to the rock 'n' roll way of life of being in hotels and living at nighttime."

At Christmastime, 150,000 lights turn Joe Cocker's adopted hometown of Crawford into a holiday extravaganza that draws visitors from around the state. Cocker's wife Pam donated the lights to all the businesses in town.

NEIL DIAMOND

Considering the ephemeral nature of pop culture, the response of Neil Diamond's fans remained astounding. For three decades, Diamond consistently was one of the biggest draws in America, setting attendance records at major venues across the country.

Diamond decided to culminate his 1999 world tour with a New Year's Eve concert at the Pepsi Center. The media prepared for big Y2K/Millennium coverage. ABC planned a marathon broadcast that girdled the globe and carried dozens of musical performances, including Diamond, from Colorado.

But Diamond's original intention was to spend the night quietly at his streamside cabin in the Rocky Mountains—he'd lived in the Roaring Fork Valley for more than twenty years.

"Colorado became my home when I wasn't touring and I didn't have specific recording obligations. I even have pictures of my little log cabin in my dressing room kit," Diamond said.

Diamond was born in Brooklyn, New York, and spent his childhood in the working-class neighborhoods of the borough. But for a couple of years in the mid-1940s, his family lived in Cheyenne, Wyoming, where his father was stationed in the army.

"I was five, but I think that experience had a big influence on me," Diamond recalled.

"That's where I got to love cowboys—they had some kind of attraction. I always thought I was one when I went back to Brooklyn.

"I loved the singing-cowboy movies—a guy on a horse with a cowboy hat and a guitar."

Traditionally, New York and Los Angeles have been the headquarters of the music industry. But the business had become decentralized by the late 1990s. In local scenes—Minneapolis, Seattle, and Athens, Georgia—it wasn't uncommon to find labels not affiliated with major companies.

Most folks in Colorado were still waiting for the Denver area to become that kind of musical mecca. While they waited, several indie labels kept busy up the road in Fort Collins.

Hapi Skratch, an independent music-production company founded by Morris Beegle, has worked with some of the region's top artists. Bruce Brodeen runs his Not Lame Recordings, a label and distribution company devoted exclusively to "power pop."

And Bill Stevenson—the drummer and songwriter of All, a spinoff of the Descendants (a near-legendary punk rock group)—is co-owner of Owned & Operated Recordings. His recording studio is appropriately dubbed the Blasting Room.

It smacks of Stevenson's days with the Southern California–based SST label, which helped develop and popularize the American punk of Husker Dü, the Minutemen, the Meat Puppets, and many others. Owned & Operated is a parallel opportunity to pull some good bands together—groups that were having a hard time finding a label to treat them right. O&O could offer experience and the studio—an opportunity to record without big cash advances.

Stevenson got his start drumming for Black Flag, the original purveyors of the D.I.Y. rock ethic. While still in high school, Stevenson co-founded the Descendants, and the influential band released eight albums before singer Mio Aukerman left in 1987 to pursue a doctoral degree in biochemistry. Stevenson then formed All with remaining Descendants Karl Alvarez and Stephen Egerton and recruited Chad Price for vocals. They stayed the punk-pop course over their eight albums.

Stevenson said, "But we left L.A. in '89 for all the obvious reasons—cost of living, pollution, crime, racial tensions, traffic."

All landed in Missouri for four years.

"But we were in the middle of nowhere," said Stevenson. "So Fort Collins was randomly chosen as a middle ground. We could just as well have landed in Austin, but the guys wanted to be in the mountains. Bands make decisions in weird ways."

They built the Blasting Room "one step at a time—'Oh, let's buy a truck, a mixing board, a bigger one ...'" When All was signed to Interscope Records, a major label, Stevenson was astute enough to negotiate for two albums. Most bands are signed for one, then dropped when they don't perform, and they wind up owing an arm and a leg. But Interscope had to pay All to leave.

The money was used to purchase a forty-eight-track board, and Owned & Operated stepped into the marketplace in earnest at the turn of the millennium, releasing punk rock CDs, several of them by Fort Collins–based bands—Wretch Like Me, Someday I, Tanger, and Bill the Welder.

"This has seemed like the progression of the earthworm. We inched our way in and somehow threw together a half-assed career," Stevenson said.

"If you had told me when I was fifteen, 'So, Bill, when you're thirty-six, you're going to co-own a studio and have a record label and your punk band is still going to be playing,' I would have just laughed and said, 'Well, first of all, I won't even be alive when I'm thirty-six because I'm going to kill myself when I hit thirty. And there's no way I'm still going to be a punker.' So all this took me by surprise."

Since making their recorded debut in 1993 with a self-titled seven-song EP, the Apples in Stereo have had a career in summery, sweetened pop music. Founder Robert Schneider, his wife and drummer, Hilarie Sidney, rhythm guitarist John Hill, and bassist Eric Allen are zealous students of the tradition—brisk tempos, brief run times, fuzzed-out guitars, and trebly vocals are their standard elements.

"When we started, everything was so heavy and dark with all the grunge stuff," Hill observed. "Although we liked that at the beginning, we were trying to do something going against that. We knew that pop songs could get across, and maybe even a lot of people would like it. We didn't set out to do anything specific other than be the best fucking band in the world."

Schneider helped start a musical collective called Elephant 6, which included like-minded groups that made jangly music reminiscent of 1960s pop acts, especially as produced by the Beatles and the Beach Boys. The innovative Schneider spent much of his time at the band's recording studio—named Pet Sounds, after the Beach Boys album—tucked away in the alleys of Denver's Golden Triangle, and forged a sophisticated sound using low-tech equipment.

The connection between Schneider's big ideas and his financial constraints was his peculiar gift for producing and engineering. He produced albums for bands including Neutral Milk Hotel, Olivia Tremor Control, the Minders, Beulah, and Elf Power.

"Our obsession has always been the best audio and production quality possible, and we've attacked it from the beginning, on our own and together," Schneider said. "We just didn't have any resources at all. We were working along at crappy little jobs. Even if we had a good bit of money, we would have done it the same way. We wanted complete control.

"It's hard being a beginning band and trying to go into any kind of studio where you don't have any real experience with it, because then you don't have any clout with what the end product is going to be. We started out on a four-track cassette deck because that's what we knew how to do. We knew we could at least get the songs across.

"We never tried to be in the 'lo-fi' scene. I don't think most people in that scene were trying to be a part of anything. They just had hardly any equipment at their fingertips."

The jovial Schneider said the Apples invented their own scene because they had been outsiders in Denver's music community.

"Not to sound snotty, but we're not really widely accepted as a local band here, and that's totally cool with us. We love that about Denver."

The Apples are well known across the United States, with write-ups in *Rolling Stone*, *Spin*, *Details*, and other national publications and in Great Britain and Japan as an indie-rock institution. They have played regularly for packed houses almost everywhere—except their hometown. Live, the band's more noisy, grinding, distorted guitar chords against trash-can drums create an undeviating power-pop romp.

The Apples in Stereo's cute, winsome outlook transformed them into a children's band when "Signal in the Sky (Let's Go)" was included on the Powerpuff Girls' souvenir album and the video aired on Cartoon Network.

In the summer of 2001, the band experienced a break in continuity. With their year-old son, Schneider and Sidney moved to Lexington, Kentucky, in pursuit of affordable housing. Allen and Hill, both members of other local bands (Hill also plays guitar for Dressy Bessy), continued to tour with Schneider and Sidney as the Apples, but they remained in Denver.

THE APPLES IN STEREO

RICK JAMES

Known for his 1981 hit "Super Freak," Rick James was on tour to promote his comeback album *Urban Rapsody* in November 1998, after serving a two-year prison term for assault.

At Denver's Mammoth Gardens, right before his first encore, the self-described king of "punk funk" became ill backstage, barely able to move. He regained his strength to perform "Super Freak," but he had ruptured a blood vessel in his neck, causing a blood clot. After the concert, James returned to his hotel and collapsed.

"I was kicking it with my security guys when I felt a funny sensation in my neck and elbow, a tightening on the left side. Rubbing it didn't help. Then my whole right side, from my head down to my toes, went to sleep. Whatever it was, I knew it was no joke," he said.

James was examined by doctors in Denver. They advised him to return to Los Angeles, where he lived, for further evaluation. The doctors performed a battery of tests and diagnosed a stroke.

"When I was onstage, I noticed it was really hot. Maybe being a mile above sea level had something to do with it. I can't really say. I played Denver before, in the '80s, and I was doing cocaine up the ying-yang and shanking it up … but I don't do those things now—I'm older."

Doctors called James' stroke the result of "rock 'n' roll neck," caused by the head's "repeated rhythmic whiplash movement."

"It's just me moving my head too fast, while I'm playing bass," James said. "Like any athlete, you shouldn't go out dry—you should warm up backstage. I don't."

Clean and sober at fifty and thinking times were promising, James was sidetracked. And the irony wasn't lost on him.

"It's God's way of saying, 'Well, me and you got to chat. It doesn't seem like you know how to talk to me, moving around like this, and I've got some things you really got to know. So let me just sit you down for a minute—bam! I'm going to give you this stroke. I'm not going to make it real heavy, but you'll feel it.'"

A recuperation period at Cedars-Sinai Medical Center was necessary before James could walk again.

Leftover Salmon formed in 1990 with the merging of two Boulder bands—the Left Hand String Band, known for progressive bluegrass, and the Salmon Heads, who did crazy Cajun music.

"It came together as an accident," front man Vince Herman explained. "The Salmon Heads didn't have enough guys to do a gig, so I got Drew (Emmitt, mandolin and guitar) and the Left Hand guys to go with us. It was strictly, 'Let's have some fun and play some rock 'n' roll folk music,' because that's what we knew."

The group lineup eventually settled with Herman and Emmitt, Mark Vann (banjo), Michael Wooten (drums), and Tye North (bass).

Serving up "polyethnic Cajun slamgrass"—bluegrass-based boogie that draws from miscellaneous influences—Leftover Salmon won an astounding national following through joyous, free-form sets at traditional events (the

LEFTOVER SALMON

Many recordings of Leftover Salmon exist—the band encourages fans to tape its shows.

Telluride Bluegrass Festival in Telluride, Colorado, and the Merle Watson Festival in North Carolina) and raucous rock jaunts (a two-week stint on the H.O.R.D.E. tour).

"That L.A. process—'Let's make a record and then try to get somebody to listen to it'—is one part of the music industry that I've never understood," Herman said of the band's devotion to the road.

"It's a very high-touch kind of music. We don't need bodyguards to get in and out of our shows. We're just geeks like everybody else, and we're interested in the same things and wearing the same clothes. We have that sharing of the culture in common."

Many recordings of Leftover Salmon exist—the band encouraged fans to tape its shows. On record, Leftover Salmon searched for ways to incorporate the variety of musical styles heard at its concerts. Leftover Salmon's album *Euphoria*, 1997's major-label debut on Disney's Hollywood Records, was at No. 3 on *Billboard*'s Mountain Regional Roundup.

But the band did better serving up bluegrass hippie hardcore in charismatic live performances for loyal followers, or "salmon heads."

"We've certainly done one or two live shows that have centered around the Led Zeppelin musical universe more than Doc Watson's," Herman said.

But, he added, bluegrass is the roots of the band.

"The bluegrass scene in Boulder is the reason I moved from West Virginia to Colorado. I held Hot Rize as a model of successful musicians. They weren't selling a ton of albums, but they were playing what they wanted to fun, interesting crowds and having a good time and making a living at it. Which I thought beat the hell out of flipping eggs at Nancy's Restaurant.

"In the '80s and early '90s, music was taking this techno direction. Kids growing up thinking about music as a career or a hobby had to feel, 'Well, I've got to go out and invest $2,000 in this synthesizer system and a drum machine.' Technology was between the music and the person.

"Bluegrass gets rid of all that, and to think we might have that influence gives us a kick in the pants—people saying, 'Yeah, my grandfather gave me this banjo and I've been thinking about picking it, but I'm definitely going to do it now!'

"That's the most rewarding stuff happening, to see that the music will keep regenerating itself in that way. Hopefully people can turn off their TVs, sit down, and look at each other and pick."

The year 2002 started out on a sad note for Leftover Salmon with the cancer-related death of thirty-eight-year-old banjo player Mark Vann.

They've never broken into *Billboard*'s Top 200 album chart or had a music video on MTV.

But the members of Widespread Panic do big business on the road. According to trade publications, the band was a Top 30 concert draw in 1998.

Since its green beginnings in the college town of Athens, Georgia, circa the early 1980s, Widespread Panic developed into a perfect example of grassroots appeal. Without radio and MTV support, the neo-hippie jam band used touring and the Internet to expand a vast, dedicated following.

In the South, Widespread Panic's influence was legendary. In 1999, the band drew a record 63,000 people to its New Orleans Jazz & Heritage Festival show, and 100,000 to a record-release party in the streets of Athens.

In the late 1990s, the sextet targeted the Colorado market, and fans were quick to get on board. The band's 2000 summer tour kicked off at Red Rocks Amphitheatre, and the three shows (some 27,000 seats total) sold out in forty-four minutes.

Red Rocks is one of the band's favorite places to play. Photos of Red Rocks were featured prominently on 1998's two-CD live release, *Light Fuse Get Away*.

"It might not be the path that everybody treads down, but it seems to be working with us," Bell said. "You just do what you feel is right at the time ... We're well-practiced at that kind of loose formula."

From the early days in small bars in Athens, the road-friendly group staked its reputation on a free-wheeling, amorphous mix of country-blues with touches of jazz-fusion and Southern rock.

Changing the set list every night, the band used standout performances at Blues Traveler's H.O.R.D.E. festival and other locales to build an enviable following.

"Back in '87, (America) was experiencing a recession. A lot of the 'hair bands' had big light shows, very flashy and effect-laden presentations—and that stuff carried such a high dollar that it wasn't really affordable," Bell explained.

"We were still in our little world, just getting our sea legs as far as touring went. We endured for a couple of years, and then there was the recognition that there was some value to what we were doing. We didn't have to be gimmicky. We could just be ourselves, and there was a market out there that would help sustain us as a band, to where we could eat once a day and play music.

"A few years later we met Blues Traveler, Phish, and Col. Bruce Hampton & the Aquarium Rescue Unit. Here were bands that had acquired established niches. We were all very different, but we all seemed to attack the music and crave what was going on—'Hey, there's a common experience in different parts of the country.'

"That was a good feeling right there. Nobody was really into hyping themselves as a band. The egos were at a minimum. You could just get on with playing music. You were satisfied with pushing yourself, and you were excited to see what other people were doing. Instead of competition, there was inspiration."

The sextet generated hundreds of web sites dedicated to the music and mission. Fans were allowed to tape concerts, and devotees followed Widespread Panic to Colorado, a level of zeal once reserved for the Grateful Dead but then applied to Panic and other neo-hippie, jam-friendly groups. Since 1990, jam band Blues Traveler has a tradition of Independence Day shows at Red Rocks, interrupted only in 1999 when frontman John Popper was hospitalized.

After playing together for more than two decades, the members of Widespread Panic have no idea what's going to happen any given night, which is why the shows remain so devotional and gladdening to the band and the fans.

"There's so much depth to being part of a band relationship," singer and guitarist John Bell said. "All of a sudden you're looking at lifelong friendships and how music plays a powerful role in communicating some of these feelings that you're going through as a human being."

STRING CHEESE INCIDENT

String Cheese Incident's approach to a musical career established the Colorado-based band as the heir to Phish's legacy. The members haven't concentrated on selling records; they've dedicated themselves to live improvisation, cultivating a dedicated fan base that follows them from show to show.

They're one of America's most popular neo-hippie jam bands based west of the Mississippi. There's a carnival-like atmosphere when they throw their festivals.

"It's always been a very interactive scene, ever since we played the first gig at a variety show in Crested Butte," acoustic guitarist Billy Nershi said.

"We always want to keep it that way. People are just as much a part of the show as we are. It takes everybody listening and being clear and involved to have a really good 'incident.'"

In 1993, String Cheese Incident was playing bars in Crested Butte and Telluride. Soon after, the five unassuming ski bums—Nershi, Michael Kang on violins, Keith Moseley on bass,

String Cheese Incident carried the positive communal vibe and idealism of the hippie era into the twenty-first century.

String Cheese Incident dates back to playing après-ski bars in Crested Butte and Telluride.

Kyle Hollingsworth on keyboards, and Michael Travis on drums and percussion—moved to Boulder to seriously pursue a career in music, a self-described "sacrilegious mix" of bluegrass, funk, and jazz with breezy Latin and African influences.

Stretching the noodly extremes of folk music, the energy and enthusiasm exuded from the stage established String Cheese Incident. Taking a page from the Grateful Dead and Phish, String Cheese Incident built a fan base so loyal and involved that it became somewhat of a phenomenon itself.

Whether it was following the group for national and international shows or collecting merchandise or trading live-show tapes, set lists, and concert reviews via the Internet, devotees made the group a way of life. They're silver-haired Deadheads, well-to-do college kids, suntanned ski bums, and middle-aged professionals, all sharing in the carefree happiness.

String Cheese Incident grossed several million dollars in revenues every year, yet the band had no major-label contract, hardly got any radio airplay, and did not have a video on MTV. As the band continued to elevate both the sound and the shows, it attracted the support of a zealous business team.

The enterprise included the band's own management and booking company. It launched its own record label, SCI Fidelity, and an in-house merchandising department. There was also an SCI-run ticketing service and in-house travel

Labeled as a neo-hippie jam band, the String Cheese Incident guys have technical mastery of their instruments.

agency, set up to help fans arrange transportation plans to "incidents." String Cheese Incident also employed a tape archivist who maintained the group's recordings from each of its shows.

All told, the String Cheese empire has two dozen casually clad staffers—and a few dogs—running around a Boulder office building.

"It's something we set out to do from the beginning—'Let's tour like maniacs and build a grassroots following, and let's start our own record company because everyone we talk to has nothing but horror stories.' It began as a dream," Moseley said.

"Then, by enlisting people to run the company, we've seen it happen. I walk through the doors here, and it's amazing it's grown into this. There's a sense of responsibility that weighs on my shoulders. I not only play in the band, I'm a part of all these different wings of the organization."

To make their tiring tour schedules more pleasant, the band members often play multiple dates in the same city so they and their dreadlocked, patchouli-soaked disciples can settle into a festive atmosphere.

For hot summer gigs, String Cheese Incident played exotic beachside locations in Jamaica, Mexico, and Costa Rica. For the band's annual Winter Carnival shows, venues near the best ski resorts were favored.

"We're doing the same thing onstage, whether we're playing to 500 or conceivably 50,000—that is, communicating as a musical unit, trying to blend five instruments into a single voice, and have some feedback from the audience … get them involved, feel their emotion," Moseley said.

While String Cheese Incident was a leader in the neo-hippie jam-band genre, others sold more records. In May 2001, String Cheese Incident's studio release, *Outside Inside,* recorded with producer Steve Berlin (Los Lobos), debuted at No. 147 on the *Billboard* Top 200 and No. 5 on the Independent Band Chart. The title track climbed the AAA charts. The band also released recordings from its massive *On the Road* CD series.

Untying the Not, issued in 2003, was an inventive and ambitious mix of progressive rock.

YONDER MOUNTAIN STRING BAND

In the late 1990s, mandolin player Jeff Austin and banjoist Dave Johnston moved from Illinois to Nederland, Colorado, where they met bassist Ben Kaufman and guitarist Adam Aijala—and formed Yonder Mountain String Band.

"The reason I moved to Nederland was the music scene," Austin said. "I knew what I wanted to do with music and I had an idea of what kind of folks I wanted to meet. Luckily, we all had the same mindset of what we wanted to do with bluegrass, the common language that we all knew.

"The musical climate was huge. At that time you could go to 'picks' and bluegrass jams five or six times a week. Leftover Salmon was playing like crazy, and String Cheese Incident was getting going, and Runaway Truck Ramp and the Tony Furtado Band were there. There was just a lot of bluegrass-influenced music going on—rock bands that had bluegrass instruments and played bluegrass songs. But one thing was missing—there was no traditional bluegrass lineup that was stretching the limits."

Yonder Mountain String Band has since experienced a meteoric rise, developing a loyal following among bluegrass and jam-band fans, playing fests in New York, North Carolina, Kansas, Oregon, and California and big summer sheds like Alpine Valley and Deer Creek. The band is known to stretch its tunes out to great lengths, and to insert surprises like Ozzy Osbourne tunes and Michael Jackson songs.

In 2002, Ryko Distribution began distributing all four of Yonder Mountain String Band's albums, which had sold a combined 100,000 records since the band's inception.

DIANNE REEVES

Born in Detroit and raised in the Denver area, Dianne Reeves knew that music was what she wanted to do since she was a middle-school student.

"When I was a kid, I went to Hamilton, and we were the first kids to be bused in. There were a lot of neighborhoods that we didn't even know existed. But I had this wonderful music teacher, Bennie Williams. In the late '60s and early '70s, the songs were very conscious politically—they meant something. From that point on, I was hooked."

Reeves was discovered by noted jazz trumpeter Clark Terry while attending the University of Colorado. After years of touring and more than a dozen recordings dating to 1977, Reeves rose to the top echelon of jazz vocalists, singing on some of the most prestigious stages of the world.

She was the recipient of two consecutive jazz vocal performance Grammy Awards, for her 2001 release *The Calling—Celebrating Sarah Vaughan* on the Blue Note label and 2000's *In the Moment: Live in Concert*. Reeves was awarded her third Grammy in 2004 for "A Little Moonlight," a lush set of ballads.

One of the few vocalists in jazz to recall the era of Carmen McRae, Ella Fitzgerald, and Sarah Vaughan while applying her own technically adept yet emotive style to the material she performs, Reeves could have sought a higher-profile jazz singing career elsewhere, but she preferred to keep her base of operations in Colorado. She moved back to Denver in 1992 after years away from home.

"No one could ever pay me to leave Denver," said the long-time Park Hill resident. "Denver is sort of in the middle, and it's easy to get to both coasts. And this is home—the place where I'm the most comfortable."

INDIA.ARIE

R&B singer India.Arie, a Denver native, is the daughter of former Denver Nuggets player Ralph Simpson.

"I was born India Arie Simpson at Rose Medical Center. It's not a stage name," she laughed.

Arie has lived in Atlanta since she was a teenager. But she found Atlanta to be less tolerant of people who were different. After a few years of being ridiculed for her dress and attitudes in Atlanta schools, she decided to move back with her father in Aurora to finish high school at Rangeview.

After graduation, she studied at the Savannah College of Art and Design in Georgia. It was there that she got a nylon-stringed acoustic guitar from her first boyfriend and began writing songs.

She signed with Motown Records in 2000 and started the eighteen-month process of writing and making her debut release, *Acoustic Soul.*

Her acoustic guitar playing has spare folk stylings but reflects soul and funk in the vocals and arrangements, a cross of Stevie Wonder and James Taylor, two of her idols. The song "Video," a track from the CD, was India.Arie's declaration of independence, with lines like, "I'm not the average girl from your video/ My worth is not determined by the price of my clothes" outlining her intentions and personality.

Arie received seven Grammy nods for the 2002 Grammy Awards—*Acoustic Soul* was nominated for Album of the Year, and "Video" was up for Record of the Year and Song of the Year. She was shut out.

"I don't get back (to Denver) very much. When I do, one of the reasons is my little sister. She knows about everything and is all excited and calls me all the time."

OTIS TAYLOR

Curiously, the 2002 winner of the prestigious W.C. Handy Award (the blues equivalent of the Grammys) for Best New Artist was a fifty-three-year-old man who began playing as a teenager in the 1960s. But both as a writer and as a performer, Otis Taylor brings a spellbinding intensity to his music.

Born in Chicago, the son of a railroad man, Taylor grew up in Denver not only listening to music but aching to create it. He spent afternoons and weekends at the Denver Folklore Center, where he bought his first musical instrument, a used ukelele. Next up was a banjo.

"I'm first-generation hip. At home, we were what some people might call a little eccentric. I was making sandals back in '64 when that hippie stuff started up. That all came out of the folk scene that I was hanging out with."

Taylor began playing folk blues after meeting such masters as Son House and Fred McDowell. By the time he drifted to Boulder, he had already led a couple of groups. He managed to save enough money to travel to London in 1969, where a brush with Blue Horizon Records lasted only a few weeks.

"They didn't get what I was doing over there. So I came back home. I was homesick anyway."

Back in Boulder, he hooked up with Tommy Bolin, who was on the rebound from the personnel changes and business chaos that surrounded Zephyr. However, Taylor retreated from the music business in 1977. During a sabbatical that lasted almost two decades, he did not perform in public, preferring to refine his gruff vocals and technique on guitar, harmonica, and banjo. He became a successful antiques dealer and then organized one of the first all-black bicycling teams.

In 1995, a friend and long-time investor in Taylor's bicycle-racing team opened Buchanan's, a coffeehouse on the Hill, and decided he wanted to do live music in the basement. Taylor and his accompanists, longtime friend Kenny Passarelli on bass (his resume included stunts in the 1970s with Elton John, Dan Fogelberg, Stephen Stills, and Joe Walsh) and Eddie Turner on venomous and ethereal lead guitar, played together and found their sound—a drumless yet driving groove, reminiscent of John Lee Hooker's one-chord boogie. It was "too cool" to disregard. Some called it "trance blues."

Taylor's scary, stinging style relies little on the standard twelve-bar blues structure and woke-up-this-morning lyric clichés. Besides thoughtful, vivid, first-person storytelling, Taylor applied fables and allegories from distant times and places. In a breathy style, he talked-moaned his dark vignettes. Some of them touched on the pain and misery of romantic infidelity, but most of the songs were peppered with vitriolic social commentary about the African-American experience.

Taylor self-released *Blue-Eyed Monster*, a mini CD. It caught just enough critical acclaim to convince Taylor and Passarelli to record a full-length CD, *When Negroes Walked the Earth*. The buzz on his 2001 followup, *White African*, eventually landed Taylor some national exposure, leading to his four 2002 Handy nominations. *Respect the Dead* and *Truth Is Not Fiction* were other intriguing, critically acclaimed albums. Augmenting the trio on several songs were Ben Sollee's evocative cello lines and the background vocals of Taylor's daughter, Cassie.

Taylor has toured with his band in clubs and at festivals. The Boulder resident sees the blues as a form for more than just good-time boogie. Through his *Writing the Blues* program, he's been sharing the genre's history and heritage.

"We still don't have much of a reputation for playing in Denver," Taylor said. "It's funny people make this excuse for stupidity. Everybody talks about how it takes a village to raise a child. And you talk to a musician, they're always saying how they get no credit in their hometown.

"The soul of humanity is the arts, and people turn their back on their own community. It's backward—it should be the community that rallies behind you. When somebody says you can't be a prophet in your own land, well, that's somebody not paying attention to their own land."

COREY HARRIS

Denver native Corey Harris is credited with revitalizing traditional Delta blues.

"But I think it would be a misrepresentation to say I was a bluesman. That's just a label that people put on me, but I don't really call myself anything but a musician," Harris said.

Harris grew up playing the trumpet in his junior high school marching band and strumming guitar on the sidewalks of downtown Denver and Boulder. After graduating from Littleton's Arapahoe High School in 1987, a scholarship took him to Bates College in Maine, which led him to postgrad work in Africa, which brought him back to America—and the blues.

"I really came into my own playing on the streets of New Orleans, because I got to play with a wide variety of musicians—people who were better than me. I learned what little music I know there."

Harris' second release, *Fish Ain't Bitin'*, won the W.C. Handy Award in 1997 for best acoustic blues album. Since that time, his critically acclaimed releases have explored new sounds that incorporate reggae, ska, hip-hop, and country.

Comfortable in the pop-rock community, he has toured nationally with Dave Matthews Band and Natalie Merchant.

"My obligation is to be fresh and to move forward with my material, which is what anyone who ever played music did," Harris said. "When people like Son House and Charley Patton were playing music, it was really something new. They were singing in part of a blues tradition, but they put a different flip on it. After them, people such as B.B. King or T-Bone Walker played modern electric guitar in their day, and people didn't like it at first. They got a lot of bad reviews.

"So whenever someone does something different, there's always some resistance. But I think that's a small price to pay compared to the cost of just sitting back and regurgitating things that have been done over and over again."

In 2003, Harris served as the guide in the first episode of Martin Scorsese's PBS series *The Blues*.

Denver Broncos players have traded their mouthpieces for microphones over the years.

Leading up to the 1977 National Football League playoffs, fullback Jon Keyworth cut a record called "Make Those Miracles Happen"—very appropriate for the upstart Broncos, who marched to Super Bowl XII. Broncos running back Melvin Bratton had a personal interest when the raunchy rap group 2 Live Crew raised a censorship issue in 1989 with the use of profanity and sexist lyrics—he was raised in the same Miami neighborhood as 2 Live Crew leader Luther Campbell, and he sang on the group's early releases. Defensive back Ray Crockett was featured on a 1999 CD that celebrated the defending NFL champions' season—he rapped the lyrics on a song titled "Salute To This." And offensive guard Steve Herndon became something of a rap star after signing with the Broncos in 2000. Herndon grew up with Georgia rapper Bubba Sparxxx, and he's maintained a close friendship with him.

"Steve's my best friend—we've known each other since we were eleven years old," Sparxxx said. "We were inseparable, from middle school on up. He left to go to the University of Georgia with a full football scholarship, and about a year later, I ended up moving on up there and did some time in community college. I stayed about seven years.

"Then we shot my first video for the song 'Ugly,' in Athens."

Herndon was front and center in the raucous music video for Sparxxx's hick-hop anthem, which received heavy rotation on MTV in 2001. It was unabashed in its stereotypical southern imagery—Sparxxx and Herndon were seen covered in pig slop on the farm, while pickup trucks rolled by like Escalades in the 'hood.

Steve Herndon made the Denver Broncos' roster in 2001 and saw his first NFL action, playing in five games and starting three.

Herndon has been a recurring video character. In July 2003, before Broncos training camp, the two pals did a video shoot for "Deliverance," the title track to Sparxxx's followup CD.

"If I wasn't playing football, I'd probably be the road manager," Herndon said. "I'd run the show and then be on the stage doing my little dance.

"We both had an opportunity to fullfill our dreams at the same time. We were two white kids who grew up in a small town in Georgia saying, 'I want to play in the NFL; I want to be a rap star.' Just to be able to stay in touch and talk about everything he's experiencing and I'm experiencing is neat."

BUBBA SPARXXX

In 2003, Stacie Orrico's major-label debut introduced her to the world of pop stardom.

"Life has definitely changed a lot since I was living in Colorado," the seventeen-year-old songstress said with a giggle.

When Orrico was a young child, her family lived in Louisville. She sang at church and in school, and at home she listened for hours to pop divas and R&B artists—Whitney Houston, Mariah Carey, Celine Dion, and Lauren Hill—while singing along in front of the mirror.

In 1998, the family decided to attend "Praise in the Rockies," a Christian-music seminar held in Estes Park. With a friend's encouragement, Orrico, who was only twelve at the time, entered what she thought was just a little competition, for the fun of it. It turned out to be a much bigger event than she or her family realized, and much to her astonishment, she won.

An executive at ForeFront Records heard her limber and mature vocal style and approached her family about signing her to a development deal. Orrico's family moved to Nashville for her career.

She had a big-selling debut release, *Genuine*, which held the No. 1 spot on *Billboard*'s national Heatseekers chart (listing titles by new and developing artists), and was a Dove Awards nominee for New Artist of the Year. The pop/R&B combo Destiny's Child took notice and invited her to be their opening act for a string of dates on their 2001 tour.

"I had my second album ready to go to the Christian market," Orrico said. "Two months before they were going to release it, Virgin came into the picture. They added a couple of songs."

The label paired Orrico with some of the top producers in the business, including Dallas Austin (TLC, Pink) and Virgin CEO Matt Serletic (Santana, matchbox twenty, Aerosmith).

"Stuck" was the first single from *Stacie Orrico*. The sassy, catchy tune had a slick urban flair—especially the hook, "I hate you, but I love you, I can't stop thinking of you"—and it was the No. 1 most-added song at Top 40 radio in its first week, according to *Radio & Records*, a trade journal—not bad for a single released to mainstream radio from a Christian artist.

"Stuck" climbed the *Billboard* Top 40 and was in the Top 10 on MTV's *Total Request Live*. "(There's Gotta Be) More To Life" also reached the Mainstream Top 40 radio airplay chart.

DRESSY BESSY

While learning his chops playing in the Apples in Stereo, guitarist John Hill moonlighted in Dressy Bessy with girlfriend Tammy Ealom. Ealom had the perfect voice for the Denver group's cartoonish charm and sugary 1960s retro-pop style—fuzzed-out twin guitars, delicious melodies, and jangling tambourines.

"It's hard to go hi-fi when you're recording your own records, and I'm into cute, colorful things visually, so we got lumped into that late-1990s bubblegum-pop genre ," Ealom said. "But we've always said we're a rock band first and foremost."

Robert Schneider, lead singer and guitarist for the Apples in Stereo, helped give a sheen to Dressy Bessy albums for several years. For 2003's *Dressy Bessy*, the band members got out of their Denver basement and traveled to a New York recording studio, retaining the hooks and simple approach but adding a harder sound.

"Before, we had always recorded ourselves—we'd overdub everything and constantly be second-guessing each other and adding things. But this time, we were able to go in rehearsed and go at things live," Ealom said.

The record got a great response from critics, with reviews in *Rolling Stone* and *Entertainment Weekly*, and it was in the Top 10 for weeks at college radio. The band also performed on *Last Call With Carson Daly*.

But it was through extensive tours beyond the Mile High City's borders that Dressy Bessy gained wider exposure and new fans.

"I've always hated the term 'local band,' because you're treated differently by club owners," Ealom said. "Not so much that they look down on you, but it's hard to get attention over touring bands because they think you're just always available.

"It's not so much like that for us anymore. We're just a band that happens to love living in Denver."

appendix

The following artists also deserve recognition for their contributions to Colorado music:

THEY SIGNED ON THE DOTTED LINE

Judy Roderick, a charismatic University of Colorado student with a beautiful voice, landed a recording contract with Vanguard in 1964. Her promising folk music got lost in the shuffle. She later married underground radio personality Bill Ashford, who encouraged her to go for it once more in 1971, fronting a funky, bluesy Colorado rock band called 60,000,000 Buffalo. The band broke up after one album, *Nevada Jukebox*. Roderick passed away in 1992 in Montana.

After spending most of the 1990s touring successfully all over the country, Acoustic Junction was signed by Capricorn Records to a national contract. At the label's suggestion, the folk-rock band out of Boulder changed its name to Fool's Progress, hoping new fans would know that it was more than a couple of acoustic guitarists. After changing the name back to Acoustic Junction, they were dropped by Capricorn and had to gradually build up their following again.

In the 1980s, vocal chemistry earned Rare Silk a major-label record deal. The women's a cappella jazz group earned three Grammy nominations and toured worldwide but always returned to Boulder.

CHART ACTION

Glenn Yarborough and the Limelighters took their name from their early stomping grounds, the Limelight Club in Aspen. They charted on the *Billboard* Hot 100 with "Dollar Down" in 1960.

The Fogcutters were a Denver University student band from 1965-1966. After a name change to the Fantastic Zoo, the members recorded mostly in California and backed Brenton Wood on his novelty favorite, "The Oogum Boogum Song," in 1967.

In the early 1960s, Van Trevor recorded for Denver-based Bandbox Records, home of drummer Ronnie Kae. He made the country charts in 1966 with "Born To Be in Love With You" (No. 22) and "Our Side" (No. 27). Tom Nix made the country charts in 1981 with "Home Along the Highway" (No. 79). Country singer Bonnie Nelson, big on KLAK in the 1970s, charted two records, "Don't Let It Go To Your Head" (No. 83 in 1986) and "More Than Friendly Persuasion" (No. 84 in 1983).

The Gentrys were one-hit wonders from Memphis—in 1965, "Keep On Dancing" sold a million. The group returned to the national listings several more times, and "I Can't Go Back To Denver," produced by Dale Hawkins, bubbled under *Billboard*'s Hot 100 in May 1968 at No. 132.

BORN AND/OR BRED

Ronnie Montrose played in a string of local bands in Denver, where he grew up. Soon after, he moved to San Francisco, where a creatively restless career saw him take on the roles of session player (Van Morrison's "Tupelo Honey"), sideman on the road (Morrison, Boz Scaggs), vanguard heavy-metal guitar hero (the Edgar Winter Group, Montrose, Gamma), and fusion virtuoso.

Pop singer, songwriter, and guitarist Randy VanWarmer was born in 1955 in Denver. In 1979, he moved to Woodstock, New York, and signed with the town's label, Bearsville. "Just When

Judy Roderick

Freddi-Henchi & the Soulsetters

I Needed You Most" was delicate, easily digestible, and a huge hit—No. 4 in *Billboard*. His career cooled, but in 1988, "Where the Rocky Mountains Touch The Sun" placed on the country charts at No. 72.

In the late 1990s, Dispatch was a pop-culture wonder—the Boston-based trio developed a large and loyal following through word-of-mouth advertising and Napster-fueled file-sharing. Drummer Brad Corrigan grew up in Colorado. Bill Frisell grew up in Denver and attended the University of Northern Colorado. He was a member of John Zorn's Naked City group, one of the most extreme noise/rock outfits of the early 1990s. The prolific Eugene Chadbourne, former Shockabilly leader and free-jazz/country/rock innovator, grew up in Boulder. Born in Capulin, Colorado, writer, composer, and producer Morris Bernstein founded Lute Records in the 1950s.

ESTABLISHED RESIDENCY

In the 1970s, when the rock 'n' roll energy of Mitch Ryder's Detroit didn't spell commercial success, he left the active performing scene and headed to Denver, working a day job for five years and honing his songwriting skills at night. After returning to Detroit, he formed a band and released the confessional, autobiographical *How I Spent My Vacation* and *Naked But Not Dead* on his own Seeds and Stems label.

Sam Bush, the founder and leader of the New Grass Revival, is so highly regarded at the Telluride Bluegrass Festival in Colorado, he's been dubbed "Mayor of Telluride." In 1989, Bush and banjo ace Bela Fleck joined Mark O'Connor, Jerry Douglas, and Edgar Meyer in an all-star bluegrass band, Strength in Numbers, at the festival.

Robben Ford, known as a touring guitarist with Joni Mitchell, George Harrison, and the L.A. Express, lived in Boulder in the mid-1970s to study guitar technique and composing and Buddhism under Chogyam Trungpa Rinpoche's direction. Slide guitar master Sonny Landreth, who currently plays with John Hiatt & the Goners, lived in Boulder in the early 1980s. Cajun fiddler Doug Kershaw is a longtime Greeley resident.

IN CONCERT

Red Rocks Amphitheatre has become a mecca for artists wanting something different for recording and filming. Neil Young's acclaimed Music in Head tour included three nights at Red Rocks on September 19, 20, and 22, 2000. His performances were featured on *Road Rocks Volume 1*, a live album from the outing. The DVD audio and video editions, titled *Red Rocks Live, Friends & Relatives*, featured more than twenty tracks captured at the famed Colorado venue.

In the 1990s, the Stray Cats' Brian Setzer did a Budweiser commercial on stage with the "guitar granny." Some of *The Adventures of Ford Fairlane*, a bomb starring Andrew Dice Clay, was shot at Red Rocks with Vince Neil of Mötley Crüe. Boukman Eksperyan's *Live At Red Rocks* was a document of the Haitian band's appearance at Reggae on the Rocks in 1998. Rickie Lee Jones released *Live At Red Rocks*.

ZZ Top performed the first rock 'n' roll concert at McNichols Arena on August 27, 1975. In the spirit of sentimentality, Denver officials scheduled the "Little Ol' Band from Texas" to play September 12, 1999, in what was billed as "The Last Rock and Roll Show" at McNichols before the bulldozers came to make room for a new stadium.

The Rumble

rock 'n' roll, with shows by U2, the Police, Pat Benatar, Cheap Trick, Journey, and many more.

Current Denver-area rock venues of note include the Fox Theatre in Boulder (one of the top-grossing clubs in industry trade journals) and the Fillmore Auditorium (formerly Mammoth Events Center).

THEY ALSO SERVED

Dusty Drapes & the Dusters, a band of hippies who cut their long hair and played pure swing-oriented country & western in the 1970s, landed a deal with Columbia Records, but their album never came out. Country musician Junior Brown was a member early on. Dan McCorison was primary songwriter for the Dusters—a progressive country stylist, he eventually inked a solo deal with MCA.

The jazz-funk band Nova, a curious mix of three Italians, one Englishman, and a black bass player from Queens, was based in Boulder. New Orleans–flavored Gris Gris was led by singer-songwriter and keyboardist Steve Conn. In the early 1980s, Conn was a regular soloist at the Hotel Boulderado's mezzanine.

Lannie Garrett, Denver's most entertaining and enduring diva, has treated fans to everything from big band shows to Patsy DeCline (her tongue-in-cheek take on country music). In the 1970s, Tim Duffy created Orchestra of Clouds—his productions incorporated a dance troupe and clowns, galactic light shows, and spaced-out monologues with his music. He's since gone the R&B route, most notably with his All-Stars. Freddi-Henchi & the Soulsetters, a great party ensemble, held court at the Good Earth, a Boulder nightclub on the third floor of a building on what is now the Pearl Street Mall.

The late Larry Wilkins, ex-Freddi-Henchi, centered Gangbusters, a funk band. Ophelia Swing Band played acoustic swing and blues in the early 1970s. Little Women was Jerry Joseph's former Colorado band. The Rockin' Rudolphs were a seasonal favorite.

The Rumble, featuring drummer Bob Rupp, won MTV's "Basement Tapes" competition in 1987. The Milkmen won a KBCO song contest but never followed through with performances. In the late 1990s,

Ebbets' Field, on the first floor of the Brooks Tower condominiums, opened in 1974. Run by Chuck Morris —a longtime local manager and concert promoter, and now local chief of Clear Channel concerts—it sat only 238 patrons, and ick-orange-and-brown shag carpeting covered the floor, the walls, and the bleacher seats. But Ebbets' hosted some amazing performances by acts on the upswing during that era, from Lynyrd Skynyrd to Joan Armatrading to Tom Waits.

The 1,300-seat Rainbow Music Hall opened in 1979 and closed in 1986. The building at East Evans Avenue and Monaco Parkway in southeast Denver is now a Walgreens, but the venue was a temple of

Lyric was managed by Danny Seraphine, former drummer for Chicago. The "folky funk" duo—Vince Johnson, a graduate of Denver's George Washington High School, and Orlando Poole, a Detroit native—grazed the adult contemporary charts with "Would I Lie To You."

Slim Cessna's Auto Club pounded out a frenzied country hybrid linking rockabilly, bluegrass, and punk rock. Jim Ratts, Jim Salestrom, and Jim Ibbotson (of the Nitty Gritty Dirt Band) hooked up to form the Wild Jimbos. Ratts and his wife Sally front Runaway Express, easily Colorado's most prolific studio outfit. Folksinger and songwriter Dan McCrimmon breathes life into western history through his songs and stories.

Ron Miles, Denver-based trumpeter, played on Elvis Costello and Burt Bacharach's *The Sweetest Punch* CD. World-renowned saxophonist Spike Robinson lived in Boulder for years and was a fixture in area clubs before relocating to the United Kingdom, where he died in 2001 at age seventy-one.

NAMES TO REMEMBER

Achilles & Frank...Action Brass...Armed Dwarf...Aviators...Baldo Rex...Bedouins...The Blitz Girls...David Booker...Bop Street... Cahoots...Ceeds...Chandels...Jon Chandler...The Chasers...The Corvairs...Dalhart Imperials...Dakota Blonde...Denny & Jay...Michael Dinner...Electric Third Rail...The Elopers...The Flatlanders...Mary Flower...Tony Furtado...The Galaxies...Gluons...Hate Fuck Trio...The Higher Elevation...Warren Hill...Blackie Jackson...Sherri Jackson... Marty Jones & the Pork Boilin' Poor Boys...Ronnie Kae...Kamakazi Klones...Karen Karsh...Kenny & the Critix...Randy King...King Louie & the Laymen...Celeste Krenz...The Lawmen...Left Hand String Band...Don Lewis...Johnny Long Blues Band...Ty Longley...Lord of Word...Love.45...Mando & the Chili Peppers...Hazel Miller...Terry Miller...The Monocles...Rich Moore...Motherfolkers...New World Mutants...Bruce Odland Big Band...Open Road...The Original Rabbits...Kat Orlando...The Other Side of Time...Timothy P. & Rural Route 3...Patrick Park...Dexter Payne...the Predictors...Psychodelic Zombiez...Chuck Pyle...The Railbenders...Ralph & Clyde...Nelson Rangell...Frankie Rino...The Rippingtons...The Road Runners...Brent Rowan...Billy Ryan...Carla Sciaky...Scott Seskind...Sick...Lee Sims... Soothsayers...Spoons...Starlight Ramblers...Nina Storey...Super Band...Paul Taylor...The Teardrops...Peter Tonks & Cowtown...The Transistors...The Trolls...James Van Buren...Sally Van Meter...Vaux... Warlock Pinchers...Dick Weissman...Bill White Acre...Halden Wofford & the Hi-Beams...Wendy Woo...Woody & the Too High Band...(Your favorite artist here).

Bibliography

This project was made much easier by George Krieger, a rock 'n' roll researcher who at every request was generous with his help. His articles in *Colorado Heritage* and *Goldmine* were irreplaceable.

For other commentary, I generally relied on selected local writers whose pieces appeared in *The Denver Post*, *Rocky Mountain News*, and *Boulder Daily Camera*. *Rolling Stone* magazine's writers got the Colorado crop of rock stars to reveal themselves in the mid-1970s.

***Billboard* Books and *Billboard* Publications were a choice source for clear, factual chart information, and Joel Whitburn's series took the guesswork out of tracking the rise and fall of the rock era's hits.**

BOOKS

Alan, Carter. *U2: The Road to Pop*. Boston: Faber and Faber, Inc., 1992.

Bronson, Fred. *The* Billboard *Book of Number One Hits*. New York: Billboard Publications, Inc., 1988.

Clifford, Mike. *The Harmony Illustrated Encyclopedia of Rock*. New York: Harmony Books, 1986.

Cole, Richard, with Trubo, Richard. *Stairway To Heaven*. New York: Harper Collins, 1992.

Crosby, David, and Gottlieb, Carl. *Long Time Gone*. New York: Doubleday, 1988.

Dalton, David. *Mr. Mojo Risin'*. New York: St. Martin's Press, 1991.

de la Parra, Fito. *Living the Blues*. Record Grafix, 1999.

Davis, Stephen. *Old Gods Almost Dead*. New York: Broadway Books, 2001.

Fudger, Dave, and Silverton, Pete. *The Rock Diary*. New York: Proteus, 1983.

Gunn, Jacky, and Jenkins, Jim. *Queen: As It Began*. New York: Hyperion, 1992.

Henderson, David. *'Scuse Me While I Kiss The Sky*. New York: Doubleday, 1978.

Hildebrand, Lee. *Stars of Soul and Rhythm & Blues*. New York: Billboard Books, 1994.

Hopkins, Jerry. *Hit & Run*. New York: Perigree, 1983.

Jancik, Wayne. *One-Hit Wonders*. New York: Billboard Publications, Inc., 1998.

Javna, John, and Shannon, Bob. *Behind the Hits*. New York: Warner Books, 1986.

Marsh, Dave. *The Heart of Rock & Soul*: New York: New American Library, 1989.

Neely, Kim. *Five Against One*. New York: Penguin, 1998.

Norman, Philip. *Elton John*. New York: Harmony Books, 1991.

Rees, Dafydd, and Crampton, Luke. *Encyclopedia of Rock Stars*. New York: DK Publishing, 1996.

Sanchez, Tony. *Up and Down with the Rolling Stones*. New York, William Morrow, 1979.

Santelli, Robert. *Aquarius Rising: The Rock Festival Years*. New York: Dell Publishing, 1980.

Shapiro, Harry, and Glebbeek, Caesar. *Electric Gypsy*. New York: St. Martin's Press, 1991.

Shelton, Robert. *No Direction Home*. New York: Beech Tree Books/ Morrow, 1986.

Stambler, Irwin. *The Encyclopedia of Pop, Rock and Soul*. New York: St. Martin's Press, 1974.

Ward, Ed, Stokes, Geoffrey, and Tucker, Ken. *Rock of Ages*. New York: Summit Books, 1986.

Whitburn, Joel. *Top Pop Artists & Singles*. Menomonee Falls, Wisconsin: Record Research, 1979.

Zimmer, Dave, and Diltz, Henry. *Crosby, Stills & Nash*. New York: St. Martin's Press, 1984.

MAGAZINES

Crowe, Cameron. "Early Byrd Finds His Wings." *Rolling Stone* (October 21, 1976).

Dexter, Kerry. "Following the Thread of Imperfection." *Dirty Linen* (February/March 2003).

Gambaccini, Paul. "Beethoven Rolls Over Again." *Rolling Stone* (May 23, 1974): 14.

Henke, James. "Dan Fogelberg has everything his own way." *Rolling Stone* (August 25, 1977).

Hickey, Neil. "Bob Dylan—whose songs so powerfully express a generation's conflicts—talks about his life and his music." *TV Guide* (September 11, 1976).

Hopkins, Jerry. "Kiss Kiss Flutter Flutter Thank You Thank You." *Rolling Stone* (November 29, 1969): 1.

Krieger, George W. "Astronauts to Zephyr: Colorado's music of the

1960s." *Colorado Heritage* (Winter 1997): 38-41, 45.
Krieger, George W. "Flash Cadillac (and the Continental Kids): America's Favorite Party Band." *Goldmine* (January 31, 1997): 72, 128-129, 132, 164.
Parrish, Michael. "Out on a Limb." *Dirty Linen* (October/November 2002).
Paynes, Steph. "Spiro's List." *Musician* (August 1994).
Rensin, David. "Dan Fogelberg: Home Free at Last." *Rolling Stone* (March 13, 1975).
Ruhlmann, William. "The Nitty Gritty on the Dirt Band: From One Unbroken Circle To Another." *Goldmine* (February 9, 1990): 26-27, 94.
Sheridan, Jim. "The Teaser Revealed—Tommy Bolin From The Archives." *Discoveries* (April 1997): 39-40.
Sims, Judith. "The Eagles Take It Easy & Soar." *Rolling Stone* (August 17, 1972): 12.
Soocher, Stan. "The Poco Reunion." *Musician* (February 1980): 94, 96.
Thompson, Dave. "Ritchie Who?" *Goldmine* (October 9, 1998): 50.
Vorda, Allan. "Zephyr: A Volcano of Dreams." *Discoveries* (April 1991): 100-107.
Young, Charles M. "Tommy Bolin dead at 25 of overdose." *Rolling Stone* (January 13, 1977): 10, 14.

NEWSPAPERS

Baca, Ricardo. "The big Cheese." *The Denver Post*, March 21, 2003.
Briggs, Bill. "Singer who sued Jackson: 'Nobody will touch me.'" *The Denver Post*, May 17, 1994.
Brown, Mark. "Ruling the Roost." *Rocky Mountain News*, August 10, 2001.
Brown, Mark. "Soul in Motion." *Rocky Mountain News*, February 24, 2002.
Callahan, Patricia, and O'Guin, Becky. "Phish fans confront the police." *The Denver Post*, August 6, 1996.
Harden, Mark. "Bluesman not really all that old." *The Denver Post*, February 26, 1999.
Hause, Butch. "Katy Moffatt back in groove." *The Denver Post*, May 12, 1995.
Katz, Alan. "Judy Collins: Her Denver years marked beginning of folk music craze." *The Denver Post*, December 2, 1987.
Kreck, Dick. "Wild Wild Weekend." *The Denver Post*, June 25, 1989.
Lehndorff, John. "Two decades on, there's a revival." *Boulder Daily Camera*, May 20, 1994.
Lipsher, Steve. "Untrussworthy: Bridge has a gap." *The Denver Post*, October 3, 1998.
Lofholm, Nancy. "Rock star Cocker lights up town with Christmas spirit." *The Denver Post*, December 24, 1999.
McAllister, Margie. "Crosby preaches against drugs." *Boulder Daily Camera*, November 8, 1989.
McQuay, David. "Subdudes have their act together." *The Denver Post*, November 26, 1989.
Mehle, Michael. "Local band casts simple 'Spell' on record deal." *Rocky Mountain News*, November 11, 1994.
Menconi, David. "Boulder's Hit Parade." *Boulder Daily Camera*, February 21, 1988.
Miniclier, Kit. "His honor 'Rubber Duck' steps down." *Rocky Mountain News*, January 13, 1992.
Mitchell, Justin. "Guercio gives CU-Denver $200,000 in recording gear." *Rocky Mountain News*, September 26, 1986.
Moore, John. "16HP cooling their jets." *The Denver Post*, October 9, 2001.
Morrison, Barry. "Beer Can Bombs and The Beatles Just Won't Mix." *The Denver Post*, August 23, 1964.
Paige, Woody. "Fans everywhere can name his tune." *The Denver Post*, June 6, 1996.
Rasizer, Lee. "Joined at the hip-hop." *Rocky Mountain News*, August 23, 2003.
Reiner, Eric L. "Hot Rize reunion rolls out bluegrass blitz." *The Denver Post*, March 6, 1996.
Rosen, Steve. "Bob Lind Bursts '60s Cocoon." *The Denver Post*, December 29, 1993.
Rosen, Steve. "Great Chemistry." *The Denver Post*, April 22, 1997.
Saunders, Bret. "Year minus CD means no third Grammy for Reeves." *The Denver Post*, October 13, 2002.
Saunders, Bret. "Reprising Johnny Smith's guitar magic." *The Denver Post*, February 26, 2003.
Sheeler, Jim. "Join The Club: Minds behind successful Boulder music venue are crazy like Foxes." *Boulder Daily Camera*, November 10, 1995.
Stonehouse, Andy. "'Red Elvis' Dean Reed back in spotlight." *Boulder Daily Camera*, April 12, 2002.

Photo Credits

The task of collecting photographs to illustrate five decades of Colorado music history was an enormous one. The author gratefully acknowledges those who took the time and trouble to search through their Rolodexes, attics, and files, especially Dan Fong, who I cannot thank enough for his many indulgences and kindnesses.

Brian Brainerd: 103, 121
Anton Corbijn: 92, 101
Henry Diltz: 34, 40
Bob Ferbrache: 78, 80, 88
Dan Fong: 28, 29, 45, 50, 52, 47, 61, 64, 71, 77, 79, 115
Michael Goldman: 93
Sharon Poteet: 118
John Preito: 127
Jim Sheeler: 123
Bill Warren: 101, 102

Courtesy of Jock Bartley: 72, 73
Courtesy of Sam Bush: 90
Courtesy of Colorado Historical Society: 2, 3
Courtesy of Paul Conly: 142, 143
Courtesy of Jerry Corbetta: 33
Courtesy of Chris Daniels: 110, 111
Courtesy of the Denver Broncos: 160
Courtesy of Steve Eng: 18
Courtesy of Tommy Facenda:
Courtesy of Barry Fey: 21, 27
Courtesy of Harold Fielden: 54
Courtesy of Nick Forster: 106
Courtesy of Sam Fuller: 19, 20
Courtesy of Jim Gallagher: 14, 15
Courtesy of Michael Jensen: 105
Courtesy of Rick Kauvar: 47
Courtesy of Kathryn Keller: 16
Courtesy of Beatrice Kemp: 36
Courtesy of George Krieger: 23
Courtesy of Robert Lamm: 62
Courtesy of Mark Lewis: 69
Courtesy of Annie McFadin: 55, 56
Courtesy of Chuck Morris Entertainment: 149, 150
Courtesy of Brian Nevin: 131, 132
Courtesy of The Michael Ochs Archives: 1
Courtesy of Shad O'Shea: 67
Courtesy of Tom Pickles: 9, 10
Courtesy of Rocky Mountain Productions: 7
Courtesy of Bret Saunders: 26
Courtesy of Bryan Sennett: 11, 12
Courtesy of Buddy Stephens: 82
Courtesy of Gary Stites: 4, 5
Courtesy of Steve Taylor: 114
Courtesy of Larry Thompson: 82
Courtesy of Kip Winger: 108
Courtesy of Jaye Zola: 141

A&M Records: 41, 140 (Ken Schles)
ABC Records: 90
ABC/Dunhill Records: 38, 44
ABC-TV: 63
Alternative Tentacles: 104
Arista Records:128
Astralwerks Records: 142 (Kevin Westenberg)
Asylum Records: 74 (Ed Caraeff), 94 (George Gruel), 95 (Gary Heery)
Atlantic Records: 8, 24, 34, 35, 70, 108 (Steven Selikoff), 135 (Melanie Nissen), 133 (Eugene Gologursky)
Blue Note Records: 156 (Clay Patrick Mcbride)
Capitol Records: 86, 122 (Bill Bernstein)
Capricorn Records: 139 (Catherine Wessel), 151 (Johnny Buzzerio)
Caribou Records: 75, 100
Chess Records: 1
Chrysalis Records: 39
Columbia Records: 23 (Don Hunstein), 62, 69, 77, 78, 89, 96, 145 (Neal Preston)
Cotillion Records: 29
Domo Records: 137 (Martina Hoffmann)
Dot Records: 36
Eagle Records: 145
EastWest Records: 112, 118 (James Calderero)
Elektra Records: 6, 25, 57, 138 (Danny Clinch)
EMI America Records: 87
Enigma Records: 96
Epic Records: 49, 84, 100, 122 (Gene Kirkland), 124 (Lance Mercer), 127 (Herb Ritts)
Epitaph Records: 146 (Stacie Lockwood)
Flying Fish Records: 106 (Steve Ramsey)
Forefront Records: 161 (Kristin Barlowe)
Frog Pad Records: 155 (Michael Weintrob)
Geffen Records: 120 (Gene Kirkland), 120 (Robert John)
Giant Records: 130
Gramavision Records: 141 (Micheal Macioce)
GRP Records: 99
Gts Records: 136
Hollywood Records: 125
Imprint Records: 134
Interscope Records: 160 (Anthony Mandler)
Island Records: 101 (Anton Corbijn), 126 (Michael Lavine)
Kindercore Records: 162
Liberty Records: 32
Life Records: 123
MCA Records: 59, 119 (Peter Darley Miller)
Mercury Records: 107 (Ross Halfin), 148
Modern Records: 105
Motown Records: 157 (Kwaku Alston)
Nova Records: 117
Polydor Records: 66
RCA Records: 13, 68, 98, 133
Reprise Records: 26, 58
Rhino Records: 83
Rounder Records: 159
RSO Records: 76
SCI Fidelity: 152, 153, 154
Select Records: 91
Silver Wave Records: 116
spinART Records: 147
Telarc Records: 158
Tumbleweed Records: 42, 43
United Artists Records: 21, 46
W.A.R.? Records: 128
Warner Bros. Records: 48, 64, 93, 97

Cover photographs by Steve Collector (xii, 163)

Index

About the Author

G. Brown considers himself a Colorado native and received a B.S. degree in journalism from the University of Colorado. For twenty-six years, G. wrote about popular music for *The Denver Post.* His work has appeared in *Rolling Stone, National Lampoon,* and numerous other magazines. He lives peacefully with his wife, Bridget, and their dog, Stella, in Louisville, Colorado.